Language Arts Activities for the Classroom

Third Edition

Pamela L. Tiedt
University of California at Berkeley

Iris M. Tiedt
Moorhead State University

Sidney W. Tiedt
San Jose State University

Allyn and Bacon

Boston • London • Toronto • Sydney • Tokyo • Singapore

Series Editor: Arnis E. Burvikovs
Editorial Assistant: Patrice Mailloux
Marketing Manager: Brad Parkins
Editorial-Production Administrator: Annette Joseph
Editorial-Production Coordinator: Susan Freese

Editorial-Production Service and
  Electronic Composition: TKM Productions
Text Designer: Denise Hoffman
Manufacturing Buyer: Julie McNeill
Cover Administrator: Linda Knowles

Copyright © 2001, 1987, 1978 by Allyn & Bacon
A Pearson Education Company
160 Gould Street
Needham Heights, MA 02494

Internet: www.abacon.com

Between the time website information is gathered and then published, it is not unusual for some sites to have closed. Also, the transcription of URLs can result in unintended typographical errors. The publisher would appreciate being notified of any problems with URLs so that they may be corrected in subsequent editions. Thank you.

Library of Congress Cataloging-in-Publication Data

Tiedt, Pamela L.
    Language arts activities for the classroom / Pamela L. Tiedt, Iris M. Tiedt, Sidney W. Tiedt.-- 3rd ed.
        p. cm.
    Sidney W. Tiedt's name appears first on the earlier edition.
    Includes bibliographical references and index.
    ISBN 0-205-30863-5
        1. Language arts (Elementary).   2. Individualized instruction.   I. Tiedt, Iris M. II. Tiedt, Sidney W.   III. Title.

LB1576 .T564 2001
372.6--dc21   00-042144

Printed in the United States of America

10 9 8 7 6 5 4 3 2 1   RRD-VA   05   04   03   02   01   00

Permission credits: p. 1: *Rasco and the Rats of NIMH* by Jane Leslie Conly. Copyright © 1986 HarperCollins. p. 53: *Dr. Seuss's Sleep Book* by Dr. Seuss. Copyright © 1961 Random House, Inc. p. 83: *Maniac Magee* by Jerry Spinelli. Copyright © 1990 Little, Brown & Co. p. 85: *Roll of Thunder, Hear My Cry* by Mildred Taylor. Copyright © 1976 Dial Books, a division of Penguin Putnam Inc. p. 123: *The Moon and I: A Memoir* by Betsy Byars. Copyright © 1996 Beech Tree Books. p. 169: From *The House at Pooh Corner* by A. A. Milne, illustrations by E. H. Shepard, copyright 1928 by E. P. Dutton, renewed © 1956 by A. A. Milne. Used by permission of Dutton Children's Books, a division of Penguin Putnam Inc. p. 187: *The Cat Who Wished to Be a Man* by Lloyd Alexander. Copyright © 1973 E. P. Dutton. Used by permission of Dutton Children's Books, a division of Penguin Putnam Inc. pp. 227 & 337: *Harriet the Spy* by Louise Fitzhugh. Copyright © 1964 HarperCollins. p. 228: *The Phantom Toll Booth* by Norton Juster. Copyright © 1961 Random House, Inc. p. 228: From *My Side of the Mountain* by Jean Craighead George, copyright © 1959, renewed © 1987 by Jean Craighead George. Used by permission of Dutton Children's Books, a division of Penguin Putnam Inc. p. 228: "Mongoose," *The Library Card* by Jerry Spinelli. Copyright © 1998 Apple. Reprinted by permission of Scholastic Inc. p. 259: From *Fast Sam, Cool Clyde, and Stuff* by Walter Dean Myers, copyright © 1975 by Walter Dean Myers. Used by permission of Viking Penguin, a division of Penguin Putnam Inc. p. 287: *Sideways Stories from Wayside School* by Louis Sachar. Copyright © 1998 Morrow Junior Books.

Contents

Preface

Language Arts Activities in the Classroom is now in its third edition. Originally published in 1978, this text has closely reflected the trends in education at each stage of its development. It is informative to observe what has remained the same over the three editions as well as what has changed in each, illustrating shifts in the perspectives in the field of language arts instruction.

Much has remained constant in this attempt to assist elementary school teachers in teaching language arts effectively. Dedicated to bringing theory and practice together, we have always espoused the best methods to support an integrated language arts program, including reading. A major strength of the presentation has been the use of outstanding children's literature to support the teaching of reading and instruction in other subject areas. A chapter on poetry, as an integral part of the curriculum, is a Tiedt trademark that teachers have especially enjoyed.

On the other hand, many changes can be noted in this third edition that reflect the influence of current theory and research. For example, in recognition of the increasing importance of incorporating literature in the elementary school curriculum, literature is presented in a separate chapter in addition to being integrated into other aspects of instruction. A strong research base clearly guides the selection of recommended instructional strategies throughout the text.

For the first time, all three Tiedts are listed as authors of *Language Arts Activities*. This unique daughter-mother-father team is comprised of teacher educators who share expertise and experience in teaching linguistics, children's literature, and instructional methodology at all levels.

We acknowledge our indebtedness to the many teachers who have inspired our work over the years. We also thank the reviewers who assisted in shaping this current edition: Richard Griffin; Alexandra LaTronica, Yeshiva of North University; and Sherry Markel, Northern Arizona University.

P. L. T.
I. M. T.
S. W. T.

1 Organizing for Learning the Language Arts

Learning is important! . . . I can't spend my whole life lying around in the sewers eating garbage.
—Jane Leslie Conly, *Racso and the Rats of NIMH*

This book is intended for use by teachers, and people training to be teachers, in grades K–8 who wish to expand their repertoire of ideas and activities for teaching reading and the language arts. In this book, the language arts will be presented as communication processes—that is, reading and writing as well as speaking and listening, for many different purposes and for varied audiences in diverse contexts. Novice or expert, all teachers can learn more about reaching students, new resources to use, and effective teaching approaches from *Language Arts Activities.* Since it is not possible to present a comprehensive list in one book, these activities have been selected to represent the best of current research and practice, make use of excellent children's literature, and provide models you can adapt to your own classroom needs. In addition, the book is based on the belief that "no one size fits all," or even that "one size fits most." The activities in this book are inclusive: They are designed to help *all* students, from students learning English as an additional language to students needing extra challenges. This book supports teachers who know that students need varied and multiple opportunities to show what they are capable of achieving.

Exploring the Foundations of Good Teaching

Recent conflicts and tensions in language arts education call into question who teachers are and what they do. It is time for a re-visioning and a re-thinking of what effective language arts instruction means, at a point when many teachers feel overwhelmed by new information and pressures to reform. From research on learning and the brain to the struggle between whole language and phonics instruction, teachers are confronted with more difficult questions than ever before.

What Is the Role of the Teacher?

The guide on the side or *The sage on the stage:* Which one are you? As we present activities designed for student-centered instruction, we create a picture of the teacher as a coach—a change from the traditional lecture-based model in which the teacher does most of the talking and student talk is limited. In some classrooms, the teacher may assume the role of *benevolent librarian,* a resource person who supplies opportunities for learning and explains problems as students encounter them. Teachers who are pulled in different directions by conflicting roles may ask if there is any place left for direct instruction. Dewey (1938), however, reminds us that the teacher will always have a powerful role to play—as a model for learning, an "expert other," an off-stage director, and a storyteller. Even as teaching moves from basal based (with all the questions and answers provided in the teacher's edition) to literature based (in which there may be no "right answer" and each student can contribute a personal response), the need for explicit instruction is still present. Teachers continue to bear significant responsibility for making instructional choices that are the most effective for their students.

What Is Literacy?

It is difficult to decide whether illiteracy rates are increasing or decreasing when the term *literacy* is used to cover such a broad area, often extending beyond print to include math, computers, and "cultural literacy." Public protests over high school graduates who are unable to read a newspaper may blame this illiteracy on instructional "fads." The solution offered, therefore, is to throw out the old programs and replace them with an approach at the opposite extreme. So we have arguments over "skills" versus "comprehension," as if we don't need to include both in our instruction, depending on the student's prior experience with literacy. And many people worry whether increased use of the computer will lead to decreased literacy, at the same time as computer technology (such as email) is responsible for a boom in reading and writing. However, as requirements for good comprehension (reading and listening) and communication (writing and speaking) skills rise, even in unskilled occupations, teachers have to pay more attention to different kinds of literacy. We must begin to acknowledge multiple *literacies,* ranging from simply knowing letter-sound relationships to *critical literacy,* or what Freire (1985) calls the ability to "read the world."

How Do Teachers Integrate the Language Arts?

How can teachers plan lessons that integrate all of the language arts when they have to spend much of their class time teaching reading and preparing students for tests? The idea of using more children's literature is appealing, and creative approaches to teaching may offset boredom, but how do teachers know they are covering the necessary material (for the next grade or for the test)? At least when teachers had a textbook they knew they were expected to "finish the book," even though they did have to rush through the final chapters. Current controversies, such as the "reading wars," have created a false dichotomy between teaching the "parts" and teaching the "whole." In fact, effective language arts teaching includes practicing the little bits *and* putting them all together in a real context (synthesis), in addition to taking apart the "whole" in order to understand its components better (analysis). No one aspect can be taught without the other, just as learning to play baseball must involve practice in swinging the bat and hitting the ball, as needed, as well as the chance to employ these skills in a full game.

How Can Teachers Reach *All* of the Students?

The more teachers learn about the influence of culture on schooling (Opitz, 1998), the effect of regional or social dialects (Ebonics), and the concept of multiple intelligences (Gardner, 1993), the more overwhelming their task seems. How can teachers do their best under the pressure of meeting so many different student needs? Teachers are expected to be the "Jack (or Jill) of all trades": a foreign language instructor, a counselor, an aide to a student with a disability—in other words, someone who is everything to everyone. However, the teacher does not belong at the center of all these activities. It is the students who need to be more involved and active at given tasks, such as writing a letter or reading a poem. Teachers can provide students with opportunities to process what they are learning, through talking and writing. *Students* can read aloud, work in cooperative groups (Slavin, 1995), teach each other ("reciprocal teaching" [Palinscar & Brown, 1984]), take on more responsibility for helping each other (Gardner, 1991), and learn to monitor their own learning (Brown et al., 1983). In fact, one key to successful teaching is: *Don't do anything the students can do.*

Designing an Ideal Language Arts Program

Research informs practice, not through programs imposed by distant experts but as practice-based research is connected to research-based practice. Teachers are naturally reflective practitioners; they can examine their own practice as they seek to learn more about the *what, why,* and *how* of teaching.

Through educational psychology, teachers can learn more about the relationship between language and culture as well as language and learning. For example, before students can comprehend what they read, teachers need to consider what knowledge students bring to the task. Aspects of the text, such as narrative structure and illustrations, and elements of culture, such as life experiences and values, all influence the reader's understanding and memory of what is read. Prereading discussion, therefore, will focus on activating students' prior knowledge by discussing similar experiences in order to predict what vocabulary might be found as well as present cultural assumptions that may be implicit in the text.

Memory is also a crucial factor in student learning. But there are different types of memory, and each serves different functions. Because space in *short-term memory* is scarce, instruction needs to include practice in paraphrasing new ideas in speech and writing. *Active working memory* is temporary and easily interrupted. Students will therefore need help with strategies and visualization to keep track of their place in the big picture. New information is eventually stored in *long-term memory,* from which it can be retrieved by connections to sensory information, organizing patterns, and paired associations. Unlike computers or dictionaries, which have linear structures, information in the brain is organized more like a web, with retrieval dependent on how the links are connected. Students can recall a fact by thinking of where on the page they read it, remembering the aroma of lunch while they read, or connecting it with an unusual event immediately before or after. Access to strategies such as *elaboration* and *rehearsal* are essential parts of students' ability to learn and remember.

Another perspective on teaching and learning comes from constructivist approaches, which replace the traditional lesson structure of teacher introducing the concept, students practicing, and then applying the concept *(deductive),* with an opposite approach: an *inductive* pattern. The teacher provides opportunities for students to discover and explore new ideas, talk about them with other students, followed by predicting and hypothesizing from these experiences, and leading to additional activities involving the concept as students have framed it. According to this developmental approach (Piaget, 1952), the students' mistakes provide significant and necessary information, because they tell us how students are conceptualizing the task internally. In addition, conflicting ideas are evidence of learning, as students constantly check new information against old ideas and then revise their understanding to accommodate and assimilate the results.

Other constructivist approaches emphasize students as *social* learners (Vygotsky, 1978). When students talk with each other, they are learning how to think—that is, to discover and comprehend ideas. And the tasks students can perform with assistance (from peers or adults) today, they will be able to do independently tomorrow. Vygotsky has called this stage of learning the Zone of Proximal Development (ZPD) or the "ripening" stage, as shown in the accompanying figure. Teachers can use "scaffolding" (providing temporary support) to work in a student's ZPD. Starting from a position of extensive assistance, the teacher gradually withdraws support so that the student takes on increasing responsibility for the work. Cooperative learning groups are a good example of activities based on social learning because they provide students of differing abilities with models and challenges that foster student development.

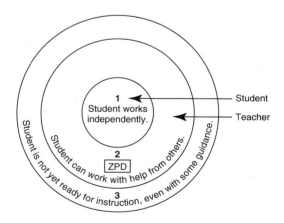

Vygotsky's Zone of Proximal Development: Learning takes place when the teacher reaches the student in the appropriate region, the ZPD (#2), not where the student can already work independently (#1) nor where the student is not yet ready for work (#3).

Howard Gardner has another perspective on how students learn. In his most recent model (Gardner, 1999), there are eight different kinds of intelligence:

- linguistic
- logico-mathematical
- musical
- spatial
- body-kinesthetic
- interpersonal
- intrapersonal
- naturalist

All kinds of intelligence are present in all people but no two people have the same blend of intelligences. Instruction can capitalize on this rich variety in the following ways:

1. Use examples from these different ways of understanding the world as entry points, or as approaches to a topic.
2. Make analogies across different domains, using the familiar types of thinking to explain the unfamiliar ones.
3. Take each aspect of intelligence and show students how all of them provide legitimate ways to represent ideas.

The traditional view of the educational enterprise has been the mastery of facts, evaluated by testing. Gardner proposes, instead, that we aim for *understanding,* and the proper way to evaluate understanding is through public performance. The teacher needs to emphasize instruction that accommodates student variation, instead of piling on more of the same kind of material, and to offer alternative paths to understanding.

Defining the Language Arts

The language arts have usually been defined as reading, writing, speaking, and listening. Both reading and listening are *receptive* modes; writing and speaking are *expressive* modes. In addition, the language arts are divided according to two channels—*oral* and *visual,* as shown in the figure.

	Receptive	Expressive
Oral	*Listening*	*Speaking*
Visual	*Reading*	*Writing*

Language arts

This traditional box, however, limits our understanding of the language arts. First, the separation of the components is artificial. In fact, reading and writing, and speaking and listening are interconnected. Each reinforces the other, in learning as well as in instruction. Because the language arts are not separable, for example, teachers do not have to complete the teaching of reading before they teach writing, or listening before speaking. They can help students "read like a writer" and "write like a reader." In addition, the division into receptive and expressive is not accurate, because reading and listening are regarded as *active* processes. As students read text and listen to speech, they are actively interpreting the information and constructing their representation of this text or speech. In fact, *thinking* is sometimes called the fifth language art, in recognition of this active processing. Instead of a box of separate skills, the language arts are more appropriately portrayed as *communication* processes, because people use talk or print according to a purpose and an audience. In addition, *viewing* and *visually representing* are sometimes considered another language art in order to include the "language" of visual "texts."

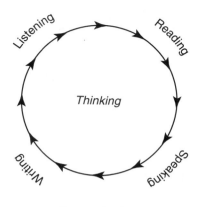

Communication

When thinking of the language arts as communication processes, it is obvious that they must be fundamental to the entire school curriculum, beyond the time explicitly allocated to the teaching of reading or writing, for example. As James Britton (1993) notes, we learn language, we learn about language, and we learn through language.

What Does an Effective Language Arts Program Look Like?

Effective language arts programs come in different shapes and sizes. For instance, an observer walks into a classroom and notices that the desks and tables are organized for flexible grouping. Obviously, this teacher expects students to work not only as a whole class, but also in small groups and individually, as appropriate. Around the room are displayed books, magazines, posters, bound collections of student writing, and student notebooks—many examples of student-written work and different kinds of text to read in a variety of categories (genres). There are areas where students can work in learning centers or on different projects, probably including a cozy Reading Corner. The many bulletin boards, charts, and posters contain, for example, student-generated lists of guidelines for revising writing or new science vocabulary. Language is found throughout the room, in such forms as labels, Word Walls, and Planning Webs. Some of the labels illustrate the varied languages represented in the classroom. *Hello,* the names for numbers 1 through 5, and *Happy Birthday* are written in languages contributed by students. Other labels on common objects are provided in English to assist the students who are learning English as an additional language (ESL). Technology is available to students and includes computers and printers for daily journal writing and publishing student work.

Now the teacher arrives with plans for the day's work. *Home* is the current focus, and he or she begins discussion by reading *How My Family Lives in America* by Susan

Kuklin, which portrays the lives of families from different ethnic backgrounds. The teacher has brought many examples of books and materials that show how different cultures, at different places and times, have solved the problem of shelter in order to incorporate this theme into reading, writing, social studies, math, science, and art activities. Later, as the teacher moves around the room, he or she is also watching and listening to the students, assessing their difficulties and their progress in order to know how to modify instruction accordingly. Because there are many alternate paths to the same goal, the teacher must draw on his or her repertoire of activities in order to reach every student. Observations of students' behaviors, such as reading miscues or story retellings, are recorded in folders for later evaluation by both teacher and student, along with samples of writing and other work.

Soon the students are working on different projects. One student is checking the calendar and writing the day's events, weather, and other news on the board for students to copy and for ESL practice. There's a buzz of conversation, reflecting the constant activity of the students who are thinking aloud and turning to others for ideas, reactions, and explanations. As they read about different habitats, small groups of students work together to plan a presentation to the class on their research. They have created posters and maps, and will perform a skit with puppets representing the animals. Students have kept a log of how they proceeded and this becomes part of their science notebooks.

Standards for Evaluating the Reading/Language Arts Program

The major professional organizations—the National Council of Teachers of English (NCTE) and the International Reading Association (IRA)—have produced a list of standards* for English language arts, predicated on the belief that all students should have the opportunity to develop to their full ability. Although these standards are presented as a list, these items are not separable but meant to be integrated parts of a whole. Teachers are expected to consider students' prior experiences with literacy, even before schooling, and to use this list as a starting point for their own knowledge and creativity as teachers:

1. Students read a wide range of print and nonprint texts to build an understanding of texts, of themselves, and of the cultures of the United States and the world; to acquire new information; to respond to the needs and demands of society and the workplace; and for personal fulfillment. Among these texts are fiction and nonfiction, classic and contemporary works.
2. Students read a wide range of literature from many periods in many genres to build an understanding of the many dimensions (e.g., philosophical, ethical, aesthetic) of human experience.
3. Students apply a wide range of strategies to comprehend, interpret, evaluate, and appreciate texts. They draw on their prior experience, their interactions with other readers and writers, their knowledge of word meaning and of other texts, their word

identification strategies, and their understanding of textual features (e.g., sound-letter correspondence, sentence structure, context, graphics).

4. Students adjust their use of spoken, written, and visual language (e.g., conventions, style, vocabulary) to communicate effectively with a variety of audiences and for different purposes.

5. Students employ a wide range of strategies as they write and use different writing process elements appropriately to communicate with different audiences for a variety of purposes.

6. Students apply knowledge of language structure, language conventions (e.g., spelling and punctuation), media techniques, figurative language, and genre to create, critique, and discuss print and nonprint texts.

7. Students conduct research on issues and interests by generating ideas and questions, and by posing problems. They gather, evaluate, and synthesize data from a variety of sources (e.g., print and nonprint texts, artifacts, people) to communicate their discoveries in ways that suit their purpose and audience.

8. Students use a variety of technological and informational resources (e.g., libraries, databases, computer networks, video) to gather and synthesize information and to create and communicate knowledge.

9. Students develop an understanding of and respect for diversity in language use, patterns, and dialects across cultures, ethnic groups, geographic regions, and social roles.

10. Students whose first language is not English make use of their first language to develop competency in the English language arts and to develop understanding of content across the curriculum.

11. Students participate as knowledgeable, reflective, creative, and critical members of a variety of literacy communities.

12. Students use spoken, written, and visual language to accomplish their own purposes (e.g., for learning, enjoyment, persuasion, and the exchange of information).

Reflecting on Trends in Education

As the new millennium begins, it is appropriate to look ahead and speculate on what the next 10 years may hold for education, especially in the language arts. Following are five areas that the authors expect will play a significantly increasing role in public discussion and educational policy, drawn from themes reflected in professional conferences and journals as well as concerns found in the popular media. All of these trends illustrate the power of social forces on education today:

1. *Diversity:* As society becomes increasingly heterogeneous, there will be a corresponding impact on teaching. Not only do students differ in the language they speak at home and their prior experience with literacy, but many other kinds of variation will be influential. For example, the mainstreaming of students with different ability levels, concerns expressed by religious groups about school celebration of holidays, and reports that girls and boys receive unequal treatment are all leading to increased pressure on the teacher

to plan instruction based on the assumption that heterogeneity is a fact and an asset. In addition, the troubling differences in race, social class, and culture between teachers and the students they teach must be addressed (Nieto, 1999). Finally, the gulf in public funding between rich and poor schools exacerbates the basic inequality of educational opportunities and access to resources, such as technology or experienced teachers (Kozol, 1991).

2. *Concern for Improving Education:* Everyone has something to say about what's wrong with education and how to improve it, especially in areas such as student reading and math scores. They can't understand why international rankings continue to show the United States lagging behind other industrialized countries, for example. This public concern is reflected in movements to increase educational options, as more parents choose home schooling, vote for voucher programs, or establish charter schools. Even teacher training programs are affected by these forces. Suddenly, attention is paid to the many teachers who don't have a credential for the subjects they teach and the massive hiring of candidates with temporary credentials. Debate over these issues recognizes credential programs as significant factors affecting the quality of schooling.

3. *Assessment:* Concern over the poor quality of public education is easily expressed in the area of assessment, as the pressure for setting high standards increases at the district, state, federal, and international levels. At the same time as educational researchers are trying to redefine assessment and turn assessment-driven instruction into a positive quality, school systems are moving in the opposite direction as they consider tying teacher pay to improvement in student test scores. To a certain extent, testing at one time served to permit upward mobility, as it allowed recognition of the abilities in high-achieving but less-privileged students. Today, testing seems to be more a tool for increasing the gap between rich and poor. In addition, there is a tendency to lowering the grade level at which content is taught, such as teaching college calculus in the high school, and offering more opportunities, such as advanced placement classes, to selected students who will therefore be prepared to perform better on standardized tests. At the same time, there is a movement among researchers and teachers to establish other options for assessment. Teachers have the chance to incorporate assessment into their own teaching with ongoing assessment and the use of rubrics to evaluate writing. And students can take a more active role in assessment by putting together portfolio folders of their best work and practicing self-assessment with a checklist.

4. *Technology:* The latest advances in technology, such as access to the Internet, have proven to have disadvantages as well as advantages. In many classrooms, computers are still being used at the level of word processing, record keeping, and drill and practice. Poor children are less likely to have access to enough computers at school or in their homes. Although some teachers are exploring having students use the Internet to look up facts and obtain pictures, the full potential of this technology has not been realized throughout the country. One of the most significant contributions the computer has made to teaching has been in writing instruction. Now, students can be evaluated on the quality of their written ideas rather than their handwriting, and they have a real incentive to revise their work because it will be "published." Over the next 10 years, it is hoped that educators will develop a better conceptualization of and experience with the full capabilities of the Internet and multimedia technology for instruction.

5. *Brain:* Increasingly, as more locations in the brain are mapped, neurological researchers have made findings of importance to teaching and learning. The latest computer-assisted scans can actually show where the different steps of reading take place and follow thought as it moves through the brain. There is also evidence that learning in the primary grades is even more important than was once thought. Teachers can put students on the right track for literacy learning by providing extensive stimuli at an early age and contact with books. Recent moves to reduce class size will also be helpful in supporting the need for more individualized instruction. Increasing research has caused educators to reject the oversimplifications of right brain/left brain divisions and differences in how male and female brains see the world. Brain research is an area where one can expect many new ideas with implications for educators.

It is interesting to compare this list of trends with the list in the second edition of this book, published in 1987. The topics of diversity, technology, and concern for improving education—appearing on both lists—continue to have a great impact. But assessment and brain research have replaced critical thinking and integrated instruction as hot topics, both as areas of public interest and potential for innovation.

Introducing This Book

The quotations from noted children's authors that open each chapter of this book illustrate what a rich resource children's literature is—a base for instruction and an opportunity for changing teaching practices. These quotations can be displayed throughout the classroom, for discussion, as a writing prompt, and as an incentive to read the book. Although the following chapters are labeled according to traditional divisions of language arts—such as reading, writing, and oral language—you will note that few of the activities included are limited to one subject area. In fact, most of the activities presented here make connections between and among reading, writing, speaking, and listening. As a result, if you want to expand your repertoire of writing ideas, for example, you will find possibilities to explore in every chapter. At the end of each chapter is a list of Discussion Questions to encourage the formation of study groups among teachers, in which they might read and discuss important material, or cooperative learning groups (CLGs) for students in teacher training programs. Exploring Further provides examples of additional instructional resources, ranging from innovative idea books to websites and CD-ROMs. Finally, each chapter ends with References, reflecting significant work and research in the field, for teachers to consult as needed to explore specific topics in greater depth.

Discussion Questions

1. Which trends do you think will influence or have influenced your career as a teacher?

2. How do you plan to incorporate constructivist methods in your teaching?

3. What implications does the theory of multiple intelligences hold for language arts teaching in a multicultural classroom?

Exploring Further

The Brain and Learning. Video series. ASCD, 1998.

Lucy Calkins, K. Montgomery, and D. Santman. *A Teacher's Guide to Standardized Reading Tests: Knowledge Is Power.* Heinemann, 1998.

Cooperative Learning. Special section of *Educational Leadership* 48 (1991): 71–95.

Eric Jensen. *Teaching with the Brain in Mind.* ASCD, 1998.

Exploring Our Multiple Intelligences. CD-ROM. ASCD, 1997.

Herb Kohl. *The Discipline of Hope: Learning from a Lifetime of Teaching.* Simon & Schuster, 1998.

Enid Lee et al. *Beyond Heroes and Holidays: A Practical Guide to K–12 Anti-Racist, Multicultural Education and Staff Development.* NECA, 1998.

Multiple Intelligences. Video series with audiotape. ASCD, 1995.

Vivian Paley. *You Can't Say You Can't Play.* Harvard University Press, 1992.

Theresa Perry and Lisa Delpit (Eds.). *The Real Ebonics Debate: Power, Language, and the Education of African-American Children.* Beacon, 1998.

Rethinking Schools. <www.rethinkingschools.org>

Maria Sapon-Shevin. *Because We Can Change the World: A Practical Guide to Building Cooperative, Inclusive Classroom Communities.* Allyn and Bacon, 1999.

Teaching Tolerance, publication of the Southern Poverty Law Center.

References

James Britton. *Language and Learning* (2nd ed.). Boynton-Cook, 1993.

Ann Brown, John Bransford, R. A. Ferrara, and Joseph Campione. "Learning, Remembering, and Understanding." In J. Flavell and E. Markman, eds. *Handbook of Child Psychology* (4th ed.). Wiley, 1983.

James Cummins. *Negotiating Identities: Educating for Empowerment in a Diverse Society.* California Association for Bilingual Education, 1996.

John Dewey. *Experience and Education.* Macmillan, 1938.

Paulo Freire. "Reading the World and Reading the Word: An Interview with Paulo Freire." *Language Arts, 62* (1985): 15–21.

Howard Gardner. *The Unschooled Mind: How Children Think and How Schools Should Teach.* Basic Books, 1991.

Howard Gardner. *The (Well)-Disciplined Mind: What All Students Should Understand.* Paper presented at AERA conference, Montreal, Canada 1999.

Jonathan Kozol. *Savage Inequalities.* Harper, 1991.

Sonia Nieto. *The Light in Their Eyes: Creating Multicultural Communities.* Teachers College Press, 1999.

M. Opitz, ed. *Literacy Instruction for Culturally and Linguistically Diverse Students.* IRA, 1998.

Annemarie Palincsar and Ann Brown. "Reciprocal Teaching of Comprehension Fostering and Comprehension Monitoring Activities." *Cognition and Instruction, 2* (1984): 117–175.

Jean Piaget. *The Language and Thought of the Child.* Routledge and Kegan-Paul, 1952.

Robert Slavin. *Cooperative Learning: Theory, Research and Practice* (2nd ed.). Allyn and Bacon, 1995.

Lev Vygotsky. *Mind in Society.* In M. Cole, V. John-Steiner, S. Scribner, and E. Souberman, eds. Harvard University Press, 1978.

2 Developing Oral Language

What is the use of a book...without pictures or conversation?
—Lewis Carroll, *Alice in Wonderland*

The apparent ease and naturalness of oral language obscures the need for its presence in the classroom curriculum. Oral language includes such activities as the speaking and listening involved in telling stories, sharing nursery or number rhymes, and taking part in a class production. Once teachers understand how children use oral language to "talk through" problem solving (Tharp & Gallimore, 1988) and how children's internalization of this "private speech" is central to their cognitive development (Wertsch, 1991), there is increased awareness of the need for providing multiple speaking and listening opportunities in the classroom (Grugeon et al., 1988). As Donaldson (1978) points out, students' talk is an essential part of their construction of meaning, the way that they make sense of the world. Many teachers restrict student talk to narration of stories and recounting of events. But this ignores the full range of talk that students need to experience, such as argument, discussion, and performance, and the different demands these genres place on students.

An effective language arts teacher will create a classroom environment that is teeming with opportunities for exploratory talk, as students talk out loud and listen to each other in order to learn about themselves and about the world. When students work in groups and engage in collaborative talk, or use language to communicate with real people in real situations (e.g., interviews), they are building the foundation for all later learning.

Working with Listening and Speaking Skills

Oral language is fundamental to reading development, as students use their knowledge of words and sounds to interpret a printed text. Students can practice and apply their sense of how the language works (phonological awareness) independently of where they are in reading instruction. Encourage students to play with the sound of language through rhyme, poetry, and making up words. Students who are learning English as an additional language (ESL) need multiple opportunities to listen to the language and engage in language-related activities before they can be expected to provide spoken or written responses. Listening to students talk—for example, during collaborative work at the computer—may give you more information about what they are learning than asking them individual questions. And a simple probe (e.g., "Can you tell me what you have been doing?") provides a better picture of their capabilities. Build in opportunities for students to reflect and report back orally so that you can assess what they are learning.

The Sounds of Silence

Is silence really silent? Have the students close their eyes and be absolutely quiet for three minutes so they can listen to silence. Then have them write down what they heard. The class can discuss what each student heard. Did the children notice more sounds with their eyes closed than they normally do? Do they think that complete silence is possible? Where might one find complete silence?

As you talk about what the students have written, take the opportunity to introduce descriptive words for these sounds. What does breathing sound like? How does a bell sound? What kind of noise do the leaves on the trees make?

A Listening Walk

Take the students for a Listening Walk around the school. Ask them to be very quiet as they listen carefully to the sounds around them. When they return to the classroom, have them write (or tell) what they heard. The class can talk about differences in the sounds people heard. Did some people hear sounds that no one else heard?

As a variation, have students pair up. One wears a blindfold and the other acts as leader. Then reverse roles.

Help the class write a group poem describing this experience. Write a beginning line on the board and have students volunteer lines until you have completed a poem. Print or type the poem to mount on the bulletin board for the class to see and to read.

> *I heard . . .*
> *cars going by*
> *dogs barking*
> *boys talking*
> *the wind in the trees*
> *people walking.*

Repeat the Listening Walk with the class after a couple of weeks. Has the students' perception of sounds improved? What other sounds did they notice? Talk with the class about how this walk was different from the first walk. What do the students think they gained from studying listening?

Sounds Around Us

What are your favorite sounds? Ask students which sounds they like best and which sounds they like least. List their choices on the board. Students can discuss why they like certain sounds and why some people dislike sounds that others like. This is an excellent opportunity to introduce more descriptive words for sounds, such as *cacophony, raucous,* and *melodious.*

Sound Pictures

Sound words can call up particular images. Make phrases for the students to complete with an image brought to mind by that sound, for instance:

As loud as . . .

> a motorcycle
> the wind when you are alone

As quiet as . . .

> an empty house
> smoke going out of a chimney

Noisy Poems

After class discussion of sound images, students may write short poems in small groups that show the wide range of sounds, from soft to loud. Each group will present the poem to the class, accompanied by appropriate sound effects and actions. Upper-grade students could perform these poems before a larger audience, such as the primary classes.

Onomatopoeia

Students will enjoy learning about *onomatopoeia,* an unusual Greek term for words that sound like what they mean. Suggest a few words, such as *squish* and *splat,* to get students started. Why are words like this so delicious to say aloud? What other words can students think of where the sound of the word adds flavor to the meaning?

> scream
> swoosh
> whisper
> plop
> choo-choo
> glug

Draw students' attention to the fact that many onomatopoetic words begin with *sc, squ, sw,* and *sl* consonant clusters.

Language Diary

Ask students to keep a record of what they listen to and what they talk about. Primary students can report on listening and speaking activities over a limited time, such as an hour of class or an afternoon on the weekend. Students with limited writing skills can make checkmarks on a chart listing possible activities. Older students can create a personal observation log with half-hour intervals to record a week's worth of listening and speaking, ranging from asking questions in class and telling stories to friends, to listening to recipe directions and having a book read aloud to them.

When students report their findings to the class, note the variety of speaking and listening types and purposes, such as:

discussing	arguing
explaining	planning
listening for new information	reporting
listening for their name to be called	persuading

Identify and Remember

Have students put their heads down and listen as you make a series of five different sounds, identifying each by number. Then ask students to list what they think each sound was. This can be done orally or in writing. Sounds to make yourself include:

striking a glass with a fork
flipping pages of a book
scratching a rock
turning an eggbeater
snapping a rubberband
rubbing two pieces of sandpaper together

As students become more sophisticated, you can increase the number of sounds they must identify and remember or vary the difficulty by preparing a tape of unusual sounds. Some sounds to use on tape include:

car starting
door closing
phone ringing
child crying
dog barking
whistle blowing

A variation is to have students listen to familiar sounds but think of different explanations or sources. For instance, a creaking chair might really be a dragon shifting his scales, and a canned soda fizz could be a spaceship of tiny aliens taking off. With eyes closed and imagination open, anything goes.

Listening with Emotion

Play a tape with a series of sounds—for example, a dog barking, a siren, symphonic music, laughing, a door bell, the ocean surf, thunder, and so on. While the tape is being played, ask students to write down how the sound makes them feel. What emotions do they connect with each sound?

Keep in Time

Teach students to hear different rhythms by clapping to the beat. Play songs with distinctive patterns, such as marches or ragtime, so that students learn to listen for the rhythm.

As a variation, have a student choose a certain pattern to clap. The class tries to reproduce the pattern. As students learn to hear these patterns, they can begin to match the beats to stressed syllables in words.

Listening to Poetry

Poetry is meant to be read aloud and to be listened to. The words of the poem create images in the minds of the listeners.

Teach students to appreciate the power of poetry to evoke images by reading poems to them. Ask them to listen for the picture words and words that appeal to the senses. After you read a poem, have them draw pictures of what they saw when listening to the poem. Talk about the words used in the poem to create pictures. Some words may be names of objects; others may only suggest particular images. Some poems create very different images for different people. Why is that?

Increase the number of poems students are exposed to and explore different styles of presentation by bringing recordings of people reading poetry to class. Students do not have to understand every word in a poem in order to appreciate the imagery used by the poet. Emphasize the creative listening necessary to understand the poet's intention.

Students are especially attracted to poems that rhyme. Play recordings of poetry for students and encourage them to memorize their favorite poems. They will have to listen carefully in order to memorize all the words.

Sound Patterns

Students are sensitive to another kind of sound pattern called *alliteration*. Often found in poetry and nursery rhymes, alliteration refers to the repetition of consonant sounds, such as the *p* in *Peter, Peter, pumpkin-eater*. Using your students' names, model examples of alliteration to create adjective-noun phrases:

Jumping Judy
Grateful Georgio
Likeable Larissa
Serious Sergei
Truthful Truong
Eager Isabella

You can also feature student names in rhyming pairs:

> Dandy Sandy
> Lady Katie

Students might also know songs that demonstrate rhyme and alliteration. Upper-grade students can write their own rap songs as study aids, for example.

Work with alliteration and rhyming sound patterns helps foster phonological awareness in children learning to read as well as vocabulary development with older students.

Listening Center

Books, games, and supplies for listening activities can be kept in a Listening Center. Provide stories on CDs and audiocassettes as well as printed versions so that students can practice listening and reading skills. This is especially useful for ESL students at any age. Also include tapes of poetry being read aloud so that students can listen to their favorites. As part of a unit of study, you can record comprehension questions for the students to listen and respond to in writing.

Tongue Twisters

These alliterative tongue twister sentences not only challenge students but they also improve the students' diction. Clear enunciation is important in effective communication.

Choose one day a week to be Tongue Twister Day. Practice the tongue twister as a group in the morning. Performance of the tongue twister could be the ticket to recess or physical education. Your students will enjoy collecting tongue twisters from parents and friends to add to the collection. Here are a few examples:

- Big Bad Bob boldly bit the bodyguard to bruise that buffoon.
- Crazy Callie couldn't collect the clickish crickets croaking classically in the creek.
- Dizzy Don delivered the dollars to diehard detectives to detain devilish doctors.
- Friendly Frieda fondly flashed a frivolous filly in front of a four-footed fly.

Humorous Listening

Many jokes need to be read aloud to have an effect. The audience has to listen closely and understand that a crucial word in the joke can have two meanings. Students love jokes and enjoy telling the same ones over and over. Provide them with some new material and, at the same time, engage their interest in listening to the language used in jokes.

Joke books are a good source of humor in different forms. Here are examples to try on the class:

- What did the ocean say when it left the shore?   (Nothing, it just waved.)
- What did one wall say to the other wall?   (I'll meet you at the corner.)

- What did the mayonnaise jar say to the refrigerator door? (Close the door, I'm dressing.)

Some suggested joke books include the following:

> *Kids Are Punny: Jokes Sent by Kids to the Rosie O'Donnell Show.* Warner, 1997.
> Dora Wood. *500 Wacky Knock-Knock Jokes.* Ballantine, 1992.

Personalized Stories

To keep student attention on a story as you read aloud, change the names of the characters to those of children in the class. This is fairly easy if there is only one character, but you will have to concentrate if you try to change more. The children will soon be able to remind you, however, as they catch on to the game.

This activity also serves as a stimulus to children to read aloud on their own or for the Listening Center. They will have fun turning Cinderella into Janet and the prince into Robert as they create a "modern fairy tale." Encourage them to make other adaptations to modernize the tale even further—for example, the chariot might become a Rolls Royce or a sleek airplane. Again, students who serve as the audience are motivated to listen attentively to catch all the changes included.

Finding the Change

When you read or tell a familiar story to your students, such as *The Three Bears,* change one of the major details of the story. See if the students can locate where you have made the change. For example, if you tell the story of *Little Red Riding Hood,* you might change the color of her hood to *blue* and see if the students notice.

What Doesn't Belong?

Recite a list of five words including one word that doesn't belong—for example: *apples, oranges, pears, airplane, grapes.* Students have to listen to the list and select the word that doesn't belong. Practice this activity as a class before students invent their own lists to challenge others in pairs or small groups. They can also tape record examples for use in the Listening Center by students who need more practice in listening comprehension.

Silly Stories

Provide more demanding listening comprehension activities as students gain in skills. One strategy for doing this is to read a very short paragraph and ask the students to discover what is wrong: What sentence is wrong? What word is wrong? What does not fit in the story? Consider this example:

> Jim and Sharon were walking along a creek in California when all at once they
> saw a large whale. After a while they ran into a small group of penguins. They fed

these tigers their peanut butter sandwiches which they had harvested from the bushes along the creek. Finally the moon came out and they knew it was time for lunch.

What Happened Next?

Another exercise to involve the students in listening is to have them finish a story. Play a recording or tape yourself reading a story. Stop it in the middle near an exciting part. Ask the students to write a suitable ending individually or in small groups. They have to have listened carefully in order to remember what has been going on and to make an appropriate contribution. After they have written their endings, ask them to supply a title for their stories. This is a good motivator for creative writing as well as practice in understanding the organization of a story.

Listening in Sequence

It is important in listening activities to develop exercises that challenge students to put events in sequence. Read a brief passage to the class and have the students relate the sequence of the events. The level of difficulty of this assignment can be varied by adjusting the length of the story.

Another activity is to prepare a topsy-turvy story with the sentences in scrambled order. After reading the story aloud, have the students rearrange the events so that they make sense. Here is an example:

- We unpacked all of our groceries.
- We were lucky to find a parking place at the grocery store.
- We checked the cupboard for peanut butter before we made the shopping list.
- The checker was very courteous and helped take the bags out to the car.

Headlines Summarize

Help students improve their listening skills by using articles from the newspaper. Students must listen carefully while you read a short article in order to write a suitable headline. They will observe that the headline is a summarizer; it contains the main idea in the article. The articles that you select can come from different parts of the paper: sports pages, local news, national/international news, or travel.

A series of several articles can be recorded on tape so that students can work with this exercise independently at a Listening Center. Provide the headlines mounted on a separate sheet of paper so students can compare their versions.

The reverse of this can also be effective. Read students a headline and have them tell you what they think the story is about. They can then check their ideas against the story in the newspaper.

Questions

To encourage listening comprehension, read or tape a short article and then ask five questions pertaining to it. After the students have had a chance to answer these five questions, reread the article so that they can make their own corrections. Make sure that you vary the types of questions.

> *Story: Three Little Pigs*
> *Literal Question:* What were the three houses made of? (The answer can be remembered from the text.)
> *Inferential Question:* Why do you think they made their houses of different materials? (The answer cannot be found in the text and more than one answer is correct.)

Listening for Ideas

Because students enjoy listening to stories, you can encourage active listening by reading a story to them and then asking questions about it. Before you read a story, tell the students that they will have to perform a specific task related to it, such as:

- Write a summary of the story.
- Act out the story.
- Draw a picture of the most important event.
- Tell why the events happened.

Critical Listening

By listening attentively, students can learn to distinguish between fact and opinion.

Students who watch television are already aware that words can be used to manipulate people. Talk about the power of words and how choice of words affects attitudes and emotions. Students can supply examples from their own experience. Introduce the word *propaganda* and explain what it means. Have students bring examples of propaganda from different sources to class and discuss them.

How do writers use words to influence people? Point out examples of slanted reporting, glittering generalities, name calling, and loaded words. A common technique makes use of what is called the "halo" effect. The name of a person who is famous or valued for one thing is used to support or endorse another idea or product. When you have developed a list of the different kinds of propaganda, play a tape of a commercial and have students identify examples of each type.

Have students collect commercials on tape. A small group can listen to such tapes as they analyze the content. Some questions to address might be: What is the commercial selling? How does it try to "sell" the customer? Is a televised commercial as effective without the visual component?

I'm Going to . . .

Play the game I'm Going to Australia with students of any age to increase their listening and remembering capacities. One student starts off with "I'm going to Australia and I'm going to take my comb." The next student will say, "I'm going to Australia and I'm going to take my comb and a jumprope." The third student must remember what has been said before and add on another object for the trip. Students will probably need help remembering all the different objects that accumulate and the sequence in which they occur, but the game will stimulate them to listen closely and with enjoyment.

An easy modification is to have the objects in ABC order. For example, "I'm going to Australia and I'm taking an apple." The second student adds a banana to the apple, and so on.

Off to Timbuktu!

"I'm off to Timbuktu, and I'm going to take along a tiger. What will you take?"

In this variation on the previous game, students take turns adding something that starts with *T*. The game can be changed by selecting a new location—for example: Zanzibar, Paris, London, or Borneo. If a student chooses a location with two names the game becomes more difficult. "I'm off to South America" will require students to use an adjective with *S* before a noun beginning with *A,* such as these examples:

small apple
slight ant
sharp asp
sunny ape
smelly artichoke

Animal Games

Other listening games include "I'm thinking of an animal." The student describes the chosen animal, feature by feature, until someone guesses the correct name.

Students can also play variations on this game in pairs. One person draws the name of a historical or book character and describes that person until his or her partner guesses correctly.

Selecting Relevant Information

Students need practice in following directions and in sorting out the important information from all that they hear. Provide examples of directions that include unnecessary or irrelevant details. Tell the students to listen closely and write down the number of the irrelevant sentence, as in this example:

How to Study for a Test
1. Have the text or workbook.
2. Get out paper and pencil.
3. Sit down.
4. Find a quiet, well-lit spot.
5. Eat an apple.

Discuss why students selected certain directions as irrelevant. A variation is to have students prepare directions and do this exercise with a partner.

Communication Is an Art

To show that verbal communication is in some ways rather difficult, try this exercise. Ask for one volunteer to be "the sender." The rest of the students will be "receivers." Place a very simple drawing in front of the sender (similar to the one shown). He or she is to give directions to the receivers so that they may reproduce the drawing that the sender has. When he or she has finished giving the instructions, the sender can hold up the drawing or project it on the wall with an opaque projector, and students can see how accurate they were in reproducing the drawing. After completing this exercise it would be very valuable to have a discussion as to the characteristics of a good sender and a good receiver.

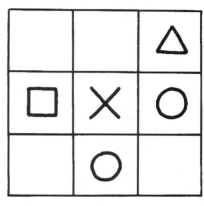

This exercise can also be done in pairs. Students may work independently to practice giving and receiving directions.

Giving and Following Directions

One concrete and practical way that people listen and speak is in giving and following directions. Give students practice in following directions for very simple paper folding. The Japanese art form of origami is an excellent technique because the students, by following directions closely, can make objects and animals that are pleasing to create. When these are completed, they make excellent room decorations hung from the ceiling as mobiles. Let students try giving directions to each other in pairs for other paper-folding activities.

Another way of sharpening a student's skill in listening is to make multiple copies of a map, or portions of a map, and have the students follow the directions on this map as they are given orally. Children can practice giving directions to their homes or to a particular building in the community: the post office, bank, or library. This activity can be carried out in the students' neighborhoods as they try to follow directions.

Remembering Directions

Give students a series of directions, maybe five in number. They are not to begin following the instructions until you have finished giving all five directions. For example, you might say, "Stand on one foot. Clap your hands. Raise your arms. Shake your head. Sit down."

Direction Game

An interesting variation on the communication activity is to give each student a square piece of paper. As you give directions, students are to respond by drawing on their paper.

For example, "Draw a line from the top left corner to the bottom right corner." Make a key on a large piece of white paper as you go along. When you have given three or four directions, students can then compare their papers with the answer key.

For more independent learners, students can work in pairs. One student acts as the teacher and prepares a list of directions and makes up a key. The other student listens carefully to the directions the first student gives and draws them on a piece of paper. The "teacher" then compares the answer key with the "student's" piece of paper. Student pairs then reverse roles.

Examples of directions might include: "Draw a line from the top to the bottom of the paper." "Put a tiny circle in the top right hand corner." "Draw a rectangle in the middle of the paper."

How Well Do You Listen?

Tell students that they are to write the numbers 1 through 10 on a sheet of paper. Next, read them 10 words associated with a topic you are studying, asking the students not to write down any word until the 10 words are completed. Then the students write as many words as they can remember. After the activity is finished, discuss how well they were able to carry out this assignment and what approaches they used to help them remember the words.

A modification of this exercise is to give only 5 words the first time, then increase it to 7, and finally to 10 words. With more mature students, it might be possible to enlarge the list even more. Since we are stressing the skill of listening in this activity, it is not imperative that students spell all the words correctly. Students find the task of remembering these words sufficiently challenging.

Discuss ways for students to remember what they have heard. If a tally was done of everyone's papers, most would remember the first, second, and the last words on the list. The closer the words are to the middle of the list, the harder they are to remember. Prepare a class graph showing the results of trying to list 10 words after hearing them once. Now read just 5 words and have students try to list them. Then read 5 more words and have students write them. Finally, graph the results. Point out that short lists are easier to remember. This can be applied to studying any type of list: spelling, math facts, and directions, for example.

Have the class try studying the spelling list by dividing it into smaller lists.

Taking Notes

Students learn to listen productively when they have to take notes on content. Have the students listen to a tape of you reading a short passage from a textbook. As they listen, have them take notes on the passage. Collect what they have written and copy excerpts from a few examples. Share these with the class and discuss why some material was included and other information was not. How did students' notes differ? How did they decide what to include? What was included that was most helpful in reconstructing the original material? What was not helpful?

Using a Visual Organizer

Help students learn active listening comprehension skills by providing them with a graphic organizer on which to record their notes as you talk. They must listen carefully to fill in the main idea boxes, which are connected by lines that represent cause and effect or chronological sequence. Have students check their work in small groups by comparing their charts.

In this exercise, students who are unable to sort through a quantity of verbal information are guided to attend to the most important facts and the supporting detail.

Talking Partners

After you have presented information to the class, ask students to work in pairs to discuss the material. Each partner has to explain what he or she thinks about the ideas and then the other person must summarize what that person said. Students will have to listen to others' ideas and understand them as well as their own in order to be effective talk partners.

Listening Teams

Have students work together to take notes on a lengthy oral presentation. Divide students into four teams and give each team the following assignment:

Team	Role	Assignment—After the Presentation
1	Questioning	Ask at least two questions about the material.
2	Agreeing	Describe at least two points that they agreed with (or found helpful) and tell why.
3	Disagreeing	Comment on at least two areas that they disagreed with (or found less helpful) and explain why.
4	Applying	Give at least two specific examples or applications of the material covered.

Allow enough time after the presentation for each group to develop its ideas. You can call on students in any order, to integrate questioning, agreeing, disagreeing, and applying. You could also create other roles for the teams. For example, one team might be responsible for creating a summary.

Techniques for Practicing Oral Patterns

Oral pattern practice helps students focus on particular sentence structures. These techniques can be used on an individual basis or in small groups with children. Each example can also be modified to suit the ability level or English language development of the student.

Repetition: Listen and repeat exactly as heard:

Teacher: Here is a book.
Student: Here is a book.

Analogy: Repeat exactly with one change:

> *Teacher:* The flowers are beautiful today.
> *Alon:* The trees are beautiful today.
> *Jie:* The bushes are beautiful today.
> *Mai:* The grass is beautiful today.

Inflection: Change the form of a word:

> *Teacher:* A bird is in the nest.
> *Alon:* The birds are in their nests.
> *Teacher:* This class is going to play baseball.
> *Jie:* These classes are going to play baseball.

Completion: Finish the statement:

> *Teacher:* Aparna will do exercises so that . . .
> *Mai:* . . . he will become stronger.
> *Teacher:* Carlos is hungry, but . . .
> *Alon:* . . . Nelson is hungrier.

Expansion: Expand the sentence:

> *Teacher:* Lanwei is sleepy.
> *Jie:* Lanwei is sleepy because he stayed up late last night.
> *Teacher:* Abby is sad.
> *Mai:* Abby is sad because her puppy is sick.

Transformation: Change the sentence to either a negative form or to a question form:

> *Teacher:* Pang would like some ice cream.
> *Alon:* Pang would not like some ice cream.
> *Jie:* Would Pang like some ice cream?

Restoration: Make a sentence out of these words:

> *Teacher:* broom, dirt, outside
> *Mai:* Let's use this broom to sweep the dirt outside.
> *Alon:* Is there a broom outside to sweep this dirt?

Response: Make a comment or response to the statement:

> *Teacher:* That dress is pretty.
> *Jie:* Yes; it looks nice.
> *Alon:* Don't you think that the colors go together well?
> *Mai:* The dress looks comfortable, too.

Once you have introduced students to these techniques, you can use them frequently when you have short intervals between other activities. You can also choose a student to be the teacher and direct the others in their responses. ESL students will especially benefit from oral practice with these structures.

People Who Talk

Using magazines and other sources, collect pictures of people talking. Mount these on the bulletin board for students to discuss. What might these people be talking about? What do you imagine this person does? Why might talking and listening be important to someone in this position? How would he or she talk?

Invited Guests

Invite people whose work involves talking and listening to speak to your class. Ask the guests how they use these skills in their lives. What do they talk about? What kinds of talking do they do or for what purpose? How is listening important in their work? Some examples of people you might ask include the following:

museum docent	librarian
another teacher	sign language interpreter
writer	physical therapist

Encouraging Discussion

As students use talk to learn about themselves and the world, they sometimes are better at telling their stories than listening to others talk. Oral language instruction will include the negotiation of ground rules for talk. Whether it is "share and pair" or group work on the computer, talk with students beforehand about what you expect from a discussion. You might ask: How can we make sure that everyone's ideas are heard? How do we show respect for alternative ideas? Students can develop guidelines for discussion that they put into their own words and display as a poster so that everyone can refer to the agreed-upon rules.

Listening Circle

Many teachers use Circle Time or Sharing Time as an activity more accurately described as "Lie and Brag." However, this activity can provide an excellent opportunity for students to practice important speaking and listening skills. Adding some structure to Circle Time will enable you to use this time more effectively. Students can take turns responding to short questions such as: What do you do for fun on rainy days? How do you make new friends?

Only one person can talk at a time. Encourage everyone to contribute something unless they want to pass. Students can also suggest possible questions for Circle Time.

Other suggestions for improving and enlivening sharing time include:

- Students exchange news in small groups or pairs.
- Students share news, then break into new groups to tell others what they have learned (jigsaw learning).

- The teacher provides feedback on specific points by drawing generalizations or highlighting a particular item.
- Students share their favorite books.
- Change the seating arrangements.
- One student acts as a reporter to ask questions after each presentation.

A pretend microphone will make playing the role easier. Model this role first yourself to show students how to ask appropriate questions.

Active Listening

This exercise promotes listening comprehension skills. Students work in pairs. Each student takes a turn at being a "speaker" while the other is a "listener." The speaker tells the other person a true story about something that is important to him or her. Here are some examples:

- The most interesting thing I have ever done is . . .
- The craziest thing I ever did was . . .
- What I really think is important is . . .
- I laughed really hard when . . .
- My favorite place to . . . is . . .

The listener's role is to listen attentively and not interrupt, except to ask questions and encourage the speaker. After the speaker has finished, the listener repeats the story as accurately as possible. The first person corrects and adjusts the story as it goes along, to make sure that the listener really understands the speaker's story. Afterwards, students switch roles.

Are You More Like the Mountains or the Ocean?

This exercise is designed to foster students' thinking about who they are and what matters most to them. Present your students with a list of paired items, some of which may be opposites. After discussing the list with the class to see that everyone knows what the words mean, ask students to circle the word in each pair that they think most describes who they are and what they are like. Remind them that some of these words will seem very strange applied to people but that they are supposed to stretch their imaginations and figure out which one most suits them. Here are some examples of possible questions:

Are you . . .
- more like thunder or lightning?
- more like the sun or the moon?
- more like cotton or wool?
- more like a butterfly or a caterpillar?
- more like a fish or a bird?

- more like red or blue?
- more like dawn or sunset?
- more like breakfast or dinner?
- more like the mountains or the ocean?
- more like fall or spring?

After students have made their selections, begin a class discussion. Ask students to tell the class what they thought were some of the differences between the paired items and why they chose the one they did. Encourage students to appreciate choices different from their own and to be interested in learning why people might have made different choices.

If some students don't want to answer certain items, they can discuss instead what types of differences they see between the items in a pair and how they feel about them. The items in each pair can be varied for any grade level. You might include favorite characters from a book.

After the class members have discussed the exercise and each student has had a chance to talk about choices made, have the students write an unsigned list of the items they circled. Have several students make a graph of the results. Post this graph on the bulletin board or give each student a copy of it.

The Speaker Commands Attention

Students select an object to represent the "speaker." While one person is holding this object, no one else may talk. The object can be passed around a circle so that students have the chance to talk in sequence, or it can be handed over to another student on request. Suitable objects for this purpose include:

beanbag
large pen or pencil
walking stick

Choosing the object to be used for a period can be a privilege given to a student.

Challenge: What Is It?

Bring in an unusual item to show to the students—something they may never have seen before, such as a carpet beater. Ask them to suggest what it might be used for. The object is not to guess the actual use but to stimulate creative talk and discussion.

Quotes and Quips

Each day write a provocative quotation on the board or on a chart so that the class can see this quotation all day. At the conclusion of the day, discuss the students' impressions of this quotation. What does it mean to them? How does it apply to their lives? What can they learn from this quotation?

At the end of the week see which quotations children remember. Encourage students to contribute quotations to be displayed. Examples that you might use include:

> *Common sense is not so common.*   —Voltaire
> *Everything has its own beauty, but not everyone sees it.*   —Confucius
> *Life is either a daring adventure or nothing.*   —Helen Keller
> *No bird soars too high if he soars with his own wings.*   —William Blake
> *I know why the caged bird sings.*   —Paul Laurence Dunbar

Brainstorming

The activity of brainstorming an idea, approach, or solution to a problem or a question is an excellent stimulus for oral language. The ground rules for brainstorming are very simple:

1. Begin with a problem or question that is as explicit as possible.
2. The emphasis is on generating as many ideas as possible; all ideas are accepted.
3. No criticism of any idea is allowed.
4. Individuals may hitchhike on someone else's idea.

Since evaluation is played down, the creative part of the brain has the opportunity to function. Students do not need to be afraid of taking risks, for there may not be any "correct" answer. In general, individuals at any age enjoy the freedom of this activity, and, after a warm-up period, it is possible to generate a number of ideas in a short time. These ideas can be looked at later with a critical eye and put in order of importance.

Some of the more thought-provoking topics, ideas, or problems that we have found include the following:

- Ask the students to think of as many different kinds of animals as they can in a period of five minutes. You can write these down or, if possible, upper-grade students can be brought in and used as scribes.
- Ask the class to think of as many different titles for stories as possible. This is a practical idea, since these titles can be used for many different activities, writing exercises, or impromptu speaking.
- Take a common object, such as a newspaper, and see how many different uses the class can find for it. You might bring the newspaper to class to help the students in their problem solving of this question.
- Brainstorm solutions to class problems, such as excessive noise during free time or arguments about sports.
- Discuss possible solutions to issues studied in social studies, such as pollution or overpopulation. After several large-group practice sessions, the class can be broken into smaller groups, which allow each individual more speaking time. Each group can select the most promising solution to present to the rest of the class.

When brainstorming, offer students a choice of materials on which to record their ideas, such as thick felt pens on large sheets of paper, small notebooks, or directly on an overhead transparency.

True Experiences

Give students a chance to retell one of their experiences: an athletic event, a trip, a visit, or any interesting adventure. Begin this activity by brainstorming possible topics with the class. These topics can be recorded on a poster or kept in a notebook.

- *Exciting experiences*
  First plane ride
  Vacations
- *Scary experiences*
  First Halloween
  Recital
- *Happy experiences*
  Birthday party
  New baby
- *Sad experiences*
  Moving
  Losing a pet

Students can include visual aids related to their experience—graphics, games, maps, pictures, objects—that would help in the explanation. You might also set a time limit for these talks.

Open Forum

Have students create a book of ideas for discussion or subjects for presentations they are to make. Make one page for each topic. This same book can be employed to suggest ideas for writing. Students can also use a box in which they place notes with ideas and concerns for further discussion.

On the Ball

Give a student a ball to hold while he or she tells a big whopper, tall tale, or story. This provides oral practice, and the fact that the students have an object to hold in their hands helps them focus. After the storyteller has finished the whopper, he or she picks someone else in the group to receive the ball, and that person tells another story.

A simple modification of this idea is a continuous story. The first student begins a tall tale, passes the ball, and the next person continues. Students will have to listen carefully to each contribution in order to be ready when their turn comes.

Table Topics

One way to structure opportunities where talking takes place is to break the class into small groups. Groups should contain no more than five students so that each individual has an opportunity to speak. Possible topics might include:

- The best pet for a small space
- Ways to conserve energy in our school
- New games for physical education
- A fair method for assigning classroom jobs

Write possible topics on slips of paper. Put them in a box and allow students to select the topic about which to talk.

After each group has had a talking time, a checklist should be used to determine whether everybody had an opportunity to talk. The class could then develop guidelines for talk etiquette.

Provocative Statements

The following topics can be used for debate, roundtable discussion, or talks to convince. Your students may want to suggest other topics as well. Display each topic as a poster in a special section of the bulletin board.

- Children should wear school uniforms.
- Some animals are as intelligent as people.
- Violence on television causes crime.
- The English spelling system should be revised.
- Young people our age should show more respect for their parents and other adults.
- Driver's licenses should be issued to people when they are 14 years old.
- No one should listen to a Walkman while riding a bike.
- Every child should have a computer.
- Students would learn more if they went to school on Saturdays.

These topics can also be used with older students to stimulate persuasive writing.

Puppets for Language Development

Many students who are shy about talking in class will open up when they can talk through hand puppets that look like different kinds of people or animals. Divide the students into small groups to work with the puppets, and give some short assignments to get them started.

The first step is for each student to introduce his or her puppet to the others. The puppets can ask each other's names and ask questions about the other puppets. All the puppets in the group can have a conversation together.

Students can also use puppets to act out events, such as the most important thing that ever happened to them, or portray favorite activities.

The group members can work together to create a play for their puppets. (Suggest topics if necessary.) After they have decided what they want to do, the students can present the puppet play to the class. If the children in a group are interested, ask them to write their play so that others can read it, and so they can present it again.

Students can also create a puppet theater to use with more elaborate productions. Using a large box, cut out an opening in one side, high enough to allow students to crouch below the "stage." Students will enjoy embellishing their very own theater.

Stick Puppets

The stick puppet is versatile and can be created easily by primary grade children. Popsicle sticks or tongue depressors form the base of the puppet. Children can cut out heads of people or animals or they may wish to create their own fully drawn figures to glue on the sticks.

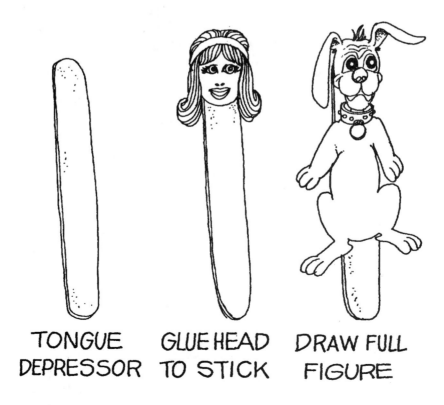

TONGUE
DEPRESSOR

GLUE HEAD
TO STICK

DRAW FULL
FIGURE

Finger Puppets

Finger puppets are also easy to make, and they can be enjoyed by the youngest of students. They can be made in various ways, as shown.

1.

BAND FOR
FINGER

ANIMAL HEAD
STAPLED TO BAND

2.

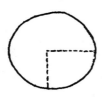  

A Simple Hand Puppet Pattern

Give students a piece of paper 8½ × 11 inches. Have them outline their hands from the tip to the wrist and add three inches to cover the arm.

The pattern is cut on the folded paper, as shown. When opened, of course, the full puppet shape looks like this:

Children may also cut two pieces of cloth using this pattern. They can sew these pieces together to gain experience in using needles and thread. Hair, ears, button noses, and other features can be added to create a character for the puppet.

Paper Bag Puppets

Puppets can be constructed quickly and easily by using readily available paper bags.

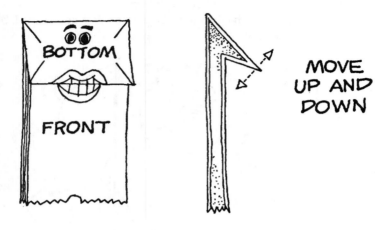

Stories for Discussion

Picturebooks make excellent read-alouds to use with all students because you can present the book to the class quickly and still have enough time for a lively discussion. Even upper-grade students will be captivated by the topics raised in these books. The following picturebooks are good examples of this genre:

> Eve Bunting. *Smoky Night*. Illustrated by David Diaz. Harcourt Brace, 1994. There's a riot in the streets where the narrator lives.
> Mem Fox. *The Straight Line Wonder*. Illustrated by Marc Rosenthal. Mondo, 1997. One line decides to become something other than a straight line.
> Margy Burns Knight. *Talking Walls*. Illustrated by Anne Sibley O'Brien. Tilbury House, 1992. Presents nonfiction stories behind different kinds of walls throughout the world.
> Virginia Kroll. *Masai and I*. Illustrated by Nancy Carpenter. Four Winds, 1992. A girl compares her city life to that of the Masai in Africa.
> Patricia Polacco. *Mrs. Katz and Tush*. Dell, 1994. Story of a friendship between an old Jewish woman and a young black boy.
> Peggy Rathmann. *Ruby the Copycat*. Scholastic, 1991. The new student dresses and acts just like the other students.
> Allen Say. *Allison*. Houghton Mifflin, 1997. Allison is adopted; she doesn't look like her Caucasian parents.
> Judith Viorst. *The Tenth Good Thing about Barney*. Illustrated by Erik Blegvad. Aladdin, 1975. A boy's cat dies.

Impromptu Speeches

The ability to give an impromptu speech is a very important skill to develop. To stimulate this type of talk, have a number of 3" × 5" index cards with a "What If" idea on each—for example, "What if a magician made you two inches tall?" The students select one of the cards, have a few minutes to study the "What If" they have selected, and then deliver a two- or three-minute impromptu talk. Have a timer ready to help students keep track of how many minutes are left. The following are additional examples of "What Ifs" to use in your file:

What if . . .
- you suddenly became 20 years older?
- there was no summertime?
- you could swim like a fish?
- you lived inside a cave?
- everything you touched turned to gold/jello/an animal/a rock/another "you"?
- you were the only person left on Earth?
- animals could talk?

- people could fly?
- you learned by taking pills?
- you could read minds?
- you didn't need food?

Rewriting Proverbs

Students can collect a variety of proverbs (or short sayings) by asking people at home and in the neighborhood to contribute examples. Select a few to write on the board. Ask students what these proverbs mean. Even if the phrases are familiar to students, there may be disagreement about the meaning or how to apply them. Through discussion and sharing ideas, they will develop a clearer idea of the significance of these phrases. Here are a few examples:

> A stitch in time saves nine. (European)
>
> An ant on the move does more than a dozing ox. (Mexican)
>
> One head does not constitute a council. (Asante)

Students can also rewrite familiar proverbs or come up with new endings for sayings. Give them some proverbs to rewrite:

> All work and no play makes Jack a dull boy.
>
> All work and no play _____.
>
> A bird in the hand is worth two in the bush.
>
> A bird in the hand _____.

Classification Game

Assign each group of students a category—such as Animals, Food, or Music—and have them write five examples of the category on separate pieces of paper. How might they organize or classify their examples? Now ask the groups to exchange papers with one another. Will the new group sort the examples in the same way? Can the group guess what the original category was that the first group received?

This activity promotes a different kind of talk as students problem solve and draw inferences from the examples they have.

Imagine an Animal

Invite students to develop an imaginary animal. In small groups, they can determine the animal's kind of body, senses, locomotion, feeding, size, and so on. Then the class can discuss how this animal would live. What would it need to have if it lived in the forest? In the air? In the ocean? Discussion questions such as these develop students' abilities to explore, clarify, hypothesize, predict, and develop ideas through talking and listening to each other.

Nonfiction Reading

Make sure that you take time to read nonfiction literature aloud to students. Because so many of the books that are read in class are stories, students may be less familiar with the conventions of different nonfiction genres, such as biography, science, and how-to books. The following are examples of nonfiction picturebooks that you can share with students at any grade level:

> Joanna Cole. *The Magic School Bus Inside the Earth.* Illustrated by Bruce Degen. Scholastic, 1987. Part of a series, this is a fantasy mixed with accurate scientific information and terminology. Also look for Cole's *On the Bus with Joanna Cole: A Creative Autobiography* (Heinemann, 1996).
>
> William Miller. *Richard Wright and the Library Card.* Illustrated by Gregory Christie. Lee & Low, 1997. Presents an episode from the early life of African American author Richard Wright, showing the racist obstacles he had to overcome.
>
> Diane Swanson. *Safari beneath the Sea: The Wonder World of the North Pacific Coast.* Sierra Club Books, 1994. Photographs and text provide information about the natural world.

What You Say

As students talk about their ideas and discuss issues, take the opportunity to record examples of their talk. Students will be interested to hear what they sound like or how others hear them. You can use these examples to motivate discussion of the importance of good speaking skills. What can students do to improve the clarity or effectiveness of their speech? Are there different ways of talking that are appropriate for different situations or audiences?

The Interview

The interview is an excellent activity to use early in the year to help the class become better acquainted. Allow the students to compile a list of 10 questions they would like to ask one another. Divide the class so that half of the students are interviewers and the other half are interviewees. After the interview is completed, students then switch roles. This gives each student a chance to interview and to be interviewed. For variety, allow the interviewer to add a few questions in addition to the class list.

This activity can be done in front of the whole class, at least at first. Have one student interview another before the class, and then switch the roles. This has the benefit of providing a model for everyone to watch the interview being carried out. You can also videotape the interviews in order to discuss them later.

With the whole-class approach, you might have only one student a day be interviewed. One rule that should be stressed is that a student always has the right to *pass* on any question. Students enjoy this activity, both asking the questions and—even though they sometimes act a little shy about it—answering the questions.

Some sample questions are:

- What is your favorite food?
- If you could have any pet, what would you choose? Why?
- What is your favorite kind of music?
- What do you do on the weekend?
- What chores are you expected to do at home?
- What do you do best?
- What would you like to do better?
- What would you like to be doing 10 years from now?
- If you were in charge of the world for a day, what would you change?

Interview Exchange

Older students can practice oral language skills by interviewing primary grade students. You can match sixth-graders with first-graders, for example. The sixth-grade class generates a list of 10 questions that they will ask. Pair each sixth-grader with a child in the first grade. Have the older children ask questions and take notes. Then each sixth-grader can prepare a simple book that tells the story of his or her interviewee's life and interests. These books make excellent gifts for the first-graders as thanks for their cooperation.

Object-ive Stories

Have children bring in all sorts of small, strange objects, and bring in some yourself. Pile them in one central area: a table, corner, or closet. When you have a short interval between activities or when students finish early, cover a student's eyes with a piece of cloth and instruct him or her to pick three objects out of the pile and guess aloud what they are. When the child has completed this exercise, he or she can tell a story that includes all the objects that were selected. Then the next child can proceed.

If the whole group is participating, each child should be blindfolded (or just have eyes closed) as he or she chooses one object out of the pile. Once each child has tried to guess what it is, he or she can take the blindfold off and share individual objects with classmates. One child can begin a story that includes his or her article and the story can be continued, round-robin fashion, with each child adding to the previous story and including the new-found object. Sample objects include:

long glove	seeds
well-chewed pencil	old-fashioned hat
horseshoe	braille book
petrified wood	shells
cookie cutter	box of buttons

Making Oral Presentations

Sharing ideas with the rest of the class is a crucial link in oral language instruction. As Gardner (1993) argues, many kinds of intelligence are being neglected in the classroom, as many teachers focus primarily on standard assessments. Instead, we need to plan for alternatives such as student performances or demonstrations of what they have learned. Storytelling is one of the simplest and oldest techniques for sharing experiences with each other. Through storytelling and other types of performance, students will communicate with others, be motivated to look closely at language, have a real purpose for developing speaking and listening skills, and develop a forum for raising issues and concerns.

Group Picture Stories

Collect magazines for pictures, getting contributions from the students, libraries, and others. Give the magazines to the students and ask them each to cut out one picture that especially appeals to them. The students can then work in small groups to create a story out of the pictures they have, using each one's picture. Have each child tape-record the story and play it for the class while holding up the pictures that illustrate the story.

Add-a-Line Stories

Telling a story provides both listening practice and oral language development. You or a student start a story by telling the title or a first line, such as, "I was on my way to . . . ." The next student adds a line or two to the story and passes it along by calling on someone else.

Primary students can read their own work if you print out the story or put it on a transparency so that the whole class can have a copy of the story they created together.

An interesting variation is to have several tales going at once in small groups. This allows greater participation and requires better listening skills.

Talk Boxes

Provide stimuli for students as they compose a story to tell to the class. Using four shoe boxes, mark each with a different label: Setting, Character, Character Trait, and Problem. In each of these boxes put suggestions written on slips of different colors, thus:

- *red:* setting
- *blue:* character
- *green:* character trait
- *orange:* problem

The student selects one slip from each of these four boxes and develops a one-minute story that she or he can relate to a small group or the whole class. (The colors of the slips make returning them to the right box easier.)

Students may choose slips presenting situations such as the following:

- *red:* small sailboat
- *blue:* magician
- *green:* stubborn
- *orange:* everything begins to shrink

- *red:* the bottom of the ocean
- *blue:* blind person and seeing eye dog
- *green:* courageous
- *orange:* all machines stop working

This type of oral activity gives students a chance to use language creatively. The structure helps by giving them some idea of where to start.

Improvisations

Improvisation provides students with experience in making up stories spontaneously. The students may choose from any of the following lists of words to make up an impromptu story in front of the class or on tape. These scrambled lists may be prepared on sheets of paper, or the words can be listed on cards to be placed in a Story Treasure Chest:

- rubber chicken, orange juice, seven, chair, jumping frog
- comet, ice cubes, prism, sinking, yellow
- eight gloves, blue face, airplane, beef stew
- moose, islands, lemon, green bag, fishing pole
- jump rope, jigsaw puzzle, chocolate cake, sack of pennies, pony
- circus tent, liars, tuba, 21 balloons, explosion
- chairs, 9 kazoos, blind, machete, fire, heavy
- three-footed, binders, Saint Patrick, fierce, telephone booth
- square, fleece, scrambled eggs, firefighter, friendly

Key Words for Stories

Write words or groups of words on 4" × 6" cards (you might select vocabulary from the current unit of study). Place the cards in a box, and ask each student to choose a card. Give each child a few minutes to look the card over, and then for three minutes (an egg timer is very handy here), the child can tell the class a story using these words. The student has the card to hold on to, which gives some security.

Here are examples of word groups that could be put on cards:

anteater	flute	letter	rainbow	book
volcano	child	tunnel	cape	shadow

| banana | danger | jar | chair | moth |
| rope | chocolate | frog | magic | laughter |

Students can also prepare cards to be used by others, possibly as a way to review vocabulary.

Small-Group Compositions

Students can compose more complex and exciting stories if you give them a little help. Show them, for example, that the essential parts of a story tell *who, what, where, when,* and *why.* Divide the class into small groups of five people each. Give each person in a group a card with the key *W*-word for which he or she is responsible. The person with the *who* card supplies the character, and the person with the *what* card describes the action. The setting, time, and motive are provided by children who hold *where, when,* and *why.*

After each small group composes its short story, the stories can be shared aloud. Usually they turn out to be very funny, so the composition experience is highly enjoyable. Repeat the experience by exchanging cards so students have to supply a different part of the story each time. Each group will create five different stories in a very short time.

This oral activity can also be developed further because students will be interested in writing down their stories. Compile a *Big Book of Short Stories* to place in the Reading Center or in your school library. Everyone will enjoy reading these humorous class-composed tales.

Improving Oral Presentations

As students create tape recordings of their stories and other oral performances, you can use this material as a base for discussion of what makes for a good story or a good presentation. Have students suggest appealing elements in the stories that they listen to. Consider such factors as tone of voice, pacing, diction, vocabulary, and expression.

As students' skills improve, you can use the taped stories to provide extra practice for ESL students or less able readers. They can listen to the tapes and follow along with a printed version. This activity can be repeated as often as needed without taking time from the whole class.

Sound Collage

Not all students are equally adept at communicating their ideas through speech. Provide varied modes that students can choose from, such as drawing pictures or acting out stories. In the sound collage, students have the opportunity to create a story through the use of sound alone. They can record a sequence of sounds—such as a telephone ringing, water running from a faucet, and someone walking slowly and heavily—that together tell a story. The audience will have to listen carefully in order to make inferences about what the sounds mean.

Broadcasting

Many schools have a public address system, which is an excellent medium to give students an opportunity to practice and refine their oral language skills. One simple way to use the system is to have students make announcements to the school. Some schools extend this idea by also allowing students to present school news or other items of interest. Students could form a broadcasting group for various activities:

- Read poems.
- Read stories.
- Read a story starter for all students to complete individually or as a class.
- Invite other classes to special performances.

Oral Commercials

Have individuals or pairs of students select from a stack of magazines and newspapers an advertisement to rewrite or remake. They cut out this advertisement, decide how they are going to redo it, and present the new advertisement as an oral commercial to the class. Students can develop some very humorous commercials. This activity gives them a chance to talk and to play different roles before the class.

Students can also select commercials seen on television or heard on radio, and modify them as oral commercials. For a different focus, you might videotape the presentation to the class and then conduct a discussion of what makes a good commercial, what students enjoy about a commercial, and what persuasive devices are used in commercials.

Students will also enjoy creating commercials to "sell" favorite books. The success of the commercial can be judged by the number of students wanting to "buy" (read) the book.

Tape-a-Letter

Instead of writing letters to pen pals, students may send a tape from the class. Have all the students tape their letters and then play the tape for the class to hear. The class members can discuss in general what they like and dislike about hearing themselves on tape and make suggestions for future recordings. The class may have other ideas for tapes to send to their pen pals, such as a class discussion or reading parts of their favorite books. Choral speaking and singing also add to this method of sharing.

Words That Talk

Use creative dramatics to introduce different ways of talking. Ask the children to demonstrate how they would try to get a friend's attention without talking above a whisper. Have the class define the words *murmur, scold, shriek, chatter,* and *mumble.* Pairs of students can act out skits to suit each word.

Pantomiming Animals

In pantomime, students can act out any kind of object or feeling they want to express, without language. Although you may want to use pantomime in any number of different contexts, a special technique would be to use it in content areas—for instance, when students are studying animals. Have students think of animals they would like to be. Each student pantomimes one animal's behavior for the other students to guess what animal she or he is pretending to be. This requires more ingenuity with smaller animals or insects. However, students can usually manage to suggest enough of the essential nature of the animal for the others to guess.

The use of pantomime or other forms of creative drama in the class allows students to shine who may be less adept at oral language skills or prefer this kinesthetic approach.

Choric Speaking

Choric speaking is an excellent activity to develop both oral language and poetry appreciation as students learn poetry in a pleasurable way. Many poems are appropriate for choric speaking. For example, "Poor Old Woman" is a poem that has all the elements (rhyme, repetition, humor) to make speaking it an enjoyable experience. Look for an attractive picturebook edition such as Nadine Westcott's *I Know an Old Woman Who Swallowed a Fly*. Older students can write their own verses for this poem or place the story in a different setting.

Help!

Use Story Starters to stretch student imaginations for class storytelling. Collect a few examples of beginnings and let students choose one to develop and present to the class.

> One day I was walking along the beach when I saw something shiny in the sand. Looking closer, I discovered it was a bottle buried in the sand. When I dug it out, I could see there was something inside. I opened the bottle to find a message. It said . . .

Wordless Books

Wordless books are very useful in the primary grades for developing student experience with storytelling. In these books, illustrations suggest the story. Here are some good examples that you can use with older students as well:

Molly Bang. *The Grey Lady and the Strawberry Snatcher*. Aladdin, 1996.
Eric Carle. *The Very Hungry Caterpillar*. Writers and Readers Publishing, 2000.
Alexandra Day. *Good Dog Carl*. Simon & Schuster, 1998.
Mercer Mayer. *Frog, Where Are You?* Putnam, 1994.
Eric Rohmann. *Time Flies*. Crown, 1994.
David Wiesner. *Tuesday*. Houghton Mifflin, 1997.

Looking at Text Structures

Older students can benefit from using wordless books to look closely at the vocabulary required by different types of fiction and nonfiction. For example, what kinds of transition words would need to be supplied for a wordless book that showed the steps in how to do something? How would these transitions be different in a book that described cause and effect or a book that told a story chronologically? Here are some examples of wordless books you can use:

Mitsumasa Anno. *Anno's USA*. Philomel, 1983.
Judy Feldman. *Shapes in Nature*. Children's Books, 1991.
John Goodall. *The Story of a Castle*. McElderry, 1986.

Role Playing

Give students the chance to act out different roles in hypothetical situations and encourage them to respond immediately, with words and action. This type of oral expression is important in a number of ways:

1. It allows students the chance to try out different roles while still being themselves.
2. It gives them a way to take risks as they create in a spontaneous manner.
3. It provides them with the opportunity to express themselves through both language and movement.
4. It demonstrates how different language forms are appropriate in different contexts.

The following are examples of situations that might be used:

- Parent explaining how to use the telephone to small child
- One person teaching another how to fly a kite
- Officer asking child to use a bicycle helmet
- Student applying for job as pet sitter for six cats
- Child apologizing to neighbor for breaking the window

Coping with Problems

Role play activities that encourage problem-solving skills can be done with the whole class or a small group. You will need to allow time for discussion afterwards. Each student can be assigned a role to play. Possible problem situations are the following:

- Guha is riding his bike and runs a red light—a police officer sees him.
- Xiana comes home too late for supper and her family has already eaten.
- Nguyen is assigned to do the family shopping and when he gets to the checkout counter he finds he forgot his money.
- Lanwei brings home a report card with Cs and Ds.

Phone Conversation

This activity encourages accuracy in oral language and develops courtesy in the use of the telephone. The materials used include two telephones. It is sometimes possible to obtain phones from the local telephone company, but toy telephones can also be used.

Develop a series of cards that give examples of phone calls that can be made. For instance, one card might require a student to make a phone call to the veterinarian to ask about a shot for a pet dog. One student can fill in the details (the dog's name and what's wrong with it), and the other student can play the role of the vet. Another card might require a student to call a local radio station requesting a particular song, while another student is the disc jockey, answering the phone.

Here are some phone conversation situations to use as starters:

- Calling video store for a particular movie
     (student and video rental clerk)
- Calling repair shop to find out if your bicycle is ready
     (student and bicycle repair person)
- Arranging class field trip to museum
     (student and docent)
- Reporting escaped tiger
     (student and zookeeper)

After the conversation has finished, the other students should analyze the conversation. What would they have added? What were the good points? What might be improved? From this experience, the students could generate a list of guidelines for phone etiquette.

Rating the Oral Presentation

Help your students develop a class rubric (or evaluation measure) to rate their oral presentations, using language that is familiar to them. You might suggest that they consider some of the following points:

- *Content*　Does the presentation:
     include enough information?
     seem appropriate for the audience?
     meet the purpose?
- *Style*　Does the speaker:
     hold attention and interest of audience?
     speak clearly?
     look at the audience?
     vary rate of speech appropriately?

The Hot Seat

Students can also role play characters from a book or individuals from a historical period. Students choose a particular character to play and prepare to "become" that person. Provide a special chair in front of the class in which the student/character may sit. The other students can ask questions of the person in the Hot Seat, such as:

Why did you _____?
What were you thinking when _____?
What do you wish you had done differently?
What really happened when _____?

Story Dramatizations

Students of all languages and reading levels will enjoy preparing a story that they know to present to the class. They can begin with any simple story, from folktale to Mother Goose rhyme. This project is especially effective when used to introduce your students to the typical West European folktales, such as *Snow White*. Everyone will have to review the story in order to bring it to life. Students can take the roles of the different characters as well as the important objects in the environment, such as a tree or a table. As students gain facility with these dramatizations, they can create their own props or backdrops to add interest to the performance.

Students in the upper grades can select a folktale to dramatize, such as *Little Red Riding Hood* or *Cinderella,* then investigate and analyze the many different versions of the story, comparing plot, characters, motivation, and outcome. They will need to discuss these differences carefully in order to decide what to include in their own performance.

Storytelling

Storytelling is an absorbing activity for people of all ages and cultures. Tell simple stories directly to the class, presenting the tales in your own words, without the aid of a book. Students are captivated by this ancient medium. They can also learn to become storytellers themselves, perhaps sharing stories with an enthusiastic audience of younger students.

Invite a professional storyteller to the class to explain the techniques of storytelling. Play tape recordings of storytellers from around the country, representing many different regional and ethnic traditions.

Sources for Storytelling

Stories to tell can come from many different sources, not just folktales. You will find possibilities for you or the students in the following areas:

riddles	personal experience
ghost stories	superstitions
family lore	tall tales
local legends	fables

Time for Stories

Many traditional storytellers were the elders of their people and were listened to with respect. Show students that it is Storytelling Time and prepare them to pay careful attention by putting on a special hat or throwing a shawl around your shoulders that you use only for Storytelling. These extra props will also help students as storytellers slip into their roles more easily.

Storytelling Sites

Today's storytellers gather their audience around websites, where they encourage interaction between teller and listener. Digital storytelling often includes text and images as well as music, voice, and animation.

Here are some examples of storytelling sites on the Internet:

<www.fray.com>
<www.storycenter.org>
<www.bubbe.com>
<www.digiclub.org>

Older students may be interested in developing their own storytelling website.

Talking about Stories

Whether students tell stories with simple puppets or memorize a dramatic presentation, they are using oral language to learn with and learn from. As they talk to each other to solve problems, to make decisions, or to try out alternatives, they are using language to think out loud and to listen to the thinking of others. Make sure that students have time to practice this "untidy" talk (or "inner speech") by encouraging them to choose their own topics and to work together in small groups.

Discussion Questions

1. How might you explain to parents the value of talking about picturebooks with upper-grade students?

2. How will you respond to other teachers who say your classroom is too noisy and the students are not on task?

3. How can you support and assess students in their use of talking as a way of exploring what they know?

4. How can you *teach* students to listen, instead of just *telling* them "Listen!"

Exploring Further

Lisa Bany-Winters. *On Stage: Theater Games and Activities for Kids.* Chicago Review Press, 1997.

Mary A. Barr and Margaret A. Syverson. *Assessing Literacy with the Learning Record: A Handbook for Teachers, Grades K–6.* Heinemann, 1999.

Choices, Choices. Tom Snyder Productions. A CD-ROM simulation designed to be used with the whole class that raises issues such as on the playground, taking responsibility, and kids and the environment

Classroom Interviews: A World of Learning, by Paula Rogovin, explains how to incorporate interviews in the primary grades as a springboard to other learning. It is accompanied by a video, *Classroom Interviews in Action.* Available from Heinemann at (800) 793-2154 or <www.heinemann.com>.

Gisela Ernst and Kerri Richard. "Pathways to Conversations in the ESL Classroom." *The Reading Teacher, 48* (December 1994/January 1995).

Susan Hynds and Donald Rubin (Eds.). *Perspectives on Talk and Learning.* NCTE, 1990.

Mac/Windows, <www.teachtsp.com> or (800) 342-0236.

Martha Mutz. *Teaching the Folktale Plays.* Curiosity Canyon Press, 1996.

Viola Spolin. *Theater Games for the Classroom: A Teacher's Handbook.* Northwestern University Press, 1986.

John W. Stewig and Carol Buege. *Dramatizing Literature in Whole Language Classrooms.* Teachers College Press, 1994.

Louise Thistle. *Dramatizing Mother Goose: The Teacher's Guide to Playacting in the Classroom.* Smith & Kraus, 1997. (Teacher's edition available)

Louise Thistle. *Dramatizing Three Classic Tales.* Smith & Kraus, 1999.

Sources for unabridged children's literature on audiotape:

Listening Library Inc.	Recorded Books Inc	Spoken Arts
1 Park Ave.	270 Skipjack Rd.	801 94th Ave. North
Old Greenwich CT 06870-9978	Prince Frederick MD 20678	St. Petersburg FL 33702

References

Douglas Barnes, James Britton, and Harold Rosen. *Language, the Learner and the School.* Penguin, 1969.

Margaret Donaldson. *Children's Minds.* Norton, 1978.

Howard Gardner. *Multiple Intelligences.* Basic Books, 1993.

Elizabeth Grugeon, Lorraine Hubbard, Carol Smith, and Lyn Dawes. *Teaching Speaking and Listening in the Primary School: Literacy through Oracy.* David Fulton, 1998.

Luis Moll. "Bilingual Classroom Studies and Community Analysis: Some Recent Trends." *Educational Researcher, 21,* no. 2 (1992): 20–24.

Roland Tharp and Ronald Gallimore. *Rousing Minds to Life.* Cambridge University Press, 1988.

Gordon Wells. *The Meaning Makers: Children Learning Language and Using Language to Learn.* Heinemann, 1986.

James Wertsch. *Mind in Context: A Vygotskian Approach.* Paper presented at AERA, San Francisco, 1986.

James Wertsch. *Vygotsky and the Social Formation of Mind.* Harvard University Press, 1991.

3 Fostering Reading

This book is to be read in bed.
—Dr. Seuss, *Dr. Seuss's Sleep Book*

Before they enter school, children may already know a lot about literacy. They imitate adults, picking up a book and "reading" it from front to back, turning the pages as they retell the story. They may recognize a few letters of the alphabet, especially "their" letter (the first letter of their name), when they see the letter in new places. They may play word games and ask questions such as, "What's that word?" And they can often "read" (recognize) signs and labels that they see at home, on television, and in the street, from *STOP* to *Safeway, Post* cereals to *Pokemon*. These are all behaviors demonstrating that literacy is "emerging" (Sulzby & Teale, 1991). Such early experiences are highly motivating (despite the complex language knowledge that underlies them, such as the alphabetic principle, word segmentation, names of letters, and predicting what comes next) because children know that they are going to school in order to learn to read, and reading is the key that unlocks the adult world.

Because they can see that reading and writing are routes to making sense of their world and to communicating with others, some children even learn to read easily, on their own and before formal instruction (Bissex, 1980). Why, then, is "school-based" learning to read so difficult for so many students? Reading instruction must address the needs of students who may not have these early experiences with literacy or understand how they are expected to apply what they already know to the task of learning to read. Without appropriate instruction, many students fall behind in their ability to read, which often leads to later school failure (Chall et al., 1990). Recent bitter controversy over instruction methods (Thompson & Nicholson, 1999) obscures agreement that the prior knowledge about literacy that students bring to school has to be incorporated into instruction (Weaver, 1998). No matter which camp you identify with in the "reading wars," you need to offer a reading program that builds on students' experiences with literacy outside of school as well as enables them to extend their ability to apply this knowledge to real-world reading and writing tasks.

Two different perspectives on how to create an effective reading program are often contrasted. Advocates of *whole language* base their approach to reading on the way children acquire (oral) language, naturally and without adult teaching (Goodman & Goodman, 1979). A fundamental assumption is that children will understand how to read if teachers provide appropriate contexts in which understanding can unfold. This model is also referred to as "top down," because instruction develops out of the whole text ("top") aspect of reading. A different lens for looking at reading comes from *phonics,* or *phonological awareness.* In this approach, understanding language at the level of letters/sounds/ words is the focus (Adams, 1994). Reading instruction, therefore, is based on students' awareness of the building blocks of language (a "bottom-up" approach). Despite the differing angles of vision, no one disputes that learning to read requires that children be able to integrate the "top" of whole text with the "bottom" of letters and sounds smoothly and navigate with ease among the complexities of different kinds of reading material, purposes for reading, unfamiliar vocabulary, and letter-sound relationships (Ruddell et al., 1994; Snow et al., 1998).

Reading instruction needs to be embedded in a context that encourages all aspects of literacy, including social and psychological ones. As a result, you will be expected to read (fiction and nonfiction) to students in every grade, talk explicitly about reading and how we do it (strategies), provide practice in taking written language apart (analysis), and putting it back together (synthesis), and invite all students to participate in responding to print.

Joining the Literacy Club

We want students to associate reading with the pleasure of sharing books with others and becoming part of a community in which literacy is valued, instead of the boredom of workbook pages that are far removed from the goal of (eventually) reading a book. Using the extensive knowledge that they already possess about literacy and texts, students can begin to "read" from the first day of school, talking about favorite books, listening to tall tales, and retelling stories. Show students that there are treasures hidden away in books and invite them to join the "literacy club" (Smith, 1992). As students read, they are more motivated to learn the intricacies of letter-sound relationships, for example, because these skills are clearly tied to the pursuit of reading. Reading should make sense. You can help students learn how to attend to the patterns of language and connect the language they know with the marks printed on a page.

Reading Aloud

One of the most important methods of supporting student reading is to read aloud to children. Although reading aloud continues to be an essential way of engaging students with literature at all levels, it is particularly important in the early years, as we establish the importance of story as a way of learning. Furthermore, through listening, the children will begin to learn the same comprehension skills they will use as they read independently. As we encourage students to respond orally or through art activities, we are consciously guiding them to respond to the work of the author, to question, and to interpret the words and illustrations presented by skilled writers and artists. Books that you will enjoy sharing include old favorites that every child should know, such as the following:

Ludwig Bemelmans. *Madeline.*
Margaret Wise Brown. *Goodnight Moon.*
Robert McCloskey. *Make Way for Ducklings.*
H. A. Rey. *Curious George.*

Include rhymes and other poetry—for example:

Glen Hay. *There Was an Old Lady Who Swallowed a Fly.* G. T. Publishers, 1998.
Dennis Lee. *Dinosaur Dinner with a Slice of Alligator Pie.* Random House, 1997.
Jack Prelutsky, sel. *Imagine That: Poems of Never-Was.* Knopf, 1999.
Shel Silverstein. *Where the Sidewalk Ends.* HarperCollins, 2000.

Introducing Mother Goose

Keep an edition of *Mother Goose* nursery rhymes handy on your desk to pick up in odd moments and read a verse to the students, perhaps as a reward for being quiet or finishing their work. Some of the students may recognize these rhymes and want to chant along with you, while others will quickly learn the short, bouncy, rhyming verses from frequent repetition. Look for a version of *Mother Goose* that includes particularly attractive illustrations, as well as a good selection of your favorite rhymes, such as the following:

Sylvia Long. *Sylvia Long's Mother Goose.* Chronicle, 1999.
James Marshall. *James Marshall's Mother Goose.* Econo-clad, 1999.
Iona Opie, ed. *Here Comes Mother Goose.* Illustrated by Rosemary Wells. Candlewick, 1999.
Tomie de Paola. *Tomie de Paola's Mother Goose.* Putnam, 1985.

"Reading" Wordless Books

Students become familiar with the concept of *story* even before they can read the printed word. They can follow a skillful author's plot shown only through illustrations in a wordless book, which can be "read" before children know much about phoneme/grapheme relationships. They will still be learning story structures and acquiring comprehension skills by telling the stories to each other. Note that all children can "read" these books, no matter what language they speak:

Marilee Burton. *The Elephant's Nest: Four Wordless Stories.* Harper & Row, 1979.
Diane deGroat. *Alligator's Toothache.* Crown, 1977.
Mercer Mayer. *A Boy, a Dog, and a Frog.* Dial, 1992.
Jan Mogensen. *The 46 Little Men.* Greenwillow, 1991.
Helen Oxenbury. *Beach Day.* Dial, 1982.
April Wilson. *April Wilson's Magpie Magic.* Dial, 1999.

Reviewing Nursery Tales

Every child can benefit from learning about the nursery tales that many of us were brought up on. In today's diverse classrooms, however, we cannot assume that all children, whatever their age, come to school knowing such tales as "The Three Little Pigs." Thus, it is essential to include many examples of these stories in your choices for reading aloud and for acting out. You can easily locate versions of these tales:

"Goldilocks and the Three Bears"
"Sleeping Beauty"
"Three Billy Goats Gruff"

Fairy Tale Study

Cinderella is a popular fairy tale motif that appears in many versions throughout the world. Older students, especially ones who may not have read Cinderella, can share in the pleasure of these simple stories by comparing several versions of the traditional tale. In addition, they are gaining practice in reading a text closely and critically. The following are some questions that students can ask as they investigate the different versions:

What impression of Cinderella and her family do you get from the illustrations in each book?
Are any elements of the plot structure different in these books, such as how the Prince finds Cinderella?
How are the stepsisters described? Do the vocabulary choices of different authors have different effects on the reader?
Which version do you prefer and why?

Check your local library and look under Charles Perrault for examples of traditional Cinderella tales. You can also find editions by different editors and illustrators, such as:

Marcia Brown, trans. *Cinderella.* Aladdin, 1988.
Amy Ehrlich, retold. *Cinderella by Charles Perrault.* Illustrated by Susan Jeffers. Dial, 1985.
Charles Perrault. *Cinderella, Puss in Boots, and Other Favorite Tales as Told by Charles Perrault.* Abrams, 2000.

Cumulative Stories

Children develop oral skills and establish foundations for comprehension and the enjoyment of good literature by retelling and acting out familiar tales. Cumulative stories (stories that include repeated lines and build on previous details) are especially good choices for such activities. "The Gingerbread Boy" (also known as "Johnny Cake") is an excellent example of a tale to read aloud and then retell. Students will join in each time you reach the Gingerbread Boy's taunting refrain: "You can't catch me...." The children can then enumerate all the characters the Gingerbread Boy meets and what happens at the end. A recent edition to look for is Richard Egielski's *The Gingerbread Boy* (HarperCollins, 1997). Another readily available tale that follows the cumulative pattern is "Henny Penny" or "Chicken Licken," which includes such funny character names as Cocky-Locky and Foxy-Woxy.

A number of modern authors have also relied on the cumulative pattern, which you can present in the same way—for instance:

Lucía González. *The Bossy Gallito/El Gallo de Bodas.* Illus. Lulu Delacre. Scholastic, 1994.
Bill Martin, Jr. *Brown Bear, Brown Bear, What Do You See?* Holt, 1985.

Books Are by People

Talk about the authors and illustrators of the books students are reading so that they understand that these books were created by *real* people. Make a point of saying, "Here's another book by the same author" or "Let's see if we can find another book illustrated by this person." Model for students the association between book title and book author (or illustrator). You can find pictures of authors and illustrators to display, or share facts about their lives and work. The list of recent Newbery (writing) and Caldecott (illustration) winners in Chapter 10 is a good place to start. Bookstores and conferences provide opportunities to meet an author *in person.*

Beginning Work on Phonemic Awareness

From the moment students enter your room, they should be encouraged to interact with words in print. Even before formal reading instruction begins, they can observe words around the room that say: *Today is Monday, Reading Table, The Writing Center,* and so on. Read these words aloud periodically, pointing to the words as you say each one so that children will associate meaning with the groups of letters that you are casually introducing as "words." Display the printed alphabet, pictures with descriptive words (*cat, dog, horse,* etc.), or a color wheel with words attached to each color. Talk about each item with the students, such as "This is called an alphabet. It is a list of all the letters that we use when we write." Or, "Here is a picture of a cat. What do you think this word is?" (Children are learning what a word looks like. They are learning to use a picture to help them "read" the word.) You might follow up with: "The word *cat* is spelled *c-a-t.* These are three letters in the alphabet. Can you find one of these letters?"

Using Children's Names

Children are very much interested in learning to read (as well as write) their own names. Place a placard on the front of children's desks or the back of each child's chair.

Timothy	Nanette	Carlos

Use these names often in incidental activities. Recite to each child the letters used to spell his or her name. You might go through the alphabet, asking: Do we have any *A*s in this class? Any *B*s? (Bobby stands up.) Any *C*s? (Carlos points to the letter that begins his name.) Use names for lining up for recess or call out letters for members on a team. Put the children's names on a Word Wall so the whole class can see them.

Recognizing Onsets and Rimes

Say to the children, "*Bear* and *pear* sound alike. We say they rhyme. Can you tell me a word that rhymes with *cat*?" Children will come up with oral answers such as *bat, hat,* and *fat*. Continue to play this game casually as children are waiting in a line to be dismissed or leave for lunch. Allow a child to be the teacher who gives a word, but the student has to know at least one rhyme before he or she can say, "I know a word that rhymes with *dog*. Do you?" Other children might supply: *log, fog, hog,* and so on. More advanced students could create their own lists.

Such constant oral practice is more effective than completing worksheets to help children become aware of sounds at the ends of words. They are demonstrating their knowledge of how sounds are put together to form words—their *phonemic awareness*. Because children hear beginnings and endings more readily, researchers separate words into *onsets* and *rimes*. The onsets are the consonantal sounds that begin each word, and the rimes are the combination of vowel sounds and final consonants.

Combinations of Consonants

Many English words begin with simple consonant sounds—for example, *pet, tame,* and *zebra*. At times, two or more initial consonants are pronounced together as *blends*. Examples of beginning blends are /bl/, /br/, /sm/, and /sn/, or with three consonants, /spl/, /str/, and /scr/. Notice that in pronouncing blends of sounds, you can still hear each separate sound. Sometimes, letters are written in pairs to form a single sound—for example, /th/ and /sh/. These combinations of two letters are called *digraphs* because two letters are used to represent a single sound.

Independent Practice

Software is available to provide supplementary practice with applications of letter/sound generalizations. Here are two suggestions; check for new material appearing each month:

> *Working Phonics.* Win95/Mac, Curriculum Associates, (800) 225-0248 <www. curriculumassociates.com>
> *Let's Go Read: Island Adventure* and *Let's Go Read: Ocean Adventure.* Win95/ Mac, Edmark, (800) 691-2985 <www.edmark.com>

Learning the Letter Symbols

Students can practice this activity independently to review the letters of the alphabet. After students have learned any 5 letters through this color-keyed exercise, use the same

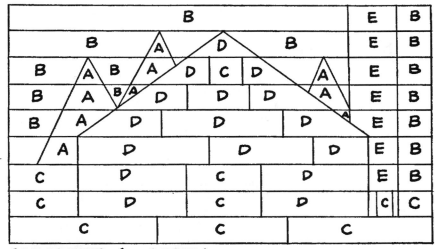

MAKE THE As GREEN.
MAKE THE Bs BLUE.
MAKE THE Cs BROWN.
MAKE THE Ds RED.
MAKE THE Es YELLOW.

technique to gradually add the rest of the letters. Later directions might read: *Make* A, G, M, *and* Z *red.*

Visual Discrimination

Ask your local library or senior center to save old copies of large-print newspapers. Give each student a page, a color pen, and an activity such as the following:

- Circle all words beginning with *f.*
- Circle all the words that are plurals.
- Underline all the words that begin like the word *bassoon.*
- Circle all the capital letters.

Same or Different?

One of the first steps in learning to read is to learn to distinguish different sounds. Students also learn to recognize the same sound when it occurs in different words. Give them practice in auditory discrimination by providing oral/aural exercises. Read a series of words as they listen carefully to the sounds in the words. Have them clap their hands or stand up when they hear the word or words that answer your question.

- Which word begins with a sound that is different from the first sound in *corner?*

  cat   teapot

  cuddle   cotton

- Which words have the same ending as in *met?*

  let   pet

  sat   roar

- Which words end in the same sound as *flash?*

  dash   reached

  jest   sash

To make this exercise more difficult, you can include contrasts such as final *k* versus *g* or *t* versus *d,* and vowel differences, such as short *i* versus long *e.*

Auditory Discrimination

For a quick review of auditory skills, read to the students a list of words in which you include one word that does not fit. Ask them to tell you the word that doesn't belong.

pound   found   (long)   round

To introduce students to this exercise, begin with rhyming work. Increase the difficulty of the task as the students gain experience and confidence.

loaf   cough   if   (bat)

blade   (mend)   sweet   time

These lists can be put on tape and kept in a Listening Center for independent review. Provide answer sheets and an answer key so that students can work alone or in small groups.

Letters with Texture

Familiarize students with letter shapes and sounds by making a textured nameplate for each student. Form the letters by dribbling glue on oaktag, then sprinkling sand or glitter over the glue. The raised letters appeal to students and the texture encourages them to trace the letter shapes repeatedly.

Labels for objects or pictures can be prepared in this fashion and mounted where students can feel the letters. Have the students copy the words on a piece of paper.

Initial Sounds

Young children need a great deal of practice associating sounds and symbols. They are especially aware of initial sounds. Try these ideas to reinforce their phonemic awareness:

- Print a large *t* on the board. Give the children five minutes to name words that begin with *t*. Everybody takes a turn suggesting words that are then printed on the board: *toy, turtle, top, table, television, telephone, tadpole,* and so on.
- Print a large *d* on the board. Again, give the children five minutes to name words that begin with the *d* sound, but this time every word must contain more than four letters. More advanced students can suggest *dandelion, determine, disaster, decorate, destination, diamond,* and so on.

The Collector

Label brown lunchbags with a beginning consonant sound. In each bag place an object or a picture of an object that begins with that sound. The bag labeled *B* might include a book and a balloon, along with pictures of birds, butterflies, and bats.

Attach the bags to the bulletin board and encourage students to contribute objects and pictures. Give a "Collector" reward to the student who contributes the most items or the most unusual object/picture.

Making Rhyme Lists

Developing rhyme lists is an excellent way of becoming aware of similarities in sounds. Using a common rime, or word ending, students can insert consonants in the initial position to test whether a word is created.

Teach children to go through the alphabet as they test these words. The letters marked out are not consonant sounds, or else they repeat sounds.

x̶b x̶ d x̶ f g h x̶ j k l m

n x̶ p x̶ r s t x̶ v w x̶ y z

Using a regularly spelled rime *at,* as in *cat,* ask students to say these combinations to themselves. Some are words to be listed; others are nonsense syllables and would be ignored.

bat	jat	pat	vat
dat	kat (cat)	rat	wat
fat	lat	sat	yat
gat	mat	tat	zat
hat	nat (gnat)		

Blends and Digraphs

Further development of these rhyme lists includes trying blends (more than one consonant sound) and digraphs (one sound written with two letters). Provide students with a chart of additional ones, such as the following:

bl	gl	sm	tr
br	gr	sn	ch
cl	pl	st	sh
cr	qu	sw	th
dr	sc	str	
fl	sl	spr	

As students try these blends and digraphs with the rime *at*, they can add *brat, flat, scat, Sprat* (Jack), *chat*, and *that* to their lists.

Chain "Letters"

This activity gives students the chance for hands-on work with onsets and rimes. Each child can manipulate this "chain" individually, and create a variety of combinations between the consonant letter and the word ending. Two strips of tagboard, 3½" × 9", should be made. On one strip print rimes, and on the other print initial consonants (see the example). Make loops with both of these strips and link them together so that the letters face the reader. Then move either circle so that different combinations of words and sounds can be made.

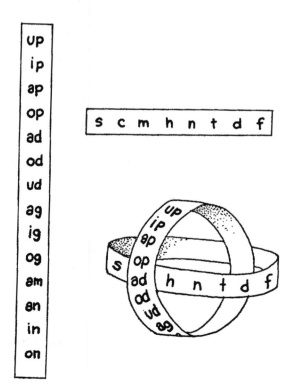

Listening for Initial Blends

As students learn to read consonant blends, prepare a tape of words that begin with the common blends. Ask students to write just the first two sounds that begin each word. This practice helps children learn to listen for blends in many different words. Deliberately include words that children probably don't know, as in this list:

spindle	broadcast
sniffle	blastoff
snapdragon	frizzy
slippery	flicker
grasshopper	pretend
glutton	transplant

Encourage students to try writing the rest of the word without fear of making mistakes. Have a list available to which they can refer to see how close their guesses were.

Word Analysis Skills

Help students maintain and improve word analysis skills by providing exercises for extra practice in the reading center:

- List all the words from this story that contain digraphs. Underline the digraphs with your favorite color.
- List all the words from this story that have long vowel sounds. Write the pronunciation symbol for this vowel after each word. (Check your dictionary for the correct symbols.)

Make several copies of different stories that students can work on, allowing for a variety of reading levels. You can increase the difficulty of these exercises as students progress:

- List all the words in this story that have suffixes. Underline the root words with a bright color.
- List all the words in this story that have prefixes. Underline the root words with a cool color.
- List all the contractions in this story.
- List all the compound words in this story. Circle the two words that make up each compound word.

First Sentences

For early primary sentence skills, make large tagboard shapes (such as a train or an elephant) and word cards with tabs that will make a sentence. Cut slots in the shape so that students can insert the appropriate word cards.

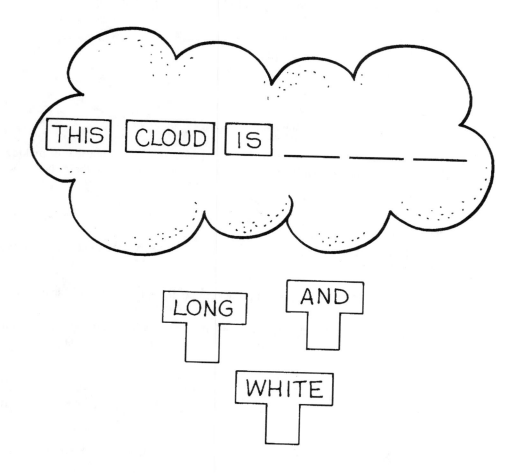

Sight Words

Provide your students with a list of sight words. Split the class into groups and assign each group a story from a basal reader. Ask the groups to list the sight words used in their story and to tally the number of times each word appears. The results can then be graphed and used as a basis for a class discussion about the importance of sight words.

You may wish to continue your sight word investigation by asking the groups to choose chapters from library books and repeat the sight word count. These results can then be compared to the basal reader graphs.

Guess the Hidden Word

Prepare sentence strips from three-inch posterboard. Try to use about the same amount of space for each word. Make sliders from two pieces of construction paper by taping the top and bottom. Attach 4" end strips to prevent the slider from slipping off the posterboard.

Divide the class into small groups. Give each group a stack of sentence strips. Each player reads the top sentence and guesses the hidden word. The slider is moved to verify the guess. If correct, the player earns a token and moves the slider to hide a new word. If incorrect, the slider is kept on the same word and the used strip is placed at the bottom of the stack.

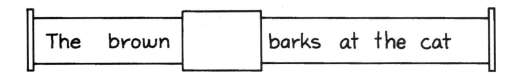

Becoming Independent Readers

A major goal of the reading program is to have students become lifelong readers. In order to accomplish this, you will need to continue reading aloud to students, provide and discuss reading materials from a variety of genres, and reward students for pursuing individual interests through reading. Even as students read more fluently and independently, the need for reading instruction remains. For example, how do you expect students to respond to the books they read? The conventional book report is only a limited model; students can reflect on and present to others what they thought about the book through a wide range of activities, such as drawing, singing, acting out, writing, and discussing in small groups. Instead of book reports, have students write book "reviews." Assemble a notebook of students' reviews in the class library or attach a comment form to each book for students to read and add to. Encourage students to consider sharing favorite books with others, as in the following: "If you like the Harry Potter books, you'll like . . ."

Literature Circles

There are many different ways to use literature circles. In a literature circle, students meet in small groups (of four to six students) and read the same book. Perhaps you will want to form literature circles for different purposes. If you have four or five groups, all could read on a similar theme—for example, historical fiction about African Americans. Students can be grouped according to reading level. In that case, you would need four to six copies of a literature selection appropriate for the reading level of each circle.

One group of fourth-graders might be reading William Armstrong's Newbery Award–winning book, *Sounder,* for example. A group of slower readers might read *Sweet*

Clara and the Freedom Quilt by Deborah Hopkinson, a short picturebook illustrated by James Ransome. A third group could read Gary Paulsen's *Nightjohn,* and a fourth might read the Newbery Honor–winning book by Christopher Paul Curtis, *The Watsons Go to Birmingham 1963.* As students in the group read their book, they can generate questions that are raised by their reading. When they have finished, they can make a list of information they gained as a result of reading this book. Finally, the groups might share their books with the rest of the class by giving a brief presentation, talking about their responses, the kinds of questions that were raised, and what they learned. Because the books are set in different time periods, students may find that other groups can help them understand what they are reading. Class questions generated by this discussion could lead to additional research.

Magazines: A Form of Contemporary Literature

Many magazines are published for children, ranging from the humorous *Muppet Magazine* to *Ranger Rick,* which focuses on nature and science. Try to locate funds for subscriptions in order to make this reading material available in your classroom. Several rooms can share a number of subscriptions by circulating the magazines from room to room, or perhaps individual students who receive a magazine might donate the copies they have read.

Talk with students about the special features of a magazine. How is reading a magazine different from reading a storybook? Using some sample copies, have groups of students read and analyze each magazine to determine the audience (age range) at which it is directed and the purpose for which it is intended. Afterwards, have students discuss how they made their decisions. What cues helped them decide? If a specific age range is given in the magazine, do they agree that this is appropriate?

Browse through the following list of magazines for children and request sample copies of those that interest you:

> *Chickadee.* Age range: 4–8. Address: The Young Naturalist Foundation, Box 11314, Des Moines, IA 50347.
>
> *Child Life.* Age range: 8–11. Address: P.O. Box 10681, Des Moines, IA 50381.
>
> *Children's Digest.* Age range: 9–12. Address: P.O. Box 10683, Des Moines, IA 50381.
>
> *Children's Playmate.* Age range: 5–8. Address: P.O. Box 10242, Des Moines, IA 50381.
>
> *Cobblestone: The History Magazine for Young People.* Age range: 8–14. Address: 20 Grove Street, Peterborough, NH 03458.
>
> *Cricket: The Magazine for Children.* Age range: 6–12. Address: Box 2672, Boulder, CO 80321.
>
> *The Electric Company.* Age range: 6–10. Address: P.O. Box 2896, Boulder, CO 80322.
>
> *Enter.* Age range: 10–16. Address: P.O. Box 2896, Boulder, CO 80322.
>
> *Highlights for Children.* Age range: 2–12. Address: P.O. Box 269, Columbus, OH 43272-0002.

Humpty Dumpty's Magazine. Age range: 4–6. Address: P.O. Box 10225, Des Moines, IA 50381.

Jack and Jill. Age range: 7–10. Address: P.O. Box 10222, Des Moines, IA 50381.

Muppet Magazine. Age range: 7–13. Address: 300 Madison Avenue, New York, NY 10017.

Muse. Age range: 5–12. Address: P.O. Box 7468, Red Oak, IA 51591–2468. <www.musemag.com>

National Geographic World. Age range: 8–13. Address: Box 2330, Washington, DC 20013.

Odyssey. Age range: 8–12. Address: Kalmbach Publishing Co., 1027 N. Seventh St., Milwaukee, WI 53233.

Peanut Butter. Age range: 5–7. Address: 730 Broadway, New York, NY 10003.

Penny Power. Age range: 8–14. Address: P.O. Box 2859, Boulder, CO 80321.

Ranger Rick. Age range: 6–12. Address: Ranger Rick's Nature Magazine, The National Wildlife Federation, 1412 16th Street NW, Washington, DC 20036.

Scienceland. Age range: 5–8. Address: 501 Fifth Avenue, Suite 2102, New York, NY 10017-6165.

Seedling Series Short Story. Age range: 10–12. Address: P.O. Box 405, Great Neck, NY 11022.

Sesame Street. Age range: 2–6. Address: P.O. Box 2896, Boulder, CO 80322.

Stone Soup. Age range: 6–13. Address: P.O. Box 83, Santa Cruz, CA 95063.

3-2-1 Contact. Age range: 8–14. Address: Box 2896, Boulder, CO 80322.

Turtle Magazine for Preschool Kids. Age range: 2–5. Address: P.O. Box 10222, Des Moine, IA 50381.

Your Big Backyard. Age range: 3–5. Address: The National Wildlife Federation, 1412 16th Street NW, Washington, DC 20036.

Reading Log

Have the students keep a record of all the material they read in a single day. Encourage them to think about the different kinds of things they read, especially outside the classroom. What might they be reading without really thinking about it? Some examples might be road signs, billboard slogans, cereal boxes, and TV advertising. The class can discuss the results of these logs. Were they surprised to see how much they read? How do they learn new words when they read?

Students can also interview adults to find out what they read in a typical day. Many adults regularly read specialized material—such as memos, reports, or instruction manuals—with which students may not be familiar.

Ad Reading

Print advertising can be an excellent source for reading activities in the classroom. Bring in examples of newspaper or magazine ads and discuss them with the students. Many ads depend on *multiple meanings* for their effect. Can students spot the different meanings involved? How are words with multiple meanings effective? Are they humorous? Attention-getting? Students can also look for *word play* in ads. How many examples can they find? Are these examples of puns? Many ads will include words unfamiliar to students. Can students guess the meaning of a word from the *context?* What clues help them guess? (There may be visual as well as syntactic and semantic context clues.)

Expanding Reading

Enlarge student horizons by showing them that reading is not something they do only in the classroom. Bring in items from the following list of free or inexpensive materials to encourage students to read and increase their ability to understand different kinds of text:

tickets	recipes
candy wrappers	comic strips, cartoons
train/bus/plane schedules	clothing tags
coupons	telephone directories
catalogs	grocery lists
restaurant menus	TV program listings
game instructions	record/cassette labels
cereal boxes	instructions for operating something
songs (songsheets)	maps

Focusing on Folklore

Have student groups select an area of folklore to explore, choosing from a list including specific countries (e.g., China) and ethnic groups (e.g., Latinos). The choices may be related to your social studies curriculum. Some of the most beautifully illustrated picture-books are found in the children's section of libraries (under Dewey Classification 398) where folklore is filed. Each group must locate at least three tales. Group members are expected to use at least two different sources of locating information. For example, encourage students to use the Internet to explore as well as visit a local library and ask the librarian for help.

After selecting their folktales, the group reads them together and chooses one to share with the rest of the class. Students can use any method for sharing that they choose. Have the class brainstorm possibilities—for example, acting out the story, inviting a guest speaker to the class, presenting a multimedia show, using the computer and other equipment, and so forth.

Celebrate Dr. Seuss

Plan a celebration on or around March 2nd, the birthday of Dr. Seuss (Theodor Seuss Geisel), who is known by most children for such books as *The Cat in the Hat.* Have older students read an outstanding picture book of their choice to children in primary grades or plan a program for the school and community featuring a range of Dr. Seuss characters. Primary-grade students can select their favorite Dr. Seuss book to share with the class.

For information about this author and Read across America Day, search the Internet <www.nea.org>.

Learning about Language through Reading

Search through your library for books about words and language. You may want to read some of the books aloud—for instance, one of Penny Parish's titles about Amelia Bedelia, who is constantly in hot water because she takes people's words literally. Others may provide ideas for comprehension activities, such as Fred Gwynne's books that demonstrate having fun with homonyms *(Chocolate Moose for Dinner or The King Who Rained)*. The following list suggests possibilities of ABC books:

> Alma Flor Ada. *Abecedario* (cassette with words and music, in Spanish). Ada/Paz, 1990.
> C. B. Falls. *ABC Book.* Morrow, 1998.
> Juwanda Ford and Ken Wilson-Max. *K Is for Kwanzaa.* Scholastic, 1997.
> Lisa Jahn-Clough. *ABC Yummy.* Houghton Mifflin, 1997.
> Ann Jonas. *Aardvarks, Disembark!* Greenwillow, 1990.
> Martin and Tanis Jordan. *Amazon Alphabet.* Kingfisher, 1996.
> Wanda Gag. *The ABC Bunny* (book and cassette). Scholastic, 1990.
> Anita Lobel. *Alison's Zinnia.* Mulberry, 1996.
> Sungwan S. Parsippany. *C Is for China.* Silver Press, 1998.
> Anne Rockwell. *Albert B. Cub & Zebra: An Alphabet Storybook.* Crowell, 1977.
> Jan Thornhill. *The Wildlife ABC: A Nature Alphabet Book.* Simon & Schuster, 1988.

Amaze Your Students with Long Words!

Display the following long words (enlarged several times with the copy machine). Encourage students to see who can find the longest word over the period of one week or perhaps a month.

Can You Read This?

- sesquipedalian
- sesquicentennial
- hippopotomonstrousesquipedalian
- pneumonoultramicroscopicsilicovolcanoconiosis
- floccinancinihilipilification
- antidisestablishmentarianism

Search for Similes and Metaphors

Introduce students to imagery, such as similes and metaphors, that adds life to the books they read. You might introduce these concepts by using George Ella Lyon's *Book,* illustrated by Peter Catalanotto (DK, 1999). Through text and illustrations, the reader encounters the question: What is a book? Imaginative metaphors provide a response to this open-ended question. Discuss this topic with students and ask them what images they would use to explain books or reading.

Have students search for similes and metaphors as they read. Then, they can try writing some like these:

- My foot is asleep and my toes feel like ginger ale.
- Color is a grease puddle: a dead rainbow.

Reading Joke Books

To encourage reading, introduce students to a wide variety of humorous books, including collections of jokes, conundrums, and puzzles. Two examples follow, with sample material from each:

> David A. Alder, *The Carsick Zebra and Other Animal Riddles* (Holiday, 1983). Illustrated by Tomie de Paola.
> **Q:** What do you call a frog that's stuck in the mud?
> **A:** Unhoppy.

> Louis Phillips, *How Do You Get a Horse Out of the Bathtub? Profound Anwsers to Preposterous Questions* (Viking, 1983). Illustrated by James Stevenson.
> **Q:** Should I purchase an automobile that has automatic drive?
> **A:** Of course not! Do you want people to think you are shiftless?

Focusing on Comprehension

What is reading? Does reading mean knowing how to *say* the words or is it *understanding* what you read? Since Durkin's (1978–1979) landmark study, which showed teachers assigning comprehension-related tasks but not teaching students how to fulfill them, there has been a concentrated effort to teach reading comprehension actively and explicitly. Round-robin reading, or having students read aloud in turn, has been called "barking at print," because we can't assume that students understand what they are reading/saying. Comprehending text is a complex task; students are asked to understand, remember, think about, compare, connect, and summarize what they read. Even fluent readers may have learned to skip difficult words and skim descriptive passages—strategies that will fail them when they encounter a heavy load of content reading, typically about the fourth grade. This change is often described as the shift from "learning to read" to "reading to learn." But students in the intermediate grades are *still* learning strategies that they will need in order to read/comprehend, as they encounter increasingly difficult forms of text, such as reports of science experiments, lists of math formulae, and primary sources for social studies. Teachers in the primary grades need to provide students with many different kinds of reading material, in addition to storybooks, to show students how reading changes depending on what they are reading and why they are reading it.

Main Idea Pictures

Teaching the skill of identifying the main idea can begin in the primary grades. Each year, students can practice this skill with longer and more complex material. Activities such as the following will help early primary students grasp the concept of main idea:

- Display an interesting picture and ask your students what story the picture is telling. Try to get your group to agree on one main idea.
- Read a simple paragraph to your students. Discuss the main idea and ask students to draw a picture of the main idea.
- Read short fables to your students and ask them to identify the main idea (moral) or draw a picture of it.
- Ask students to draw a picture of the main idea of a story in their reading books. Discuss the pictures and help the students write a sentence to amplify their picture. Group discussion will help those still having trouble identifying the main idea.
- Ask your students to suggest possible titles for a picture. Write suggestions on the board and have the group decide which comes closest to stating the main idea.

Writing Main Ideas

Asking students for the main idea in various stories will help them learn to apply the concept. For basal reader stories, book reports, and discussions following read-aloud sessions, ask students questions such as the following:

- What was the most important idea of this story?
- What was the moral of this story?
- What did you learn from this story?
- What do you remember most about the story?
- If you had to tell the whole story in one sentence, what would you say?
- If you were asked to draw the cover for this story, what would you draw?

Story Analysis

Read your students a short story. Write the following column headings on the board. Ask the students to retell the story as you fill in the chart. Here is an example:

Somebody	Wanted	But	So
Cinderella	to go to the ball	no dress or coach	Fairy Godmother helped

Tell your students that many stories have this logical mapping, and that they can use this chart both to analyze and to remember stories.

Provide your students with a Somebody/Wanted/But/So form each time you read a story aloud. After students become proficient at completing the form as a class, have them begin to map stories independently.

Cause and Effect

Introduce students to the concept of cause and effect by asking simple questions about familiar stories. Folktales and fairy tales work well, as in the following example from *Snow White:*

- The dwarves think Snow White is dead. Why do they think that?
- The mirror says Snow White is the most beautiful woman in the kingdom. What effect does that have on the evil witch?

Ask your students to listen for examples of cause and effect relationships throughout their day.

Cause and Effect Sentences

Have students list events from the story you are reading aloud. Show them how to make cause and effect sentences from these events. It is helpful to point out that either the cause or the effect may begin the sentence. After reading *James and the Giant Peach* by Roald Dahl, they might develop the following:

- James went to live with his awful aunts (effect) because his parents were eaten by a rhinoceros (cause).
- James tripped (cause) and spilled his magic potion (effect).

Discuss the importance of cause and effect relationships in the plot of a story.

Matching Cause and Effect

You can prepare simple matching exercises for independent practice, to monitor and expand student comprehension of cause and effect relationships. The following example is based on *Pippi Longstocking* by Astrid Lindgren:

Cause	Effect
_c_ **1.** Pippi Longstocking rescues two boys from a burning building.	**a.** Pippi takes a ride on the bull to teach it a lesson.
_a_ **2.** The bull chases Tommy and he falls.	**b.** The tramps decide to break into Villa Villekulla.
_b_ **3.** The tramps see Pippi counting her gold pieces.	**c.** The townspeople cheer Pippi.

A variation is to give your students only half of the cause and effect relationship and have them complete the blanks. You can accept any answers that make sense.

Cause	**Effect**
1. _____ _____	1. Pippi Longstocking draws on the floor when she goes to school.
2. _____	2. Two police officers come to see Pippi.
3. Pippi is invited to a coffee party at Tommy and Annika's.	3. _____ _____
4. Pippi's mother is dead and her father was lost at sea.	4. _____ _____

Question Practice

Divide the students into small groups for more practice in asking and answering questions. Select a short passage from a book and have each group write a list of questions about it. Then have the groups exchange their lists so that another group must answer the questions.

Discuss the questions produced by the groups. Ask students to categorize the types of questions. Were both literal and inferential types of questions represented, or only literal questions? Which questions required more thought? Which questions had more than one answer? What makes a good question?

Following this discussion, repeat the exercise with a new passage so that the students can immediately try out what they have just learned. This skill of asking and answering questions on material read is fundamental to higher-level comprehension.

Levels of Questioning

Help students develop skills in asking and answering different types of questions, by modeling both literal questions (where the answer is explicit in the text) and inferential or evaluative questions (where the student must interpret or apply the material). For example, after reading the first two chapters of *The Phantom Tollbooth* written by Norton Juster, ask the students the following questions:

1. Why was Milo dejected as he walked home from school?
2. Did Milo have friends he usually played with after school?
3. What were the Doldrums?
4. Why were the Lethargians afraid of the watchdog?
5. How did Milo get out of the Doldrums?
6. Do you think the watchdog is going to be an important character in the rest of the story?

Discuss the questions and how students can answer them. For some questions, the answer appears in the book—students can underline it or point to it, even if they have to look in more than one place. Usually there is only one right answer. Other questions require students to think about what they read and develop an answer based on their own ideas and experience. In this case, several answers may be equally correct. Have students sort the questions into these two categories, justifying their selection as they make it.

In the Text	**On Your Own**
Q#1. Two to three lines; several possible answers	**Q#2.** No mention in the book; students must interpret information given
Q#3. One line	**Q#6.** Prediction; students answer based on their experience of reading books
Q#4. Information given in two places; students must connect these	
Q#5. One line	

Jigsaw Sentences

An excellent activity that requires minimal reading ability is this game to play with the class as a whole or in small groups. Each student puts four sheets of paper together and cuts out a large shape. Still keeping the four copies together, each one cuts the shape in half, using some kind of irregular line. Now, separating the copies, each student writes the first half of a sentence on the top half of the shape and the second half of the sentence on the bottom half, so that when the shapes are put together properly, they make a sentence.

Have the students exchange their sets of eight pieces, all mixed up, with the other students in the group or the class. The object of the game is to find two pieces that fit together and also make a sentence.

If you prepare the game in advance, you can create more difficult sentences to test reading ability and knowledge of what makes sense. If you cut shapes from tagboard, students can use them over and over again for practice.

Basic Cloze

The cloze procedure, a popular informal diagnostic tool, can be easily used by any teacher with any group of students. Typically, in order to assess student reading level, you must choose a passage of approximately 250 words that is unfamiliar to the students. Leave the first and last sentences intact. For the rest of the passage, systematically delete every fifth word. (Leave a space the same size for every blank.) Ask students to fill in the word that was deleted.

To obtain a student's score, add up the responses that are *exactly* the same as in the original. Interpret scores as follows:

57% correct (and above)	Independent Reading Level	Student can read easily at this level.
45–56% correct	Instructional Reading Level	Student can read with teacher assistance.
44% correct (and below)	Frustration Reading Level	Student cannot read at this level, even with assistance.

These scores can be used to give you a quick estimate of the reading levels in your class.

Cloze Variants

Alternative forms of this fill-in-the-blank technique also provide excellent strategies for monitoring reading comprehension. The following are examples of cloze variants:

- Delete only words of a particular category (for example, prepositions or nouns).
- Allow synonyms (or words that fit the sentence) as correct responses.
- Give the passage orally and have students respond either orally or in writing.
- Provide multiple-choice options from which to select an answer (sometimes called Maze).
- Cue students by giving part of the word (for example, all consonants, prefix, first letter, etc.).
- Let students read the passage first without blanks, or give them a cloze exercise on a passage they have seen before.
- Discuss why students chose particular completions.
- Use cloze as a pretest/posttest to check student comprehension of a topic.

All of these exercises help students develop and practice their ability to use syntactic and semantic context clues in interpreting what they read.

Cloze Practice

The following is a sample cloze, taken from the children's literature classic *The Velveteen Rabbit* by Margery Williams (Doubleday, 1926). Have the students read the sample over once and then try to fill in the missing words. Score the students' responses according to the list of correct answers below.

The Boy was going to the seaside tomorrow. Everything was arranged, and _____ it only remained to _____ out the doctor's orders. _____
1   2   3
talked about it all, _____ the little Rabbit lay _____ the bedclothes, with
4   5
just _____ head peeping out, and _____. The room was to _____
6   7   8
disinfected, and all the _____ and toys that the _____ had played with in
9   10
_____ must be burnt.
11

"Hurrah!" _____ the little Rabbit. "Tomorrow _____ shall go to the
12   13
_____!" For the Boy had _____ talked of the seaside, _____ he
14   15   16
wanted very much _____ see the big waves _____ in, and the tiny
17   18
_____, and the sand castles.
19

_____ then Nana caught sight _____ him.
20   21

"How about his _____ Bunny?" she asked.
22

"That?" _____ the doctor. "Why, it's _____ mass of scarlet fever
23   24
_____! Burn it at once. _____? Nonsense! Get him a _____ one. He
25   26   27
mustn't have that any more!"

Answers:

1. now	8. be	15. often	22. old
2. carry	9. books	16. and	23. said
3. They	10. Boy	17. to	24. a
4. while	11. bed	18. coming	25. germs
5. under	12. thought	19. crabs	26. What
6. his	13. we	20. Just	27. new
7. listened	14. seaside	21. of	

Story Graph

Graphing the plot of a story often helps students see the relationship between one event and another. You may wish to add a graph like the one shown on page 77 to your literature program.

STORY GRAPH

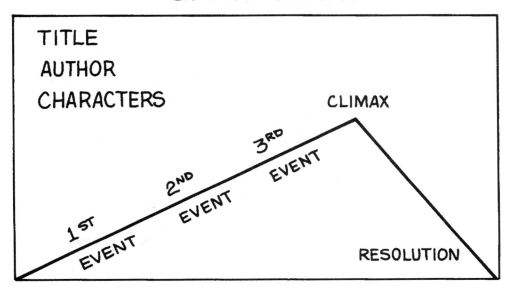

Sentences in Sequence

After the students have read a story, lead a discussion of story events, in order, and write down each major event as a sentence. Later, to review the story, duplicate the set of sentences in mixed order and ask the students to cut them out and arrange the sentences in sequence.

Talk with the students about what cues they used to arrange the sentences as they did.

5. The wolf tries to eat little Red Riding Hood.
3. Little Red Riding Hood arrives at her grandmother's house.
1. Little Red Riding Hood's mother gives her a basket to take to her grandmother.
6. The woodsman rescues little Red Riding Hood.
4. Little Red Riding Hood thinks the wolf is her grandmother.
2. The wolf eats little Red Riding Hood's grandmother.

Examining Various Genres

Students need to be familiar with the characteristics of the various forms that literature can take. They will then know what to expect from a specific book, which will help them better direct their reading strategies. Students can analyze the characteristics of each genre after reading a few examples and develop a list of features that define the genres. Discuss with students how they might have to modify reading strategies—self-questioning, speed, rehearsal—according to the kind of book they are reading. Include some of the following examples:

Short stories:	Michael Cart, ed. *Tomorrowland: Ten Stories about the Future.* Scholastic, 1999.
History:	Ruby Bridges. *Through My Eyes.* Scholastic, 1999.
Play:	Aliki. *William Shakespeare and the Globe.* HarperCollins, 1999.
Informational:	David Schwartz. *If You Hopped Like a Frog.* Illustrated by James Warhola. Scholastic, 1999.
Narrative:	Christopher Paul Curtis. *Bud, Not Buddy.* Delacorte, 1999.
Memoir:	Rachel Field and Rosemary Wells. *Hitty: Her First Hundred Years.* Illustrated by Susan Jeffers. Simon & Schuster, 1999.
Folktale:	Simms Taback. *Joseph Had a Little Overcoat.* Viking, 1999.
Poetry:	Rebecca Kai Dotlich. *Lemonade Sun and Other Summer Poems.* Illustrated by Jan Spivey Gilchrist. Wordsong/Boyd Mills. 1998.

Where and When?

Select a portion of dialogue from a story or write a short passage yourself. Present the dialogue to the class either on the board or on duplicated sheets. After the students read this conversation, discuss it together, asking for suggestions about what might have preceded the conversation and what might follow, who is speaking, what kinds of people the speakers are, and so forth.

Each student then composes a story and fits this dialogue in as appropriate. Comparing the results will impress the students with the many possibilities for developing a story from a single situation. Here is a sample dialogue:

"Quick, duck down behind these boxes," Bess hissed. "Who knows what will happen if they catch us here!"

Using Suspense

When reading a book to the class, use high points in the book to create suspense. Choose an exciting moment or decision point, stop reading, and ask the students what they think will happen next. Have them discuss various possibilities and what clues affected their choice.

Narrative Story Map

Use a familiar story (e.g., "Three Billy Goats Gruff") to create a group story map on the board. You may need to prompt with questions like: *What did the goats do first?*

Setting: Bridge

Characters: 3 billy goats, troll

Problem: Goats want to cross the bridge guarded by troll.

Goal: To reach greener grass.

Events: First goat tells troll to wait for fatter brother. Second goat tells troll to wait for fatter brother. Third goat vanquished troll.

Resolution: All goats feast on greener grass.

Supporting Understanding

Mapping activities help students understand stories they have read. Introduce such activities to students through the use of short stories that can be read relatively quickly and easily by students. At first, you may demonstrate a method by reading a picture book aloud to the whole class. You might select *Sam, Bangs, and Moonshine,* which won the Caldecott Award for author/illustrator Evaline Ness. Before beginning to read, have students consider the meaning of the title. Identify *Sam.* What does *Bangs* refer to? And what about *Moonshine?* Students will be amused to discover how misleading this title is after they learn the truth: Sam is a little girl, Bangs is her cat, and moonshine refers to the lies this lonely young girl tells. After reading the story aloud, talk about the events and how the plot is developed. Also discuss the character and how she comes alive as you read about her. Have students map this story using a frame like this:

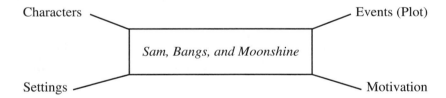

Remind students of the methods used that helped them understand the story: thinking about the title, listening to the story, and mapping the story.

Discussion Questions

1. What are the different positions regarding the teaching of phonics and teaching with whole language? Can these positions be reconciled?

2. How can you best engage parents as partners in the process of teaching their children to read?

3. How does the shift in focus from *reading readiness* to *emergent literacy* affect instruction in the primary grades? In the upper grades?

4. How can you teach reading effectively so that you support students' learning about the written language as well?

Exploring Further

Susan M. Glazer. *Phonics, Spelling, and Word Study: A Sensible Approach.* Christopher-Gordon, 1999.

Michael Graves and Bonnie Graves. *Scaffolding Reading Experiences: Designs for Student Success.* Christopher-Gordon, 1994.

Diane Lapp et al. *Content Area Reading and Learning: Instructional Strategies.* Boston: Allyn and Bacon, 1996.

Daniel Meier. *Scribble Scrabble—Learning to Read and Write.* Teachers College Press, 2000.

William Nagy. *Teaching Vocabulary to Improve Reading Comprehension.* International Reading Association, 1988.

Susan B. Neuman and Kathleen A. Roskos, eds. *Children Achieving: Best Practices in Early Literacy.* IRA, 1999.

Reading/Language Arts Framework for California Public Schools: K–12. Curriculum Development and Supplemental Materials Commission. California Department of Education, 1999.

Timothy Shanahan. "Good Ideas for Teaching the Language Arts." *The California Reader, 32,* no. 2 (Winter 1999):16–23.

Dorothy Strickland. "Reinventing Our Literacy Programs: Books, Basics, Balance." *Reading Teacher, 48,* no. 4 (1994/1995).

Ruth Helen Yopp and Hallie Kay Yopp. "Sharing Informational Text with Young Children." *Reading Teacher, 53,* no. 5 (2000): 410–423.

References

Marilyn Jager Adams. *Beginning to Read: Thinking and Learning about Print.* MIT, 1994.

Isabel Beck, Margaret McKeown, Rebecca Hamilton, and Linda Kucan. *Questioning the Author: An Approach for Enhancing Student Engagement with Text.* IRA, 1997.

Glenda Bissex. *Gnys at Wrk: A Child Learns to Write and Read.* Harvard University Press, 1980.

Jeanne Chall, V. Jacobs, and L. Baldwin. *The Reading Crisis: Why Poor Children Fall Behind.* Harvard University Press, 1990.

Marie Clay. *Becoming Literate: The Construction of Inner Control.* Heinemann, 1991.

Dolores Durkin. "What Classroom Observations Reveal about Reading Comprehension Instruction." *Reading Research Quarterly, 14,* no. 4 (1978–1979): 483–533.

Anne Haas Dyson. *The Social Worlds of Children Learning in an Urban Primary School.* Teachers College Press, 1993.

Ken Goodman and Yetta Goodman. "Learning to Read is Natural." In L. B. Resnick and P. B. Weaver, eds. *Theory and Practice of Early Reading Vol I.* Erlbaum, 1979.

Robert Ruddell, Martha Rapp Ruddell, and Harry Singer, eds. *Theoretical Models and Processes of Reading* (4th ed.). IRA, 1994.

Frank Smith. *Joining the Literacy Club: Further Essays into Education.* Heinemann, 1992.

Frank Smith. *Understanding Reading: A Psycholinguistic Analysis of Reading and Learning to Read* (5th ed.). Erlbaum, 1994.

Catherine Snow, M. Susan Burns, and Peg Griffin, eds. *Preventing Reading Difficulties in Young Children.* National Academy Press, 1998.

Dorothy Strickland. *Teaching Phonics Today: A Primer for Educators.* IRA, 1998.

Elizabeth Sulzby and William Teale. Emergent Literacy. In R. Barr, M. Kamil, P. B. Mosenthal, and P. D. Pearson, eds. *Handbook of Reading Research Vol II.* Longman, 1991.

G. Brian Thompson and Tom Nicholson, eds. *Learning to Read: Beyond Phonics and Whole Language.* IRA, 1999.

Constance Weaver. *Reading Process and Practice* (2nd ed.). Heinemann, 1994.

Constance Weaver, ed. *Reconsidering a Balanced Approach to Reading.* NCTE, 1998.

4 Expanding Vocabulary

For the life of him, he couldn't figure why these East Enders called themselves black. . . . The colors he found were gingersnap and light fudge and dark fudge and acorn and butter rum and cinnamon and burnt orange. But never licorice, which, to him, was real black.

—Jerry Spinelli, *Maniac Magee*

In the early grades, students need to learn approximately 3,000 new words every year—a feat that is impossible through direct instruction alone. In addition, a student's vocabulary knowledge is expected to double in grades 4 through 8, as a direct result of how much the student reads. By the eighth grade, students should recognize and know the meaning of well over 80,000 words. That many students fall behind in academic performance in the famous fourth-grade slump is not surprising, then, when you think of the heavy increase in content reading (Chall, Jacobs, & Baldwin, 1990). Students must acquire a proficiency in the "language" of texts—a task that is especially difficult for those who are learning English as an additional language. Such pressure from reading comprehension requires an equal increase in vocabulary knowledge. Consider the following: If there are 65,000 words in the average school dictionary, a student would have to learn 5,416 words every year for each of the 12 years of schooling. The major source for students' vocabulary learning comes from their independent reading. In addition, knowledge of vocabulary benefits students in their writing as well as in speaking and listening activities.

In order to be able to process this weight of new vocabulary, teachers must pay particular attention to how they teach vocabulary. Students must hear new words, speak and write them, and talk about the context in which they appear. Reading aloud to students also builds vocabulary and language. The more a teacher models analysis of new words and prediction of word meaning, the more students gain in vocabulary and comprehension (Dickinson & Smith, 1994). This chapter presents a sampling of activities that support student vocabulary learning by enjoying working with words, looking at word patterns, and exploring the meaning of words.

Taking Pleasure in Words

Vocabulary teaching often consists of direct instruction of new or unfamiliar words before a reading or writing activity (Scott & Butler, 1994), which can become boring for teachers and students. But it is not possible to teach students every word that they will encounter. An alternative approach is to focus on imbuing students with a love of words so that they will be eager to explore the fascinating words that they are learning every day.

Say and Savor

Students enjoy playing with the sounds of words: long words and short words, rhyming words, and alliteration in words. Encourage this playful manipulation of language as part of the process of learning vocabulary. The ABC framework stimulates thinking and challenges students to come up with new possibilities. Taking each sound (letter) in the alphabet one at a time, they can create names, phrases, and sentences that begin with the same sound, such as *luscious lollipops* and *menacing monstrous mealworms*. Share with students a book such as Mordecai Gerstein's *The Absolutely Awful Alphabet* (Harcourt Brace, 1999), which takes alliteration to new heights.

Word Images

Help students learn to visualize words and their meanings through unusual phrases. Again, the ABC frame can provide an effective structure to guide students' creativity. Read some of the examples presented in *The Accidental Zucchini: An Unexpected Alphabet* by Max Grover (Harcourt Brace, 1997). Students can talk about the mental images created by such odd combinations from the book as *umbrella underwear* and *octopus overalls*. As they invent more examples, students can illustrate their phrases and collect them in a book for others to enjoy.

Count on Words

In addition to ABC books, many interesting books about words are available that encourage students to look at words in new ways. One classic work, popular with children and adults, is *Ounce, Dice, Trice* by Alastair Reid (Abrams, 1991) and illustrated by Ben Shahn. The title of the book refers to creating alternative ways of counting. Invite students who are bored with the old *one, two, three* to invent their own new words for counting. Notice how Reid selects real words that are somewhat similar in sound to the words they replace, so that students have no trouble understanding what they are counting. This book is also a rich source of old, new, and always interesting words. For example, the author plays with names for twins, using words that come in pairs.

A Rich Language

Teachers can model an enthusiasm for words and a curiosity about them. As you read aloud to students, take the opportunity to savor the interesting words that you encounter. Students will become involved with the sounds, meanings, and structures of words if you show them your own pleasure in words. For example, as you read the following passage from Mildred Taylor's *Roll of Thunder, Hear My Cry,* use your voice expressively to emphasize the rich qualities of the words used:

> "Cassie, stop that," Stacey *snapped* as the dust *billowed* in *swirling* clouds around my feet. I looked up *sharply,* ready to protest. Christopher-John's whistling increased to a *raucous,* nervous *shrill,* and *grudgingly* I let the matter drop and *trudged* along in moody silence, my brothers growing as *pensively* quiet as I.

Teacher as a Source of Vocabulary

Students will be more likely to remember new words if you try to use them when talking to the class as often as possible. In fact, you are a major source of new words. "Advanced" words quickly become part of the student vocabulary when you use them in contexts where the meaning is clear. This makes new words sound more interesting, and students will enjoy discovering the meaning from the context. Make the introduction of new vocabulary part of your daily routine, thus:

- People who *procrastinate* never get their work done.
- What *loquacious* students you are this morning!
- I want some volunteers to clean up the *chaos* in the Learning Center.
- Can anyone tell me why Robert's experiment was a *fiasco?*
- You should try not to provoke students when they're *pugnacious.*
- Please line up with *alacrity.*
- Let's try to think of a solution to end this *controversy.*

Vocabulary Growth through Listening

When students are listening to a story or poem, they will frequently hear words they don't know. They don't find the strange vocabulary intimidating, however, because the meanings of the words are usually explained by the context. This is an excellent way to introduce new words. Discuss the new words when you have finished reading. Students will probably be able to suggest an approximation of the correct meaning. Talk about how they know what the author means when they can't understand all the words. Also talk about what clues they might use to gain the meaning of the words.

Find the Secret Word

At the beginning of class, announce that you have a secret word for the day and that you will use this word once every half hour. Students are to listen carefully and try to guess the word. When students think they've got the word, ask them to share it with you secretly. If no one gets the word, tell the students what it was at the end of the day. Vary this listening exercise by having the first student to discover the secret word contribute the word for the next time.

New Words

Always be alert for the opportunity to introduce a new word, whatever subject the class is studying. If the discussion is about health, you could supply the word *ailment* as a synonym for illness. Ask if anyone knows the word and have a student write it on the board as you discuss its meaning. Have the class develop a definition for the new word and ask a volunteer to record it in the class Word File. Provide a sentence using the word in context or an illustration to further clarify the meaning.

A Class Word File

As your class becomes more interested in words, the students can maintain a class Word File. Each new word that is talked about or introduced or that children find necessary in their writing can be put in this file. The box contains words on cards with a simple definition and the word used in a sentence.

Students can use this file for writing assignments. They can also develop various word games where they can ask each other a word and see if they can spell it or define it. Students have the opportunity to see their class Word File increase as the school year progresses.

Vocabulary Word Lists

Have students compile word lists centered on specific topics. Students can work alone to develop personal lists or as a small group to stimulate discussion and vocabulary development. Suggested topics are:

> *Animals:* horses, cats, dogs, tigers
> *Places:* school, home, playground, city
> *Media:* TV, books, movies, music
> *Jobs:* teacher, president, doctor
> *Recreation:* games, toys, parks, sports

These lists develop children's knowledge of categories. Encourage students to help build each other's lists.

A Personal Word Bank

Students can develop their own resource file of words that they can use in speaking and writing activities. They can collect lists such as favorite words, onomatopoetic words (words that sound like their meaning), or words for different ways of talking. Students can keep these words in a small file box or a shoe box, for easy reference. Encourage them to share their words with other students.

A Word a Day

A special section of the bulletin board can be devoted to featuring a new word every day. These words should be discovered by students, although you may occasionally feature a word that is especially relevant to a current topic of study. Have the student who provides the word prepare a card with the word and its pronunciation and definition.

Mount the card on the bulletin board and have the class discuss it. At the end of the week, review the five words that have been presented. Throughout the week, try to slip some of these words into your conversation with the class. Reward students who use any of these words, in speaking or writing, by putting their name on the board. Keep these student-produced word cards in the Word File, for easy student reference and review.

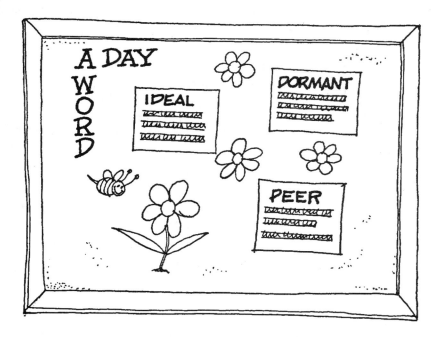

What's That Word?

Here is a game designed to increase student vocabulary and to help review words that students can play in small groups and on their own. Using a stack of 3" × 5" cards, print a word on one side and its definition on the other. To play the game, divide the cards randomly into six stacks. The players roll a die and pick up the card on top of the stack corresponding to the number on the face of the die. They read the word aloud and then give a definition. If the definition is correct, which they check by looking at the back of the card, they get to keep the card and the turn passes to the next person. If they gave the wrong definition, the card is replaced at the bottom of the stack. When a stack is depleted, any player who rolls that number gets a second turn. The game ends when all the cards are used.

You can make a basic set of these cards and add to them every time you introduce new vocabulary. If there are words on the cards that no students can define, you may want to review these words with the class. This game is most useful when the students play it frequently.

Hidden Words

Challenge students to smuggle new words into their speech. Give each student a slip of paper with a secret word written on it. As other students ask them questions, they have to incorporate the secret word into their response, while keeping the others from guessing which word is their secret one.

This activity works well with words taken from reading and writing exercises as well as content area studies.

Make a Sentence

Have each student draw four words from the class Word File. He or she then has to make up a sentence containing all four words. How many different sentences can the class come up with?

This activity can be used for review on an individual or small group basis in a learning center.

Vocabulary Inventory

Another technique for reviewing new words is the Vocabulary Inventory. This simple vocabulary quiz can be compiled by several students. Inventories can consist of questions such as these:

- If you made a *serendipitous* discovery, would you be (1) pleased or (2) disgusted?
- A *neophyte* is a person who is (1) young, (2) pretty, or (3) new.

Students will gain useful knowledge about words by creating these inventories as well as by answering them. Duplicate the sheets for the learning center so students can complete them independently.

What a Card!

This game is best played in teams. Pin to each student's back a card with an interesting word printed on it. The object of the game is for each person to guess the word on his or her back. Each student is allowed a specified number of questions that can be answered *yes* or *no*. The player who guesses the right word in the fewest number of questions wins. If someone cannot guess the word in the time limit, the others on the team are allowed to give clues.

Use this game to encourage students to remember new vocabulary words. You can also play the game with titles and authors of books as students guess who they are.

Guess My Word!

In another game, one student writes a selected word on a sheet of paper that is shown to the audience. Then a panel of five students takes turns attempting to guess the word selected. The panelists ask questions that can be answered only *yes* or *no,* for example:

Word chosen: Python
- Is it a noun?   *(yes)*
- Does it have more than one syllable?   *(yes)*
- Does it begin with a vowel?   *(no)*
- Is it in this room?   *(no)*

The panelists get 20 chances to narrow down the field so they can guess the word. If they do not guess correctly, the other team wins.

Word, Please

Give students a word that is easily defined and allow a short period of time for them to prepare as many specific questions as possible with that word as the answer. For example, for the word *carrot,* some questions might be:

- What is Bugs Bunny's favorite food?
- What is orange and grows underground?
- What vegetable is rumored to improve eyesight?

If you wish to adapt this activity for small groups, give each leader a pile of word cards with a sample question written on the back. The first player to create three correct questions becomes the new leader. Word cards can be sorted by categories (vegetables, state capitals, etc.) to review specific vocabulary.

Do You Know?

For a fast word game, prepare cards with a word on one side and the definition on the other. Divide the class into two teams. A student from one side reads the definition on the card and the other team has three minutes to guess the word. Each team gets a point for coming up with the correct word. Examples are:

- What's the word for the last car in a train?   (caboose)
- What do you call the place where hunters hide and wait for birds?   (blind)

Students will enjoy developing these cards on their own. Keep a supply in the learning center for student practice.

Name That Group

Give your students short lists with something in common and ask them to label the similarity. (There will usually be more than one right answer.) Students will enjoy small or large group discussions of possible answers. Here are a few suggestions:

> whale, dolphin, seal, otter
> ice skates, skateboard, roller skates, skis
> spring, summer, fall, winter
> ghost, bat, vampire, witch
> rain, snow, hail, sleet

Students who are able to identify the relationship quickly can be challenged to suggest another item that belongs with the group. Students can also create their own examples for use in the learning center.

Find the Oddball

Give your students short lists with all but one word sharing a similarity. Ask students to label the relationship that unites the similar words and circle the oddball word that does not belong, such as:

> ball, globe, box, grapefruit, orange   (All the objects are round except the box.)
> fog, mist, haze, ice, smog
> tiger, bear, jaguar, lion, panther
> carrot, cheese, potato, onion, radish
> shirt, sweater, shoes, jacket, coat

These problems can be adapted to challenge even your most able students, for example:

- tiger, lion, jaguar, leopard, ocelot   (The lion's coat is not patterned.)
- carrot, potato, onion, cucumber, radish   (The cucumber does not grow below the ground.)

Analogies

Once students have become adept at identifying relationships, they can move on to the more complex task of completing analogy pairs. To introduce students to the concept of analogies, you will need to go through several examples with the class to show them how it works. Provide cards with more examples for them to work on for practice. Read the first example: *Finger is to hand as toe is to what?*

> finger : hand   ::   toe : _____foot_____

car : road	::	train: ___rails___
lamp : light	::	___radio___ : sound
kitten : cat	::	___puppy___ : dog
book : library	::	horse : ___stable___
window : glass	::	___table___ : wood
chair : leg	::	tree : ___branch___
cat : animal	::	rose : ___flower___
sugar : sweet	::	lemon : ___sour___

At first, students may need help verbalizing the relationship between the items in order to be able to complete the blank.

Of course, students should be encouraged to use the dictionary when they do not understand a word. In some of the examples, several answers are possible. As the students become accustomed to this exercise, provide more difficult examples.

Looking at Word Patterns

There are two kinds of vocabulary: One is the group of words that people use actively and frequently in speaking and writing. The other, a much larger group, contains the words that people are expected to recognize when they see the words in print. Knowledge of word patterns plays a major part in the ability to understand the words one encounters as one reads. This section shows how you can model this approach to vocabulary learning and help students draw on this knowledge.

ABC Challenge

Have students make lists of words that follow the order of the alphabet. This is a good small-group or individual activity for expanding vocabulary, motivating students to use the dictionary, and also for practicing spelling.

Easy Words		*Longer Words*	
ant	nail	accordion	nonsense
bed	owl	butterfly	ostrich
cap	pin	crimson	pinnacle
doll	quit	dolphin	quotation
ear	run	eclipse	rainbow
foot	star	fantastic	saxophone
goat	top	glitter	tarantula
hair	under	harmony	umbrella
ice	voice	imagine	vampire
jacks	whale	jungle	wintergreen

kite	x-ray	kangaroo	xylophone
light	you	luminous	yearling
mouse	zoo	magician	zigzag

Vary the word lists by focusing attention on a particular subject, for example:

Plants	*Animals*
acacia	aardvark
birch	buffalo
calendula	cougar
dahlia	deer
endive	emu

Other categories might be titles of books, names of characters, boys' names, girls' names, adjectives, nouns, cities, and countries. A math alphabet may be found in David M. Schwartz's *G Is for Googol* (Tricycle, 1998).

Other examples of ABC books that stimulate interest in different words include:

Robert Bender. *The A to Z Beastly Jamboree.* Dutton, 1996.
Seymour Chwast. *The Alphabet Parade.* Harcourt Brace Jovanovich, 1991.
Kathy Darling. *ABC Cats.* Walker, 1998.

Hidden Word Puzzles

In a hidden word puzzle, students look for words horizontally, vertically, or diagonally. The words to look for can be printed at the bottom of the page or the directions might read: "Thirty-four pieces of clothing are hidden in this puzzle. See how many you can find."

Hidden Words

stockings	vest	shorts	hood	leotards
shoes	scarf	jacket	slippers	tie
blouse	shirt	coat	nightgown	camisole
pants	sandals	thongs	purse	slip
sash	skirt	nylons	bag	cap
ribbon	dress	boots	sweater	parka
socks	mittens	hat	gloves	

Encourage students to work together to create puzzles as well as solve them. Use the example "Hidden Clothing" on page 93 to show students how this type of puzzle works.

Creating Puzzles

Duplicate a puzzle frame (see page 94) so that students can make their own puzzles. Use a smaller number of squares for younger children and make the whole frame larger. Possible topics for a Hidden Word Puzzle or a Crossword Puzzle are:

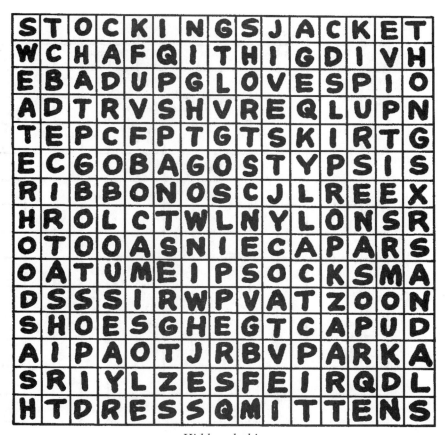

Hidden clothing

cities	song titles
authors	space
countries	transportation
students' names	plants
musical instruments	food
colors	vocabulary words

Riddle

Many riddles must be read aloud, because they depend on word play. Try this one on your students:

What's black and white and read (red) all over?   (a newspaper)

Did your students think of both meanings for the homonym *red/read?* How did the riddle influence them to interpret the word as a color, *red?*

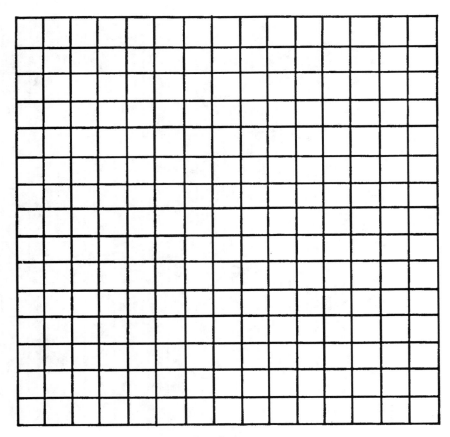

Puzzle frame

Read other riddles to the class to encourage them to pay attention to the sounds of words, as well as the meanings. Here are some books to get you started:

John Bierhorst, ed. *Lightning inside You: Native American Riddles.* Morrow, 1992.
Izhar Cohen. *ABC Discovery: An Alphabet Book of Picture Puzzles.* Dial, 1998.
Joanne Cole and Stephanie Calmenson. *A Pocketful of Laughs: Stories, Poems, Jokes, and Riddles.* Doubleday, 1995.
Susan Joyce. *ABC Animal Riddles.* Peel, 1999.

Sound Power

Draw the students' attention to the following words/phrases:

humpty-dumpty
roly-poly
helter-skelter

Ask the class what these words have in common. They should be able to recognize that these words differ only in the first letter/sound and that they rhyme. Ask them to suggest similar sets of words.

A related list of word pairs is the following:

thick and thin
spic and span
chitchat
knickknack

Can students identify the difference between the first list and the second? All of these words are examples of *reduplication,* where a word or part of a word is repeated and sometimes changed slightly. If only the beginning is changed, the words rhyme. If the ending is changed, the words are alliterative. Examples of simple reduplication are *choo-choo* and *boo-boo.* The reduplication gives the words a humorous effect and makes them appealing to say aloud.

Hinky Pinky

This activity is also called Jingo Lingo or Terse Verse. Students come up with pairs of rhymed words that create a humorous picture, for example:

cow chow
bog fog
bloom room
hefty lefty
bitter quitter

(One-syllable pairs are call Hink Pinks.) As students think of more examples, they can challenge others by providing two-word definitions:

- What's a *puzzle fad?*   (maze craze)
- What's a *nasty robot?*   (steel heel)
- What's a *burglar alarm?*   (crime chime)

Students will enjoy using rhyming lists to create more examples.

Word Display

Use the bulletin board to feature words in groups. A good way to emphasize knowledge of syllables and to stretch vocabularies is this display, called Five Syllables (see page 96), using words that children have discovered. Naturally, children will be intrigued about the meaning of these different words. The person who discovers the word can print a short

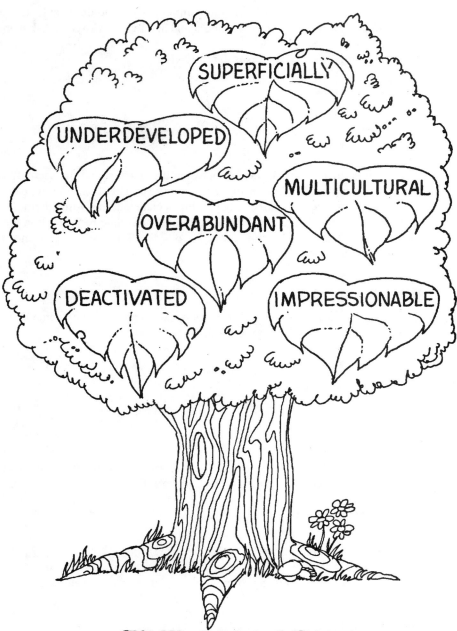

FIVE SYLLABLES

definition on the back of the leaf. If leaves are pinned on the tree, students can easily remove them while they read the definition and replace them when finished. Notice that emphasizing five-syllable words stresses prefixes and suffixes because that is one way of producing long words. Students will pore over the dictionary to discover words that begin with *un, pre, ex,* and other prefixes they know.

Speaking in Monosyllables

Many new words that students learn are polysyllabic, composed of more than one syllable. Draw students' attention to the rich stock of one-syllable words that make up the core of the English language. Challenge the students to write a sentence using only words of one syllable, such as:

I ate soup and cheese for lunch.

Older students can make the activity more challenging by writing a paragraph of monosyllables or maintaining a conversation using only one-syllable words. They will be surprised at the variety of words available.

Compound Lingo

Compound Lingo is a Bingo game with a twist. It will provide students with lots of fun, plus good exercise with compound words. You can prepare in advance some cards in Bingo form.

Let the children select the cards of their choice. Then inform them that you will read an unfinished sentence, and they must listen and try to see which word will fit the sentence. The twist in this game is that after each sentence is read, each player passes his or her card to the left, and continues the game on the card that was just passed. (It would be helpful to have the players sit in circles, either in small groups or as one class.) The first player to cover words in a straight line calls *Lingo,* and if all the answers are right, that player wins.

Examples

bathtub	foursquare	toolbox
toothpaste	railroad	halfway
faraway	seaweed	washcloth
leapfrog	hardware	foxhole
farmland	pawnshop	moonlight
midday	automobile	popcorn

1. A tub that you can take a bath in is a _____.
2. Cleaning paste to scrub your teeth with is _____.
3. Looking away to a far place makes you look _____.
4. A game in which you leap like a frog is called _____.

5. Good land that you can farm is _____.

6. The middle of the day is sometimes called _____.

7. One ball game that four of you can play in a square is called _____.

8. A road that is built for the rails of a train is a _____.

9. A green weed that grows in the sea is _____.

10. The wares that you can buy to do hard work with are _____.

11. A shop in which you can pawn your goods is a _____.

12. A mobile that drives automatically is an _____.

13. Your tools can be stored in a box called a _____.

14. If you've gone only half of the way, you've gone _____.

15. A cloth to wash yourself with is a _____.

16. A hole for a fox to hide in is a _____.

17. The light that is shining from the moon is _____.

18. The corn kernels that can pop make _____.

Place the words in different arrangements for various Lingo cards. You'll also need to provide something with which the players can cover their words. In addition, the children will learn the concept of "winning with the winner," since everyone is contributing to everyone else's cards.

Picturesque Words

Invite children to play with language as they observe the potentially funny meanings of compound words such as *horsefly* or *catfish* (see page 99). They can create a humorous poster illustrating this type of play with words. Other words that you can suggest include *boardwalk* and *wristwatch*.

ANTics

ANTics is a good way to expand student vocabulary while having fun. You can play this game with the class divided into small groups or you can give each student a list of questions to fill in. Here is an example:

Student A: What kind of ant would you like to have?

       B: Plant. What kind of ant is something to wear?

       C: Pants. What kind of ant is something you would say?

       A: Chant. What kind of ant is on a diagonal?

       B: Slant. What ant means barely enough?

       C: Scant. What ant means something given?

       A: Grant.

Have you ever seen a horse fly?

Other words that can be used in a list are *can't, rant,* and *implant.* You can also vary the game by encouraging the use of such words as *lantern, mantel, shanty, frantic, plantation,* and so on.

Outrageous Definitions

Sometimes students find new words especially funny because they see funny meanings in analyzing the parts of the word. You can catch your students' interest to motivate the learning of new vocabulary. Give them words they may or may not know and ask them to write a humorous definition based on the parts of the word. Afterwards, they should look the word up in a dictionary just to see how outrageous their definitions were. Here are some examples to get you started:

> *Extent:* when you've given away your camping equipment
> *Hallucination:* the country of people called halluces
> *Mushroom:* a place to store oatmeal
> *Enterprise:* an award for attending
> *Cannibals:* what you need to play tennis
> *Shamrock:* a fake stone
> *Palindrome:* a place where they keep elephants

In many cases, knowing the meaning of the parts of a word provides a clue to the meaning. This kind of exercise will encourage students to be aware of meanings of the parts of new words (morphemes) that they encounter.

Giving the Students a Hand

Give students this exercise to increase their vocabulary. They will have fun figuring out the words to answer each question.

1. What you learn after you learn to print   Hand_____
2. A good-looking person is   Hand_____
3. Someone who is good at repairs around the house is   Hand_____
4. Something you did yourself is   Hand_____
5. When someone talks about you behind your back, you say they are _____hand_____
6. Clothes you get from your older brother or sister are   Hand_____ or _____hand
7. A very generous person is called   _____hand_____
8. When you hear about an event from someone who was there, the account is _____hand
9. A person who works on a farm is a   _____hand
10. The square of material you use to blow your nose on is a   Hand_____
11. A purse is also a   Hand_____
12. What the police put on prisoners   Hand_____
13. Where you would look for information about the basic rules   Hand_____
14. Embroidery, needlepoint, and knitting are all   Hand_____
15. If you stick your fingers in a bag of candy and pull out as much as you can hold, how much do you have?   Hand_____
16. What might you do if someone gives you what you most want in the world? Hand_____

Students can make up quizzes like this using other words, such as *pan* or *car.*

Answers:

1. handwriting
2. handsome
3. handyman
4. handmade
5. underhanded
6. hand-me-downs or second-hand
7. open-handed
8. firsthand
9. fieldhand
10. handkerchief
11. handbag
12. handcuffs
13. handbook
14. handicrafts, handiwork
15. handful
16. handsprings

Palindromes

A palindrome is a word that reads the same backward and forward. You have probably noticed some of these words, which are intriguing to students. Share these examples with students:

> level
> eye
> Hannah
> madam

Even young children will be able to think of a number of palindromes.

Mom	dud	Bub	pop
did	bib	Bob	nun
Dad	Sis	gag	pep
wow	Nan	tot	tat

Older students may come up with these examples:

> Anna
> ewe
> deified
> radar
> kayak

Another use of palindromes is to create sentences that read the same forward and backward. Challenge students to create their own palindrome sentences. Some examples are:

- Able was I ere I saw Elba.
- Madam I'm Adam.
- A man, a plan, a canal: Panama!
- Too bad I hid a boot.

Students will enjoy *Sit on a Potato Pan, Otis* by Jon Agee (Farrar, 1999).

Word Puzzles

Keep a file of interesting and unusual language puzzles on cards for students to answer. (Newspaper columns are often a good source of examples.) Paste the questions on cards and put the answers on the back for students to check.

Students can work on these individually or in pairs. They can also bring in their own examples to share with the class. Start with the following:

- What sentence reads the same backward and forward? (RISE TO VOTE, SIR.)
- What sentence, when printed in capitals, reads the same upside down? (NOW NO SWIMS ON MON) *(James Thurber)*
- Reconstruct this English word: The first two letters signify a male; the first three letters signify a female; the first four letters signify a great man; and the whole word signifies a great woman (heroine)
- What word, when printed in capitals, reads the same forward, backward, and upside down? (NOON)
- What five words, written in capitals, read the same forward, backward, and in the mirror? (TOOT WOW MOM TOT OTTO)

Word Challenge

Give the class a word and ask them to write down as many words of five or more letters they can find within the given word. For example, in the word *improvisation* the following shorter words can be created:

impart	provision	stair	vision
import	ration	strain	visit
maroon	smart	strap	visor
mason	snort	strip	
ovation	spoon	tapir	
piston	sport	train	

Root Families

Groups of words are related in meaning through their root. Students can expand their vocabularies just by learning a few common Latin and Greek roots. Give them a root and a few examples and see how many other words they can find, as shown here:

- *ped*—Gr. *foot*
  pedestrian
  pedestal
  impede

- *port*—L. *move*
  import
  transportation
  portable

- *scribe*—L. *write*
  inscription
  scribble
  prescribe

- *graph*—Gr. *write*
  autograph
  grapheme
  graphic

You can also give them definitions of several words with the same root and have them figure out the meaning of the root, such as:

Pentagon—a figure with five sides
Pentangle—a five-pointed star
Pentameter—a line of verse with five feet

Pent means five. Can students think of other words that contain *pent?*

The Word Tree

This bulletin board display will arouse interest in word families. Use a large tree shape for the display, and at the bottom place a root word such as *scribe* written on a piece of construction paper. Branches of the tree hold examples of English words derived from this Latin root: *describe, inscribe, prescribe, subscribe, transcribe,* and *scribble* (see page 104). Students can discover new examples of derivatives to add to the tree.

There are many common Greek and Latin roots for you to explore with the class. Some of these are:

Auto: automatic, automobile, autobiography, autograph
Mal: malady, malpractice, maladjusted, maltreated, malice
Photo: photogenic, photography, photosynthesis, photosensitive

Root!

Make sets of four cards based on roots and derived words, such as:

scope: telescope, microscope, periscope, stethoscope
graph: phonograph, photograph, telegraph, autograph
meter: diameter, perimeter, kilometer, millimeter
cent: century, centigrade, percent, centipede

A set of 52 cards is enough for four players to play Root. This game is played like Fish, with each player trying to complete sets of 4 cards, which are laid down as a book. Each player in turn calls for the root desired—for example, *graph*—while other players turn over the cards that go in that set.

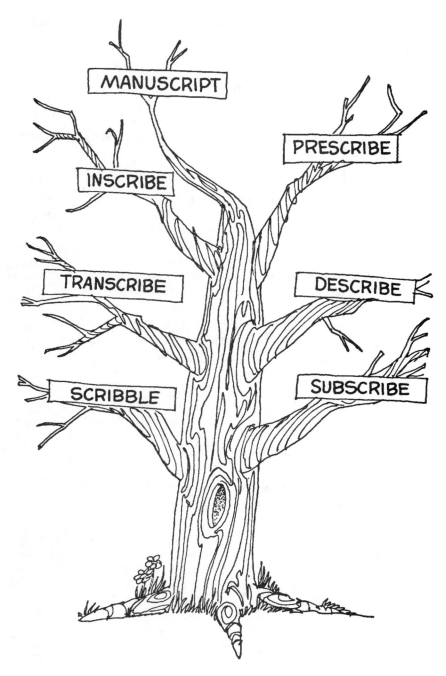

MANUSCRIPT

PRESCRIBE

INSCRIBE

TRANSCRIBE

DESCRIBE

SCRIBBLE

SUBSCRIBE

SCRIBE

A more complicated version of Root requires students to pronounce each word by asking for a specific card. Holding the card below, a player might ask, "Teresa, do you have *equinox* from the *equi* family?"

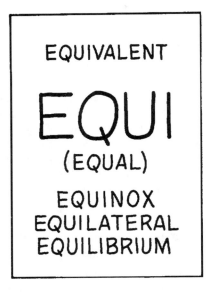

EQUIVALENT

EQUI

(EQUAL)

EQUINOX
EQUILATERAL
EQUILIBRIUM

Math and Science Roots

As students study subjects such as geometry, weather, biology, and astronomy, they will encounter quantities of new vocabulary. They can often learn the meaning of these words by looking at the roots with which they are composed. As students find new words, they can add more roots to a poster on the bulletin board. Then have students check this list to remind them how the words they already know will help them understand the new words they come across.

> *hydroponics: hydro (water) + ponics*
> *quadrilateral: quadri (four) + lateral (sides)*
> *thermometer: thermo (heat) + meter (measure)*

Greek and Roman Mythology

The stories of the Greeks and Romans have also influenced many words in the English language. Give students examples of phrases, such as the following:

> Herculean task
> Midas touch
> world atlas
> panic attack

In small groups, students can investigate the origin of these phrases and what they mean now. Each group then reports its findings to the class.

Students can also investigate the original meanings of familiar words such as the days of the week and the months of the year.

Inventing Scientific Terms

Students can participate in the delight of developing a word that is just right for something. Talk about important scientific inventions and what they are called. How was the name invented? If it comes from Latin or Greek roots, what do the roots mean?

Many inventions expand on the possibilities introduced by previous inventions. The *telephone* was an example of the expansion of communication, an advance over the *telegraph,* and *television* was a step beyond. Talk about current popular terms, such as *modems* and *video games.* What possible future inventions might grow out of these? What might these inventions be called?

Provide students with lists of useful prefixes, roots, and suffixes from which they can construct their words:

manu	graph	istic	trans
andro	port	tion	able
neo	fact	ness	vert
sub	scope	ator	ortho
phobia	bio	ology	retro

Prefix-Root Wheel

Help students build vocabulary by manipulating a Prefix-Root Wheel (see page 107). As students move the prefixes, they will form such words as *pretend, discover,* or *unfold.* Make the outside wheel 9" in diameter. The inside wheel is 5" across.

Students will learn a lot by making these wheels themselves. They need to use the dictionary to check on possible words because not all combinations form new words. They will also encounter new words, such as *depose* and *deduce.*

The Con Game

This game reviews prefixes orally and helps develop vocabulary. A class leader says a prefix, and then quickly counts to 100, while a student names as many words as possible that begin with that prefix. The leader might say *con,* for example, and then point to a student. The student then names words such as *convict, contender, conduit,* and *conclusion.*

The class can be divided into teams and the score can be kept by counting one point for each word mentioned. Make a list of common prefixes to use during the game. Lists of words beginning with prefixes can also be developed.

Here is a useful list of prefixes for this activity (as well as others):

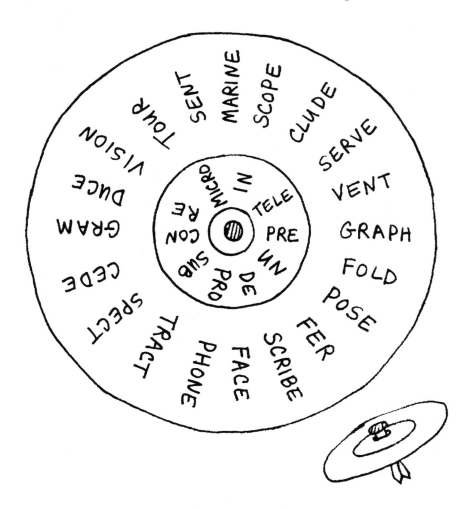

auto	fore	post	sub
bene	im, in	pre	semi
contra, counter	mis	proto	trans
de	multi	re	un
ex	ob		

Word People

No matter how many words there are in the English language, new words are always needed. Often, a scientific discovery is named after the person who found it or developed it, such as the *Shoemaker-Levi* comet and the *bougainvillea* plant. In addition, people's names are given to ideas that they are associated with, such as *boycott, bloomer,* and *quisling.* As new ideas and technologies evolve, people alive today have the opportunity for lasting fame (or infamy). Ask students what they would like to have named after them (An insect? A skating technique? A new kind of musical instrument?). Or perhaps something they will accomplish can be named for them. Students can discuss what they want their name to mean and why they chose it.

Seeing Relationships

Students are accustomed to sequences of words in alphabetical order or to numbers that have clear relationships—for example, 1, 3, 5, 7. Provide exercises in which one word, letter, or number is omitted and see if the students can supply what is missing based on the relationship they see.

a e i _ u

1 2 4 8 _

apple bear candy _____ elephant

farm cow zoo tiger ocean _____

cub bear _____ duck colt horse

lazy industrious happy _____ old young

bone crowd baby corn _____ cork

O T T F F S S E _ T

Answers:

(o)	(duckling)
(16)	(sad)
(any word that begins with *d*)	(any word beginning with *b*)
(any animal seen in the ocean)	(N; letters begin words for numbers 1–10)

Exploring the Meaning of Words

Being able to grasp the meaning of a word in context is not enough to enable students to use the word independently and with precision. Students need practice in understanding what words mean and how words are organized, in categories such as synonyms and antonyms, and in levels of generality. The typical instructions to "Look it up and use it in a sentence" result in mechanical exercises that do not have an impact on students' receptive (listening or reading) or productive (speaking or writing) vocabulary knowledge. Instruction should focus, instead, on presenting a word as part of a larger web of connections and connotations.

My First Dictionary

Early primary students will enjoy creating personalized dictionaries to illustrate new vocabulary words, examples of environmental print, and labels of objects around the classroom. On each page, have them put the word, a simple definition (created by the class), and a picture (drawn or cut out). These dictionaries can be prepared individually or as a class, with each student contributing a particular word. Putting the pages in order as new words are added throughout the year is good practice in alphabetizing. Future writing activities can be based on the words in these dictionaries.

ESL students will also benefit from bringing in pictures from magazines and other sources and labeling the objects in them. Other students can help them with the vocabulary or check the spelling.

Dictionary of the Month

Each month is characterized in many different ways: by the color that the month is indicative of (Spring—green—April), the holidays of each month, school activities, and so on. This focus can be used to help increase students' vocabulary and can also be used as a good resource for writing stories.

The class can make a dictionary that is divided into the months of the school year. Within each month, words can be included that have something to do with that month, and the paper used can be the color of that month. Words can be added to the lists according to the needs of the children or their interests. Children should be encouraged to use this dictionary as a writing tool as well as an alternative dictionary. Here is an example:

January (white)	*February (red)*	*March (green)*
winter	correspondence	tulips
sleet	blizzard	emerald
evergreen	torrent	spring
icicle	marshmallows	hibernation

Visual Dictionary

A model for a dictionary that older students will enjoy is *Star Wars: Episode I, The Visual Dictionary* by David West Reynolds (DK, 1999). Students will note that each page features a specific topic and lists elements, labels objects, and explains the background. Following this format, students can prepare their own dictionaries on favorite topics, individually or in small groups.

The Dictionary Game

This challenging game for older students helps them use their knowledge of word meanings and dictionaries. Have the students divide into groups of about five. Each group selects a leader to begin playing. The leader uses the dictionary to choose a short, simple word that no one knows—for example, *hovel.* (You may prefer to hand out a list of possible words to choose from in order to save time.) The leader reads the word to the group members and asks them to write down a suggested definition, while he or she writes the correct one. Guesses usually range from obvious to outrageous. Set a time limit and have the leader collect all definitions. The leader then reads each definition aloud, including the real dictionary definition, and the group votes on which definition they think is right. After everyone has voted, the leader surprises the group by telling them which definition was from the dictionary. One point is awarded to the leader for each person who does *not* guess correctly and also to the member(s) who fools someone with a definition. Two points are awarded to the person who guesses the *correct* definition. Then a new leader is chosen to begin the next round.

Besides encouraging dictionary use and vocabulary development, this game challenges students to make intelligent guesses about the meaning of words, and rewards them for writing definitions that sound like reasonable dictionary entries. You can adjust this game to play with the whole class if you keep the number of suggested definitions small. Vary the difficulty of the game by choosing longer or shorter words. In general, the shorter words are more difficult because there are fewer clues to their meaning. For example:

> *Calumny:*   Vote for one of the following definitions:
> 1. a mythological Greek god
> 2. a lie meant to injure someone
> 3. a mineral form of calcium
> 4. having a relaxing effect

In Other Words

Instead of having students use new words in a sentence, have them use their own words to rewrite or paraphrase the meaning.

Give students sentences such as the following and ask them to rewrite the sentences so that their meanings are clear:

- The servant smiled *obsequiously* at his master.
- The servant smiled *in a sickeningly respectful way* at his master.

A Herd of Children

Particular words used for groups of objects can be surprising and amusing. Have students list examples of familiar phrases:

> school of fish
> herd of elephants
> flock of birds
> pack of wolves

Some less common terms you might add include:

> rabble of butterflies
> pride of lions

covey of quail

gaggle of geese

brace of partridge

Once the students understand the idea of these collective nouns, invite them to think up their own. Start them out by giving them phrases to fill in:

a _____ of teeth

a huddle of _____

a _____ of students

an entanglement of _____

a _____ of dragons

a shushing of _____

a _____ of penguins

Students can continue to create phrases of their own, individually or in small groups. Have them illustrate their suggestions for a display that others can appreciate. Maybe your class will think of a term that everyone will adopt.

An Exaltation of Larks by James Lipton (Penguin, 1984) contains a multitude of examples of these group words, with illustrations. Students will enjoy poring over the book and discovering unusual phrases.

Go-Together Words

Ask students if they can guess the word that goes in each blank:

day and _____

salt and _____

knife and _____

table and _____

back and _____

Do they all agree on the correct word? Can the students think of other Go-Together Words? Have them create more examples to try out on the class.

Word Webbing

Illustrate the semantic connections of a word by writing it in the center of the board and drawing a circle around it. Ask students to suggest related words. Place examples provided by students around the circle and draw lines to connect related words.

This graphic representation of a word helps students remember new words and incorporate these words into their working vocabulary. Use this activity regularly in your reading program to expand student awareness of word meanings.

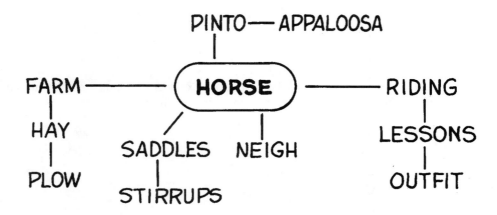

Stale Words

Tell the students that they can't use the words *say* and *said* for one day. Brainstorm a list of possible substitutes, such as:

whisper	mutter	shout
holler	cry	murmur
call	question	complain
ask	grumble	giggle
proclaim	assert	promise

Another word that could be retired is *walk.* Have students suggest synonyms, or other ways of expressing the same idea. Students then act out a synonym and challenge the class to guess which word best describes their *walk.*

Ways of Saying

Upper-grade students can use the newspaper as a source of alternatives to the word *say.* Give groups of students different pages from the news section of the newspaper. Have them draw circles around all the different synonyms for *say* that they can find. How many different words are used in the newspaper? Post examples of these words on the bulletin board to encourage students to incorporate them in their speech and writing.

Thesaurus

The word *thesaurus* means *treasure* in Latin; a thesaurus, then, is a *treasury of words,* an invaluable list of synonyms for most common words.

Pass a copy of a thesaurus around the class and demonstrate how the book is organized. Some editions have the words listed by subject, so that you have to look up the word in the index first and then find it in the book. Others are alphabetical and are used like other dictionaries. Always have a copy available to students for use during writing periods or to look through in their spare time. A class set or at least a set of 10 inexpensive editions is recommended in classrooms from fourth grade up for vocabulary development. Try George Beal's *The Kingfisher Illustrated Thesaurus* (Kingfisher, 1996) and *Beginning Writer's Thesaurus* (Scott Foresman, 1994).

Making a Class Thesaurus

After the class has been introduced to the use of a thesaurus, have students compile a personalized version for class use. Each student can take one word that has been overused in class writing and develop a list of 10 synonyms for it. Examples are:

see	nice
red	eat
girl	like
hot	old

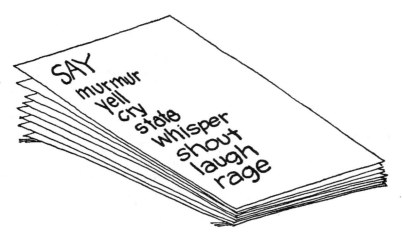

Collect the individual pages and place them in a notebook in alphabetical order for a Class Thesaurus. Then encourage students to consult the thesaurus and share the words they find. They will learn more from compiling their own synonym dictionary than if they had just copied lists of words from another source.

The Synonym Wheel

One way to focus student attention on synonyms is to display them on the bulletin board. Cut a wheel from brown paper or use a real wheel, if you can get one. At the center, place a common word, such as *little*. Have the students write synonyms—*small, tiny, diminutive, miniscule, petite*—for this overworked word on slips of paper and mount them on the spokes and the rim of the wheel. New words can be featured on the wheel as you study vocabulary for reading and writing. Other words to use on the hub are *big, pretty, run, like,* and *good.*

Attach the paper wheel to the bulletin board with a thumbtack so students can turn the wheel to read new synonyms. Display a different synonym every week, helping students find new words to use instead of the common ones.

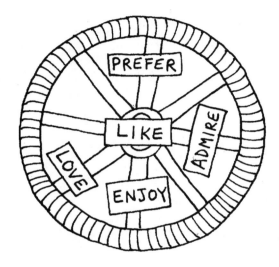

Synonym Poems

Students can use their examples of synonyms to write short rhyming couplets. The first line is a series of four adjectives, nouns, or verbs, all synonyms. The second line is a statement that rhymes with the first line. Here is an example:

> Gracious, polite, well-mannered, kind,
> Why is it so hard to find?

Students can work on these poems in small groups or this exercise can be assigned as part of their vocabulary review.

Painting Pictures

Students can put their knowledge of synonyms to use and make their writing more precise, interesting, and colorful. Provide students with a short passage, such as the following:

> They were cleaning out the house that day. The carpets smelled bad and the windows were broken. There was a lot of work to do. It would take a long time.

Have students work in groups to suggest alternatives to the underlined words. Each group can share its version with the class.

Color Me Red

Color words are useful for students of all ages. Have the class work in small groups to brainstorm all the words for different shades of one color—for example, red, yellow, blue, or green. Notice all the different kinds of *red* that are listed here:

scarlet	ruby	claret
vermilion	garnet	russet
crimson	maroon	magenta
cerise	rust	carmine

Have students bring in pictures of red objects. What color words would they use to describe the objects? When students write after this exercise, they will be able to provide a more exact picture for the reader.

Antonyms

Antonyms are the opposite of synonyms. Students are very familiar with pairs of opposites. Have students think of as many pairs as they can, such as:

over—under	tall—short	rich—poor
old—new	thick—thin	slow—fast
full—empty	cheap—expensive	happy—sad

Antonyms can also be expressed in the form of a ratio or an analogy, as shown here:

$$\frac{old}{new} :: \frac{thin}{?}$$

The analogy is read: "Old is to new as thin is to _____?" The first step in solving the ratio is to determine what the relationship is between the first two words. Since they are opposites, the second pair must be opposites as well. The answer may be *thick* or a synonym of *thick,* or it might be *fat.* In some cases, there are many right answers when there are many synonyms for a particular opposite.

$$\frac{add}{subtract} :: \frac{?}{little}$$

Here, the answer could be *big, gigantic, immense, large, huge,* or *tremendous.*

Students can create their own analogies to challenge the class. Keep examples of analogies on hand in the learning center.

Jigsaw Opposites

Primary students can practice using opposites with this game. Select a simple jigsaw picture puzzle and turn it over. On the pieces, write pairs of opposites so that the opposites touch. When the students play the game, they try to match the opposites to complete the puzzle. When finished, they turn the puzzle over, and they will have a complete picture.

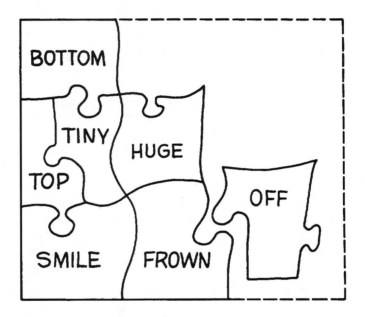

Word Volley

Have students line up in two rows so that they are facing one another. The first group starts out by selecting a word, such as *good*. Then the first person on the other side must give a synonym for the word *good*, such as *excellent*. As in volleyball, the word passes back to the first team, and they must think of another synonym for *good*. Synonyms are bounced back and forth until one group cannot give another synonym. If you wish to score this game, the team giving the last synonym would have a point. (You may need to enforce a time limit for answering and have a judge to decide if words are acceptable.) The group that was successful in coming up with the last synonym selects a new word, and play continues.

This game can also be used for antonyms of the same words or word chains. It can be played without keeping score but with the two teams seeing how long they can keep the "volley" going.

Borrowed Words

Another way to encourage vocabulary development is to introduce the students to the many words in English that are borrowed from other languages. Develop this aspect of language in connection with the study of a particular country or language as you feature words borrowed from that language.

For the study of French words, place a map or outline of France on the bulletin board. To this map attach yarn leading to words mounted on pieces of paper around the bulletin board. Possible words to display include:

chic	nation	azure
cuisine	liqueur	ennui
embarrass	à la mode	ballet
compliment	silhouette	

Discuss how borrowed French words are sometimes pronounced differently than English words. An example is *massage,* in which the final sound (spelled *g*) is different than it is in *message.* Here are two phonemes: /j/ and /ž/. For *garage,* you may hear people using either of these phonemes. The word *page* has been completely anglicized, so only /j/ is used by speakers of English. Words that were borrowed from French recently show less adjustment to the usual patterns of English pronunciation than those borrowed some time ago.

Have a small group of students create a world map illustrated with borrowed words from many different countries. Encourage them to discover words from such unexpected languages as Japanese *(bonsai),* Hindi *(khaki),* and Dutch *(yacht).* The students will also enjoy figuring out where some of these languages are spoken. Here are some examples:

Spanish: cargo, alligator
Aztec (by way of Spanish): tomato, chocolate
Dutch: cruise, landscape
Persian: bazaar, caravan, sugar
Arabic: syrup, algebra
Hindi: bungalow, shampoo
Russian: samovar, steppe
Italian: cello, crescendo

Acronyms Create Words

Some acronyms have become words and are no longer capitalized. The most familiar example is *radar,* originally from *radio detecting and ranging.* Many of us have forgotten that these words were once acronyms. Other such examples are:

laser: **l**ight **a**mplification by **s**timulated **e**mission of **r**adiation
snafu: **s**ituation **n**ormal: **a**ll **f**ouled **up**

scuba: self-contained underwater breathing apparatus

Loran: long range navigation

sonar: sound navigation and ranging

New English Words

Have students prepare a list of words that are new in the English language. Words that have been invented recently include:

debug   hacker

byte   chip

frisbie   marsquake

sol (a day on Mars)   yuppie

Eponyms

Eponyms are words that come from someone's name. Challenge students to research how these words originated.

diesel: Rudolph Diesel

guillotine: Dr. Joseph Ignace Guillotin

leotard: Jules Léotard

nicotine: Jean Nicot

sandwich: John Montagu, 4th Earl of Sandwich

silhouette: Étienne de Silhouette

Invented Words

Invite your students to try to match these words with the authors who created them:

1. scrooge   a. Francois Rabelais
2. ogre   b. Karel Capek
3. robot   c. Charles Perrault
4. moron   d. Molière
5. gargantuan   e. Charles Dickens
6. serendipity   f. Horace Walpole

Answers: (1e, 2c, 3b, 4d, 5a, 6f)

Challenge advanced students to put these words in order of invention. They can check their hypotheses against an unabridged dictionary.

Creating New Words

Using made-up words to spur children in creative writing is a good way to bring out the individuality in every child, since more conventional words (i.e., *happiness, friendship,* etc.) sometimes bring very conventional compositions.

Write the made-up word on the board and pronounce it for the students. Have them think about the word through their senses: What does it smell like? Can you eat it? What does it taste like? How does it feel on your cheeks? Does it make a noise? Can you do anything with it? Here are some sample words:

shoop	oversnod
glunch	jengier
salagango	poubalistic
erpted	

Students can also identify objects or ideas that don't have a name and need one. What areas in their experience are difficult to think or talk about because there is no word for it? They may suggest topics such as family relationships, clothes, and body language.

Warm—Hot—Boiling!

This activity requires students to determine the relationship between the words given in order to select the correct word that completes the sequence, such as:

cool, warm, _____	(tepid, hot, cold)
sand, pebble, _____	(mountain, rock, salt)
large, gigantic, _____	(enormous, big, small)
tree, sapling, _____	(forest, seed, pine)

Playing with Words

There are many interesting ways to represent words. Explore the meaning of words through illustration, as seen on page 120. Encourage students to discover new ways to represent their favorite words.

Malapropism

This type of word play is named after Mrs. Malaprop, a character in *The Rivals* (a play by Richard Brinsley Sheridan) who was always getting her words just slightly mixed up. Examples are "John is not in school because he is *guaranteed* with the measles" and "She took the *subscription* to the druggist."

Malapropisms are humorous because the intended word is replaced by another word with a similar sound. Have students underline the malapropism in each of the following sentences and write the correct word above.

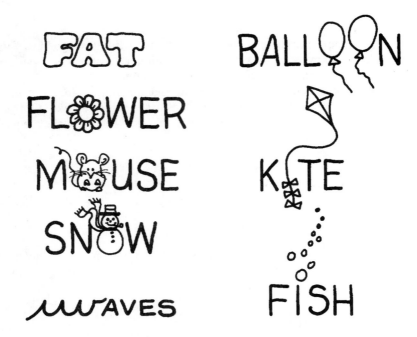

- Don't take everything so liberally.
- Forget it. It's irrelevant. It ain't German to the conversation.
- Whoever sent them obviously wanted to remain unanimous.
- You're invading the issue.
- It's a proven fact that capital punishment is a known detergent to crime.
- Well, goodbye and good ribbons.

Older students can create their own malapropisms to share with the class. They can try to trick the other students who have to spot the malapropism and supply the correct word.

Discussion Questions

1. Some students seem to pick up new words faster than other students. How can you provide sufficient instruction and practice for these students without leaving out the rest of the class?

2. Is there a difference between teaching vocabulary to ESL students and students who are below grade level?

Exploring Further

The American Heritage Student Dictionary. Houghton Mifflin, 1994.

Blurt! The Webster's Game of Word Racing. Board game for 3 to 12 players. Patch Products, (800) 524-4263 or <www.patchproducts.com>

Nancy Lee Cecil. A Plethora of Pink Poppies. *The California Reader* 26, 3 (Spring 1993).

Encarta World English Dictionary. CD-ROM. Microsoft, 1999. Also available in print from St. Martin's.

50 Wonderful Word Games: Easy and Entertaining Activities That Build Important Language Arts Skills. Scholastic, 1998.

Merriam-Webster's Intermediate Dictionary. Merriam-Webster, 1994.

Reading Skills Activities Library (3 vol, grades 1–3). Center for Applied Research in Education.

Scholastic Children's Dictionary. Scholastic, 1996.

Vocabulary Development. CD-ROM. Optimum Resources. Mac/Windows.

Vocabulary University. Comic strips, interactive word puzzles, and other activities to expand vocabulary for elementary through high school. <www.vocabulary.com>

Webster's New World Student's Dictionary. Macmillan, 1996.

Word Games through the Year: Challenge Your Mind. Instructional Fair, 1998.

References

Janet Allan. *Words, Words, Words: Teaching Vocabulary in Grades 4–12*. Stenhouse, 1999.

Jeanne Chall, V. Jacobs, and L. Baldwin. *The Reading Crisis: Why Poor Children Fall Behind*. Harvard University Press, 1990.

D. K. Dickinson and M. W. Smith. "Long Term Effects of Preschool Teachers' Book Readings on Low-Income Children's Vocabulary and Story Comprehension." *Reading Research Quarterly, 29,* no. 2 (1994).

Judith A. Scott and Cynthia E. Butler. *Language Arts in the 1990s: A Survey of General Practices with an Emphasis on the Teaching of Vocabulary in Literature-Based Classrooms*. Paper presented at AERA, New Orleans, 1994.

5 Beginning Writing

When I type a title page, I hold it and I look at it and I think, I just need four thousand sentences to go with this and I'll have a book!
—Betsy Byars, *The Moon and I: A Memoir*

Awareness of the importance of writing has grown considerably over the past decade. On the one hand, students are expected to do more writing, from primary grades to university, as well as later, in their professional lives. On the other hand, there is increased public concern over tests that show high school graduates still lack what are considered basic writing skills. The *writing process* approach (Graves, 1983) has had a major impact on improving writing instruction in the schools. Students are not expected to sit down with a blank piece of paper and produce perfectly polished "products." Instead, they are guided as they move through the stages of planning, drafting, revising, and editing. Not only are students encouraged to write more but they also practice more different types of writing and write for different audiences. Students begin to see themselves as real "authors" when they publish their own writing and connect it with the authors of books that they read. Teachers have learned to incorporate activities that support these processes, such as prewriting warm-ups, response groups for revising, daily journal writing, and writing to learn across the curriculum. The evaluation and assessment of writing has been rethought; today, because student writing is often evaluated by following a writing piece from beginning to end as it takes shape (as in portfolio assessment), teachers are no longer responsible for correcting *every* error in *every* paper that their students produce.

In the ideal language arts program, students will write every day. The writing will range from assigned topics or timed writing to personal narratives or topics they choose themselves, including short and long pieces, stories, reports, and project logs. Only a limited number of these compositions will be selected to revise and polish in order to make them ready for a real audience.

Getting Started

Writing is more than putting a pen to paper (or a hand to keyboard). In fact, writing often begins with speaking and listening as students warm up with prewriting activities such as brainstorming, clustering, and sharing ideas. These oral thinking and composing processes come into play as students begin to write and again when students return and rethink as they draft their ideas. The earliest stages of writing are social. As students talk with one another about what to write, they compose group stories. As they gain experience and fluency in writing, they continue to use talk to plan and compose independently. Throughout, the teacher provides structure and support by writing along with students, talking about writing, and analyzing writing models. This teacher *scaffolding* allows students to benefit from helpful formulas, such as the five-paragraph essay, as they need the support, yet move beyond this restrictive structure as they gain in writing experience.

Clustering

Introduce students to the idea of *clustering* before writing. They can write a word or a topic, such as *friendship,* in the middle of a piece of paper. Then, around the word, they note all the related words and ideas that they can think of. They can add examples, associations, synonyms/antonyms, and so on. They can also draw lines linking ideas to show how they are connected. Do this activity first as a whole class so that everyone is involved in suggesting connections and students can "piggy-back" on each other's ideas. Have each student select a part of the group clustering. Students can continue their clustering individually and then use the ideas that they have come up with as a base for writing a paragraph.

As a prewriting activity, clustering helps students generate ideas to write about, make connections between ideas that will lead to improved writing, and use writing to find out what they think.

Write from the Start

For classes with students of diverse language and writing abilities, you need to provide varied meaningful and interesting learning activities that will help students learn to link oral and written language. Select a theme and collect a wide range of materials that will stimulate student discussion and engagement with language, as in the following:

> *food:* examples of menus, canned food, cereal boxes, shopping lists, measuring cups, recipes
>
> *growth:* different seeds, flower catalogs/order forms, student growth chart, linear measure, calendar, plant food/fertilizer containers
>
> *weather:* thermometer, rain measure, solar calculator, barometer, wind direction vane, balloons

Student involvement in talk around these topics will lead naturally to writing activities, as a class, in small groups, or individually.

Story Scribes

Even the youngest students can "write" a story if they have someone to whom they may dictate it. Use aides, parents, or even upper-grade students to sit with students and type or write the story as it is told. If you establish a special "story chair" for this purpose, students will vie for the opportunity to have their words recorded.

Since the student composed the story, it is easy for him or her to read it back. At the same time, students are learning the conventions of writing without having to worry about correct spelling. Duplicate the stories for reading material or staple them together in book form for pride of authorship. Story dictating will help students develop a positive attitude toward communicating through writing.

Beginning to Write Independently

As soon as first-graders learn the rudiments of printing, they are fascinated by printing words. They can soon compose a sentence or two, for example, expressing ideas they have drawn or painted. They can also compose sentences based on a topic introduced by the teacher:

- *What do you like to do?*
  I like to play soccer.
- *What do you like to eat?*
  I like to eat ice cream.

Help the students with writing by printing words they need on the board. Encourage them to write words down the way they sound ("invented" spelling) rather than worry about the accuracy of their spelling at this point. At this age, the ideas students express are more important than the form they use. Interest and need will lead to greater awareness of meaning and proficiency in spelling as the student gains fluency in writing.

All about Me

This inventory can be given to students of any age. Have them write their responses or tell them to the class. Each item can be used separately and carried out over a week. The inventory can also be used at the beginning of the year and at the end of the year, as children compare their responses. Here are some suggestions:

- What are three things I enjoy?
- What are three things I don't enjoy?
- What are three things I like to do alone?
- What am I proudest of?
- What would I like to change about myself?
- What would I change about the world?
- What job do I do best?

- What person do I admire the most?
- What special talent would I most like to have?
- If I had one wish, what would I wish for?

Students can also use these questions to interview each other. The written responses are collected in a notebook that may be titled "Our Classmates."

Group Dictation

The dictated group story or poem also lends itself to beginning writers. Students can compose sentences, telling personal news or describing class experiences. As an imaginative teacher, you may extend this technique to record more creative expression by introducing such phrases as *Snow is . . .* or *The funniest thing happened to me . . . .*

Group dictation can also result in a story or poem that a class composes orally. Record this story as it develops sentence by sentence. Begin by asking the class members what animal they would like to write about. Introduce the idea of prewriting activities by having students first talk about the selected animal. If they choose a hippopotamus, for instance, they might discuss places they have seen hippos, and then decide on a specific one in terms of size, color, name, location, and habits. The story grows as each child is encouraged to participate. Then it can be typed or printed on a large sheet for use in further reading activities.

A "Holey" Story

Give each child a piece of white construction paper, 9" × 12" or larger, in which you have cut scattered circles of various sizes. Have the students draw a picture around the circles, utilizing them in some way (see page 127). They can then write or dictate a sentence(s) about their pictures. Have them discuss their pictures with the class. Put finished drawings on the bulletin board for use with additional reading and writing activities.

Use Your Senses

Use this idea at the beginning of the year to stimulate students' awareness of their senses: hearing, seeing, smelling, tasting, and touching. Ask the children to brainstorm or jot down their responses to the following questions:

- How many bright red things can you name?
- Name two sounds that make you feel happy.
- What tastes make you think of summer?
- What is the fuzziest thing you can think of?
- What smells would you most like to find when you go home tonight?
- What makes you feel really cold when you see it?

A "holey" story

Story Skeletons

This writing prompt reinforces student awareness of story structure. Have students complete a set of sentences that form a story when read in sequence. Use a pattern such as the following:

- One morning I was on my way to _____.
- I saw a huge _____.
- It was sleeping under _____.
- I didn't want to wake it because _____.
- Suddenly, I heard _____.
- I began to run toward _____.
- Just as I got there _____.
- I'm lucky that _____.

Students can work individually or in small groups to compose their story. After all the sentences have been completed, tell the students to add a title at the top of their papers. They can read their versions of this Story Skeleton to the class. For use in the learning center, duplicate this structure and allot several lines for the completion of each sentence.

Circle Writing

Another way to motivate students to write is to present something that is totally different from what they're used to doing. "Take a piece of paper out and start writing" is a pretty ordinary instruction, but "Draw a circle in the middle of the sheet and start writing around in circles" intrigues children. The circle in the center could contain a picture of what the story is about or it could be the title of the story. Instruct the students to write in a circular motion, so that the reader has to turn the sheet around to read the story.

Public Writing

Children love to write on the board, especially with colored pens. Designate a corner of the board for free writing where children can write a riddle to mystify their friends, a favorite line of poetry, or a question they wonder about.

At times, you might label the corner for a specific activity, such as:

- Animals and their babies
- What does *tree* make you think of?
- Words of four syllables

Creative Writing

Encourage students to write more, try out different types of writing, and use their imaginations for writing by having a class Treasure Chest. Students can submit any of their (anonymous) literary gems to the class collection. Periodically, you or a student will draw a selection and read it aloud. Students will be motivated at the thought of an audience for their work. Types of writing they might include are:

poetry	stories
songs	jokes
concerns	dialogues
riddles	essays

Suggest that students select pen names for their contributions. Do not reveal who is behind the pen names until the end of the year.

Pictures Tell a Story

Ask the children to bring in pictures of people who are happy, sad, angry, and so on. It is helpful if some pictures are large and colorful. The pictures can be mounted on a sheet of paper placed on a bulletin board. Depending on the space available, 5 or 10 pictures can be mounted.

As a daily oral exercise, students can contribute descriptive words about each of the pictures. You can write down the students' words or a scribe from the class can perform this task. Words are then placed under each picture.

At the end of the week, each child has the opportunity to select one of the pictures and to create a story, giving his or her ideas about what might have led to the picture and why this person is acting this way. Of course, the descriptive words are available to aid the children in writing their stories. Each student writer has the option of utilizing these words or thinking of new ones.

The advantage of this approach to writing is that the students can exercise their ability to "read" pictures. They develop a vocabulary for each of the pictures. It might also be interesting for the children to discuss why they selected certain pictures about which to write.

Photo Prompts

Collect photographs for students to use as story starters. Students can select a photo that interests them from the collection and write about it and/or give it a caption. If the photos are blurred or obscure, students will have to use their imaginations to describe the picture or tell what is going on in the picture.

You can accumulate extra photos quickly if you can get two sets of prints developed for the same cost as one set.

Photo Portraits

The availability of inexpensive cameras makes student photography possible. Have students brainstorm a list of important people (or pets) in their lives. They have to consider what makes that person special. Then they must plan how to represent the character they have chosen. What will the person be doing? How will he or she be dressed? Where will they take the photo and what will be in the background? They may need to take a number of shots, with different lighting and from different angles, before they find one that seems exactly right for the person.

Creating and interpreting photographs or pictures is a visual kind of literacy as well as an opportunity for students to exhibit a different kind of intelligence. Students are learning how to "read" and "write" this visual text. This photo project can be the base for more writing about the person featured as well as interviews with people involved.

Hot Air Stories

Give each student a balloon to blow up. Have the students pretend they are inside the balloons and write group or individual stories. Here is an sample story:

> Something strange is happening. I can't hear anything. I wonder where I am? The last thing I remember is blowing up the balloon Mrs. Richardson gave me. I was glad that she handed me a red one since that's my favorite color. Wait a minute! That's why everything looks so rosy. I'm INSIDE THE BALLOON! It's sort of fun in here: really slippery spots and (yuk!) *damp* in other spots. I think I'll slide down to the bottom. Whoops! It's hard to stop! Hey! I can jump on the bottom and touch the top. This is more fun than a trampoline. Oh, oh the walls are starting to cave in. I'd better get out of here before I'm smothered!

Shapes and Things

Provide children with a sheet of paper that has objects drawn on it (or draw objects on the board) and ask them to write about the objects. You can also ask children to think of objects and draw them in front of the class to entice their classmates to write. For example, see the top of page 131. These objects have been adapted from Native American artwork illustrated in *Authentic Indian Designs,* edited by Maria Naylor (Dover Publications, 1975). (Up to 10 illustrations can be reproduced free and without special permission.) Look for other Dover Publications for more examples of art in the public domain.

For a variation on this exercise, have students write a description of an object. Each child passes his or her written description to another student who tries to draw the object based on the writing. Students will enjoy comparing the original objects to the ones drawn by their classmates.

Peculiar Animals

Have the students draw a picture of the most peculiar animal they can imagine (see the bottom of page 131). Then they can write stories about the adventures of their animals. What is the animal's name? Where does it live? What does it like to eat? Would it make a good pet?

  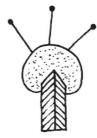 

Native American art (adapted from Authentic Indian Designs)

This is also a good activity for oral conversation. After a student has described the animal to the class, the other students can ask questions about the animal's habits and adventures.

Snabbit

Peculiar animal

Class Mascot

Choose a stuffed animal to join the classroom, perhaps a Teddy Bear or a Beanbag Frog. Students can work together to decide on a name for their animal. Give students the opportunity to take this "classmate" home over the weekend. When they return, they will have to explain to the class how their animal spent the weekend, as recorded in its diary. Each student can write a chapter in the continuing adventures of the animal.

Creature Features

One day after school, cut giant "footprints" out of heavy paper and arrange them across the walls, floor, and ceiling of your classroom. When the students arrive, have them try to imagine what kind of creature made these prints. What does this creature look like? Where does it live? What does it eat? They can write stories about the creatures they imagine.

Post the stories on the board and use them to extend the learning experience. Give students an exercise sheet with questions on it such as the following:

- List four synonyms for *scary.*
- List five synonyms for *big.* Circle the one that's the *biggest.*
- Give a recipe for your creature's favorite dish.
- How does your creature celebrate a birthday?
- Look up the following words and circle the one that best describes your creature: *herbivorous, carnivorous, omnivorous.*
- What's your creature's favorite color and why?
- If a movie was made about your creature, what would it be called? Who would star in it?
- Write a bedtime story for your creature.

For older students, vary the activity by asking them to imagine that this is an *extraterrestrial,* a visitor from another planet. What kind of planet does the alien come from? Why is it here? What is it like and what does it do? What does it think of this planet? Students can write lengthy descriptions or stories about the alien they imagine.

The Touch Box

Inside the Touch Box is a hidden object. From what the children imagine the object to be and from its texture, they can begin to create a story or poem. An ordinary shoe box can be the Touch Box. Cut a hole in the front of the box big enough for a child to reach inside to feel the object. Attach a sleeve around the hole so the child cannot see what is inside the box. Write "Touch Box" on the lid. Print instructions with a felt pen on a 12" × 18" sheet of paper or tagboard, as shown in the illustration.

After three days, open the box. What is it? An unusual candle? A funny-shaped sweet potato? A sock filled with interesting objects? Let the children discuss their guesses.

The Touch Box

Put your hand in the box.
Feel what is inside.
What do you think it is?
Write your answer on a sheet of paper.
Tell what the THING looks like.

What If?

A favorite writing prompt is the "What if?" question that encourages students to use their imaginations. Read a few of these to students:

What if...

- everything you touched turned to gold?
- you could buy gills to breathe underwater?
- everyone looked exactly the same?
- you never needed to sleep again?

Encourage students to suggest other "What if?" ideas that can be used.

And Then What Happened?

Older students will ask what might happen if people could have their dreams come true. Many folktales revolve around the granting of three wishes. Students can discuss the possible consequences and then write their ideas about what happened next. For example, King Midas has second thoughts after turning his daughter to gold in Lynne Reid Banks's *The Adventures of King Midas* (Morrow, 1992). *The Frog Prince, Continued* by Jon Scieszka (Viking, 1991) explains what happens *after* "and they lived happily ever after."

Trading Places

Here is another activity that combines writing and imagination. Pose some questions for your class, beginning with the phrase, "How would you feel if . . . ?" and have them write down their responses. Try to provide some illustrations of each question so that the children can visualize the situations, for example:

- How would you feel if you were looking at your pet dog and all of a sudden you became the dog wagging his tail, and the dog was looking at *you?*
- How would you feel if you woke up one morning in a strange bed in a strange house and then looked in the mirror and realized you had turned into someone you had never seen before?

Cat Tales

Make a bulletin board display of cats. Include Story Starters that are related to cats, such as:

- Last night my cat jumped up on the table and said _____.
- My neighbor's cat has the funniest pet.
- I think that my cat is getting much smarter since I showed him how to turn on the computer.

Each child should choose one of these sentences to begin a story. Attach the completed stories to the bulletin board display or compile a *Big Book of Cat Tales.*

Plot Situations

Here are some Story Starters put in a plot situation form. This technique immerses the child in a situation, encouraging the student to become totally involved.

Easy

- Angela got an animal for her birthday. What is it and where will she keep it?
- Yosen hates to eat cooked carrots. Today he has decided to pretend the carrots are something else. What will he do to fool himself? Will his trick work?
- While Tracy was eating breakfast, a bird began to peck on the window. What does the bird want Tracy to do?
- While Justin was taking a bath today, he thought of a nice thing to do for his sixty-year-old neighbor. What will he do? What will his neighbor do?
- Robin looked out the window today and was so happy that it was raining. She knew that she'd do her favorite thing in the rain. What is it?
- The ice cream man said that he had a new flavor today. What is it? How does he make it?

Hard

- When Aimee got dressed this morning, she noticed that her clothes were much too big. Why is Aimee getting smaller? Can she do anything to stop shrinking?
- Alex painted a picture of two horses. When he showed the picture to Sasha, they noticed a shadowy boy standing next to one of the horses. As Sasha examined the painting, the boy in the painting began to look more like Alex and the real Alex

began to become transparent. Why is this happening to Alex? Can Sasha save Alex? Does Alex want to be saved?

• When you woke up this morning and walked out the door to go to school, a crowd of people was waiting outside to get your autograph. What are you famous for?

• Last night, Atish baked some magic cookies that would grant any wish that a person had, but warned everyone against eating too many of them. What *would* happen if you ate too many?

• Every day, Jenny ate her lunch in the park by a statue. Today, the statue tapped Jenny on the shoulder. What did the statue want? How did the statue communicate with Jenny?

Character Cards

Make up a set of story cards for use with students in developing characters for their stories. Older students can help create cards for the class. On one set of cards, list possible occupations, activities, or jobs, such as:

>   doctor
>   computer programmer
>   chef
>   engineer
>   animal trainer
>   musician

On the other set, list possible (including outrageous) behaviors, such as:

>   always wears purple
>   never speaks
>   likes to ride a bicycle
>   is more than six feet tall
>   dyes hair orange
>   has no sense of direction

Students can select a card from each pile in order to create a character for their story. Use two different colors of cards for these piles or write the information in different colors of ink so that students can replace the cards they use in the correct pile.

Writer's Notebook

Have students keep a special notebook for their writing. They can decorate the front with drawings or pictures. Allow at least 10 minutes a day for students to write in their notebooks. Perhaps you will want to provide specific topics to write about, such as:

- List every place that you have lived in and describe each one.
- What did you think about when you were younger (5 years old)?
- What smells do you remember from your childhood?

This activity works well on the computer, as students can easily add to their writing file.

Quick Write

Students need a great deal of practice with writing. Provide frequent short opportunities to write throughout the day. Set a time limit and give them focused topics, such as:

> 10 things that make you happy
> 10 things that make you unhappy

Unfinished Stories

Prepare a series of exercise sheets on which Unfinished Stories are printed. The first paragraph sets the stage and suggests what might happen, but students can produce different endings. Here is an example:

> Leona wanted to show her friends her brother's new motor scooter. She sat on the scooter and began to explain how it worked. As she was talking, the scooter suddenly began to move. Soon it was rolling quickly down the hill. Leona was terrified. She tried desperately to remember what her brother had said about stopping the scooter.

- Did Leona manage to stop the scooter? How?
- What did her friends think?

Leave space for students to illustrate their story if they wish.

Supposing

Encourage students to write intriguing paragraphs that begin with "Supposing . . . ":

- Supposing I fed some cows cocoa beans and all the milk came out chocolate.
- Supposing I woke up in the morning and I was smarter than everybody, including the teacher.

Students can collect their paragraphs in a class book.

An excellent book that presents many examples of these ideas is *Supposing* by Alastair Reid (Little, Brown, 1960).

Last Lines

Last sentences can also serve as Story Starters and, just like beginning sentences and titles, stimulate interest and motivate writing. Place last lines in a notebook or box where students can look at several and select one that suggests a story. The following are examples to start you off:

- Suddenly the wind stopped and everything was still.
- Tia thought she saw the cat wink as it left.
- The music faded away as the sun rose.
- "I guess it was only a dream," thought Sean. Then he noticed the purple feather on his pillow.
- Niamh blinked twice and the mouse vanished.

Students can brainstorm new ideas whenever the supply runs low. These endings could also serve for an impromptu storytelling session.

A Day in the Life of . . .

Invite students to imagine what their backpacks would say if they could talk. This technique of giving human characteristics to an object or idea is called *personification*. How would students personify their backpacks? Would all backpacks talk and act the same way? Could they have different personalities? After students have discussed their ideas and written examples, point out that this is a device used by many writers. They can look for more examples of personification in the literature that they are reading.

"Me" Collage

Here is a creative way to get acquainted with your students. Have students make a collage about themselves—who they are and what they like. Ask them to bring in materials for everyone to share as they make the collage. Have magazines, newspapers, pictures, paints, and pens on hand. They can cut out pictures and words, illustrating their ideas any way they want. Give students large pieces of cardboard on which to mount their collages so that you can display the results for everyone to appreciate.

After they think about what they want to express through their collages, have the children write something about themselves. They can write a short description or a series of phrases in poetry form. If they feel comfortable talking about what they write, you can have students read what they wrote as they show their collages. Students are curious to hear what others wrote and what kinds of things everyone thought of. This is also a good way for students to find out what their classmates are interested in.

"Me" collage

What I Would Miss Most

Ask the students to think for a minute about what they would miss most if it were taken away. Anything they wish to ponder can be used: an object (television), an idea (friendship), a person (Grandma), and so on. The purpose of this activity is not only to have students think but to motivate them to write about their own lives, their values, and what is important to them. After a brief discussion, they write on the topic "What I Would Miss Most." (If students feel comfortable, they might share their ideas.) Students can explain why they would miss this thing, or idea, or person in some detail, and why it is important to them.

My Favorite Food

Ask students if they have a favorite food in their family. Does their family have a special recipe for some dish? Have students write the recipe for their favorite food or describe their special meal. Discuss how to write recipes and directions for the preparation of food. Students will practice explaining a process and organizing their ideas into a set of procedures as they write their recipes.

Share books about food, families, and recipes with students so they can connect their writing to what they have read. The following books are suggested:

Ina Friedman. *How My Parents Learned to Eat.* Illustrated by Alllen Say. Houghton Mifflin, 1984.
Anna Grossnickle Hines. *Daddy Makes the Best Spaghetti.* Clarion, 1986.
Marjorie Winslow. *Mud Pies & Other Recipes.* Macmillan, 1961.
Audrey Wood. *Sweet Dream Pie.* Illustrated by Mark Teague. Scholastic, 1998.

Almost Like Me

Sometimes, in our urge to have students write "creative" stories, we forget that they are also interested in everyday activities. Students often enjoy writing adventure stories about children their own age. The fictional character might live in your town, go to your school, and perhaps even meet the author of the story. The use of familiar experiences often helps the novice author become comfortable with the art of writing. Students will find it easy to create a hero/heroine by exaggerating their own strengths and interests. Writing about someone the same age and sex as themselves will also make it easy for students to insert a note of reality into their story. You may wish to prompt your students with titles like these:

The New Student in Room 14
The Day I Moved to San Francisco
The Soccer Player
The Video Game Champ of Fairmeadow School

Class Log

Students can work together to keep a written class record of activities, discussions, and assignments. Choose a student to be the recorder for a day or a week. All students must contribute ideas to be written in the log. When students have been absent, you can refer them to the class log to help them keep up with what the class is doing.

Mail Box

Provide a special container, such as a large box with a slit in the top, for students to use in writing letters to each other. Once a week, one student can be the designated letter carrier and deliver the letters to students. You can have students make envelopes for their letters and practice writing an address. They can even design their own postage stamp for the mail. A Secret Pal program will ensure that every student receives some mail.

Stationery

Students enjoy using special paper especially made for writing letters. Computer graphics and duplicating machines make it possible for teachers and students to design different kinds of stationery for class correspondence. You can create headings *(From the class of . . .),* borders (leaves), and shapes to cut out (a pumpkin for autumn). Students can also personalize stationery by drawing, rubber stamping, or printing out their own design. This special paper motivates students to continue with their correspondence.

A Letter to Myself

Some teachers have had students write special letters to their future selves. At the end of the year, ask students what they would like to say to themselves five years from now. They can write about what they are doing in school, what they enjoy now, what they think is important, and how they imagine their future selves. Students who write letters when they are in third grade, for example, will be surprised and pleased to read these time capsule letters when they are eighth-graders.

A Potpourri of Titles

Develop a file of provocative titles or topics that you and the students can add to periodically. The student who needs an idea for writing can consult this source.

The Cave	Kitchen Chemistry
Dreams for Sale	Lost in the Computer
Walk into the Future	The Homework Machine
Forbidden Island	Storm of the Century
Fur or Feathers?	The Great Science Experiment
The Worst Day of My Life	The Hundred-Year-Old Egg
My Undersea Adventure	Ice Cream Madness
Alone on a Sunny Beach	The Cosmic Zoo
My Strange Friend	The Magic Coat
The Best Time I've Ever Had	Inside the Outside
Why I Always Wear a Hat	No More Room
The Ticklish Fish	Factory of Fun
Adventures of a Banana Slug	Sneaky Sneakers
The Secret Life of Plants	Flying High
The Caterpillar's Secret	The Teacher's Room
The White Tiger	Always Winter

A book of unusual illustrations, titles, and first lines that will encourage student writing is *The Mysteries of Harris Burdick* by Chris Van Allsburg (Houghton Mifflin, 1984). Houghton Mifflin has released a new edition with just the individual drawings, including ones not found in the original book, called *The Portfolio Edition of the Mysteries of Harris Burdick* (1999).

Developing Writing Skills

Students are learning about putting their ideas into words and on paper even before they can spell correctly or read fluently. Early spelling attempts illustrate students' desire to express themselves in writing before they have a grip on correct spelling. By accepting this "invented" or "temporary" spelling as an example of developmental processes, teachers demonstrate the value of students' personal expression. Dictated stories show students that what they write can be read by others, over and over again. Reading aloud to students and talking about books helps students discover the differences between *written* and *spoken* language. As students struggle to put their ideas into writing, the mistakes they make are evidence of the learning process (Shaughnessy, 1977). Specific conventions—such as the use of dialogue, punctuation, verb tenses, and commas—are taught in context, as the need for this information arises. In addition, as students revise and polish their writing, they are motivated to put their knowledge of spelling, grammar, and usage into practice. Because different types of writing require different skills, students need experience with all types, from narrative and descriptive to persuasive and expository. In both instruction and assessment, teachers will focus on one specific topic at a time, such as:

 clear organization
 word choice
 sentence variety
 development of a central idea
 student voice
 adapting writing to a different audience

A Commonplace Book

Start students off on the right foot for writing by encouraging them to think like writers. A Commonplace Book is a journal or log that professional writers use to record ideas for stories, notes (of characters, details, etc.), or bits and pieces of writing to include in future work. Like an artist's sketchbook, it is a collection that a writer can refer to later to construct longer, more polished writing.

Give students some time every day to write in their Commonplace Book. They can record potential story titles, story starters, what ifs, and other imaginative stimuli as well as unusual names for characters, interesting details, special words, and snippets of conversation. They can also experiment with different forms of writing, from letters or descriptions to poetry or jokes. If students have difficulty thinking of subjects to write about, you can put a topic on the board as a suggestion. Every two weeks or so, have students select a passage from their notebooks to revise and polish up to turn in.

Regular writing develops fluency and increases the quality of student writing. Students write more freely when they are not afraid of being corrected. They can communicate thoughts, ideas, and feelings that are usually not shared with others.

Endless Writing

Divide the class into four or five teams. At the instruction "Go," every member of the class begins to write. The purpose of this game is to see how many words each person can write in his or her story during a set period of time. (Five minutes might be a good time to start with.)

When you call, "Stop," have each student total up the number of words in his or her story, and then add them together for a team score. The team with the most words wins. If the students find that they are running out of ideas during this time period they can repeat the last word that was written until a new idea comes along, or they can write about what they're thinking when they can't think of anything to write.

For the first few times, list several suggestions on the board before the game starts, for instance:

- A funny thing happened to me on the way to school this morning.
- What if we could read other people's minds?

Sentence Strategy

Write five letters on the chalkboard. Challenge students to write several sentences using only words that begin with those five letters. Here is an example:

S   O   A   E   M
- Many sweet oranges are enormous.
- Ellen stepped on a mouse.

Set a time limit and see how many sentences students can create. Students will also enjoy competing to produce the funniest or wildest sentence.

The "I's" Have Had It

One of the problems that children have with writing is falling into the trap of starting each sentence with *I: I* went shopping, *I* went downtown, *I* went to the show, *I* went to the ball game. The object of this activity is to develop new ways of starting sentences so that students have the opportunity to read and observe a variety of sentences. Encourage them to experiment with new ways of writing *I* sentences. *I went to the show,* for example, might be rewritten: *Bill and I went to the show, My friend and I went to the show, Going to the show with my friends was great fun.*

Have your students see how many different ways they can write the sentence: *I saw my friend.* Samples include:

- My friend looked nervous at the band concert!
- My dog licked my friend when we met downtown yesterday.
- While I was eating breakfast, my friend jogged by the window.
- Yesterday my friend was playing soccer in the park.

Fortunately and Unfortunately

A good motivation for writing sentences is the Fortunately and Unfortunately game. Read a few of these examples to your students to get them started with this humorous approach to writing:

- Fortunately, I bumped the car in front of me very gently.
  Unfortunately, it was a police car!
- Fortunately, I found my dog before it turned dark outside.
  Unfortunately, he was chasing a cat up a tree!
- Fortunately, I stopped the egg before it hit the floor.
  Unfortunately, I stopped it with my foot!
- Fortunately, there was an ice cream shop nearby.
  Unfortunately, it was closed!
- Fortunately, I stopped the door from slamming.
  Unfortunately, I stopped it with my finger!
- Fortunately, my grandfather's antique radio works.
  Unfortunately, it gets only one station.

An illustration of this pattern is Remy Charlip's *What Good Luck, What Bad Luck* (New York: Parents Magazine Press, 1964). The book takes the reader through a stream of occurrences that are classified as good luck and bad luck. You'll find that children will turn the pages faster and faster to see how Ned will get out of the *next* one!

A Strong Lead

Write an active sentence on the board—for instance: *The horses dashed madly across the field.* Encourage students to speculate about the story situation that might follow this sentence. Does this sentence make them want to read the story? Why? Students can then use the sentence as the first line in a story. Other sentences you might wish to include:

- The flames crackled ravenously through the forest.
- The prairie dog scurried frantically into the grass and dove into a hole.
- The coiled rattlesnake struck with deadly swiftness.
- The hissing kittens tumbled down the hall in a blur of fur and claws.

Collect examples of strong leads from picturebooks. Encourage students to consult these books as references to see how other writers have solved this problem.

Headliners

Give the students stories from the newspaper with the headlines cut off and have them write the headlines. Keep the real headline so students can compare their suggestion with the one the reporter wrote. Or give each student a headline and have him or her write a news story to accompany the headline. Discuss with students the features of a good headline. What information is included in a headline?

Story Grammar

Use the story structure chart on this page to stimulate writing ideas. The elements found in typical narrative stories are called the grammar, or the structure of the story. Students can pick one item from each column and write a story. When students exhaust this chart, have them make up new charts for different combinations.

Setting	Character	Plot
Dark basement	Scientist	Character suspects foul play.
Space shuttle	Panther	Character is lost and hungry.
Museum of Natural History	Secret Agent	Character is given the power to become invisible.
Island in the tropics	Unicorn	Character discovers two others in danger.
Fire station	Dalmation	Character finds a time machine.
Orchestra pit	Bassoon player	Character is trapped by an enemy.
The 99th floor of a building	Explorer	Character has to do three good deeds before dawn.
Jungle	Detective	Character must act quickly to prevent disaster.
Airport	Alien being	Character wants to play a trick on friends.
Vacant lot	Mystery writer	Character loses a vital object.

Using the Newspaper

Select several short interesting items from the newspaper. You can use an example for a discussion with the whole class or assign one item to each small group. Have students read their item and then think about how they might change the story. They could put the story in the past or the future, turn it into a mystery, make it humorous or serious, or pretend it is a fairy tale. Students can read their versions to the class. What elements did they have to change from the original piece?

Comic Strips

One way to rewrite a news story or a familiar children's book is to turn it into a comic strip format. In order to create a comic strip, students will have to focus on the action of the story and on developing appropriate dialogue for the characters. A comic strip format provides useful practice in finding the heart of the story.

The Iliad and the Odyssey by Marcia Williams (Candlewick, 1996), a comic strip retelling of the famous epic poems, is a good example to share with students.

Filling in the Plot

You can use the chart on page 144 or have students write their own examples of plot situations. A typical plot sets up a problem that the characters must solve. However, the path to the solution cannot be easy in a good story. Have students generate possible roadblocks to the characters' success, such as:

Problem

How can you get out of the library after being locked in at night?

Roadblocks

the telephone doesn't work

your parents think you are studying with a friend

it's the custodian's day off

you're getting hungry

Solution

You manage to set off the fire alarm so you are finally rescued.

Naming the Characters

Professional writers are always looking for good names for their characters. Students can collect their own examples to place in a file to use for future stories. Brainstorm with students sources of possible names. One useful resource is the newspaper. Students can find interesting names in every section of the paper. How will they classify their examples? Some possible categories are: Good names for—

heroes

animals

villains

beings from another planet

first names

last names

nicknames

Point of View

Selecting a point of view for your tale is a key decision in writing a story. Have students imagine a familiar story told from a different point of view. What if the three bears told their side of the incident with Goldilocks? Or Cinderella's stepmother tried to explain her cruel behavior? They can choose a story to rewrite from a different perspective. This is a good activity for heterogeneous classes in which not all students know the traditional fairy tales. Students will be motivated to investigate the original version in order to change the point of view effectively.

The True Story of the Three Little Pigs, by Jon Scieszka (Putnam, 1997), is an excellent model for this writing activity. In this version, the wolf gets to tell his side of the story. Not surprisingly, his version is different from that of the three pigs.

Characterization

Establishing a fully rounded character is a crucial part of a story. Help students understand the role of detail in developing a character by having them analyze picturebooks for examples of good writing. What does each character look like? How do their actions tell us about their character? Have students imagine where the character lives and in what kind of house. You can reverse this activity by describing a room and having students guess which book character might live there. When students are writing a story, they need to help the reader see this level of specific detail.

Character Study

Help students understand how to move beyond stereotypes or cardboard characters in their writing. They can combine elements and features from many different sources to create interesting characters. Before writing a story, or when revising a draft, have students cluster or brainstorm about the character. What makes this person unique? What does he or she wear? What would this person carry in his or her pockets? How would this character react to a sudden shock? This information does not have to be included when writing the story. Tell students that television and movie actors often try to imagine a "backstory" for their character in order to bring that person to life. The student writers' process of thinking about their story character will help them present a more rounded picture in their own writing.

Writing for an Audience

Often, students have trouble understanding how *audience* affects their writing. Have students share personal experiences or incidents and then select one about which to write. Divide the class into three groups. One group writes a diary entry describing what happened to them. Another group writes a letter to a close friend on the same subject. The third group writes a letter to their parents as if this had happened to them. How do the three writing samples differ? Can students tell who the audience of the diary/letter was intended to be? How might each version differ in vocabulary, in the details included?

A News Story

Have students select a story or poem that they have read. Tell them to rewrite this piece of "fiction" as a newspaper article—for example:

Woodcutter's 2 Children Missing

Hansel, 12, and Gretel, 9, have been missing since last night. Hansel was wearing a red shirt and blue pants and Gretel had on a blue striped dress, according to their mother, who said she had seen them going for a walk toward the forest just after lunch. Friends searched for several hours but found no tracks to follow before it became too dark to continue. The children's father, the woodcutter, said they liked running off to the woods. A neighbor commented that they seemed like such a close family. She couldn't imagine how worried they must be.

What are the different requirements of each form? What can one communicate in a poem but not in a newspaper article? Is information needed for the newspaper version that was not present in the original story? Students can discuss these differences in order to understand how the choice of type of writing affects what they write.

Fiction or Nonfiction

Older students can analyze and compare different forms of writing. For example, they can compare a fictionalized picturebook biography to a nonfiction version. What is the basis for each book? How do we know which one is "true"? Is it important to have both kinds of biographies? Why would a writer choose one form over another? Have students discuss these questions in small groups and write their responses. An interesting set of books to compare is:

Ann McGovern. *"Wanted Dead or Alive:" The True Story of Harriet Tubman.* Scholastic, 1998. Nonfiction.
Faith Ringgold. *Aunt Harriet's Underground Railroad in the Sky.* Crown, 1992. Picturebook story using Harriet Tubman as a key character.
Alan Schroeder. *Minty: A Story of Young Harriet Tubman.* Illustrated by Jerry Pinkney. Dial, 1996. Fictionalized picturebook biography.

Writing with Feeling

Use a class writing period to motivate students to explore new ways of expressing familiar ideas. Have students brainstorm words associated with a topic, such as *cold,* while you suggest a few more advanced words:

icicle	chill
frost	shiver
numb	frigid
glacial	snow

Students can move on to complete the sentence:

- It was so cold that _____.

They can also find words to replace *cold:*

- It was so _____ that _____.

Showing, Not Telling

Give students opportunities to practice writing that allows the reader to experience a feeling or an idea. Instead of *telling* the reader what to feel, *showing* leads to more vivid writing. Read examples of "showing" writing from children's books, especially picturebooks. Have students discuss what qualities make this writing effective, such as:

- It puts you "inside" the action.
- I can feel what's happening.
- I know what it's like inside the character.
- It uses action words.
- It refers to all the senses.
- Dialogue communicates the sense of being right there.

Show Me

Students can create their own short examples of "show me" writing. Brainstorm some simple descriptive statements, such as:

- Her room was messy.
- He talked a lot.
- They were good friends.
- He didn't like his little brother.
- We enjoyed the movie.

Have students select a statement and write a paragraph that communicates this idea without telling which one they chose. Students can share their paragraphs with the class and the others can guess what idea the writer is trying to express.

Sensible Language

Stimulate students to think about how they perceive objects through their senses: sight, hearing, touch, taste, and smell. Select an object such as a strawberry and place it in front of the class so that everyone can see it. Now have the students suggest words that describe how they *see* the strawberry, how they *hear* the strawberry, and so on, through the senses. Write the suggestions on the board, thus:

Strawberry
sight: red, green, spotted
touch: soft, bumpy
hearing: squishy, plop
taste: sweet, juicy
smell: fresh, sweet

Notice that words such as *sweet* can be applied to more than one sense.

Everyone has trouble distinguishing the role the different senses play in perception. Some senses are used much less frequently than others. People almost always use the sense of sight, but they exercise their sense of taste less often. Discuss with students the effects being blind or unable to smell might have on the rest of their senses. Other objects for class exploration of the language of the senses include:

raisins	watermelon
cloves	coconut
almonds	mint leaves
chives	garlic

Painting Word Pictures

To stimulate the use of adjectives and adverbs, discuss with the class how terribly dull writing would be if all colorful words were eliminated from language. No one would bother to read stories if they sounded like this:

Yesterday I went to the beach. It was cold. There were waves. I saw some birds. I played in the sand. I found a shell. Then I came home.

Give the students a worksheet with several ordinary, colorless sentences written on it. Have them add color, sparkle, and excitement by substituting more interesting words and phrases, such as:

- The bird flew into the tree.
  (What kind of bird? How did it fly? What kind of tree?)
- The truck went down the street.
  (What kind of truck? How was it being driven?)
- They were eating ice cream.
  (Who is *they?* Describe the ice cream. How was it being eaten?)
- The butterfly sat on the flower.
  (What did the butterfly look like? What kind of flower?)

You might then ask the students to write three ordinary sentences and exchange them with another student who can rewrite the sentences to make them more vibrant.

Colorful Words

After students have written a paragraph describing someone or something, have them assess their use of sensory vocabulary. Have students circle the "seeing" words in blue, the "hearing" words in red, the "feeling/touching" words in yellow, the "tasting" words in green, and the "smelling" words in orange. They can look at their passage and see immediately whether they have used too many words of one category or not enough examples in another category. This is an effective activity for teaching students to read their own work and revise it.

Improving Word Choice

For additional practice in the importance of word choice, give students sample paragraphs for editing. Select a passage and underline words that may be replaced because they are trite, vague, or nondescriptive. Provide a list of possible substitutions that includes a variety of synonyms for each word. As students read over the story, they can search the list for a synonym that fits the story. Since they can use each word only once and some alternatives may be more appropriate than others, students will have to consider the possibilities carefully.

Students will learn editing skills to apply to their own writing when they perform this activity as a class, individually, or in small groups. Advanced writers will also enjoy creating sample passages for the class to work on, particularly developing the list of synonyms.

Whale Hunt

When I woke up that morning, the ocean was <u>calm.</u> I <u>got</u> out of my bunk and <u>got</u> into my clothes. I took a glass of orange juice and <u>went</u> up on deck. The sun felt <u>good</u> on my back and the breeze was <u>warm.</u> I pulled out my binoculars and began to <u>look</u> for spouts. I felt sure that today I would find my first whale. Then I <u>saw</u> a thin line in the distance. I told the captain to <u>go</u> to the left. As we got <u>closer,</u> I was sure I had finally <u>found</u> a humpback. Then a <u>large</u> body <u>came</u> out of the water. It was in the air long enough for me to snap a picture. Then it <u>fell</u> back into the water. What a <u>noise!</u> I was glad our boat had not been any closer to that <u>big</u> show of strength. I <u>saw</u> my whale spout once more as our <u>small</u> boat rocked in the waves the humpback had made, but I was too busy <u>holding on to</u> the rails to take any more pictures!

Words to choose from:

serene	splashed	reaching for	huge
spotted	clinging to	occupied	drew near
suddenly	balmy	climbed	racket
steer	scrambled	soothing	encountered

tiny	leapt	streaked	enormous
observed	scan	titanic	approached
suspended	identified	slipped	clambered
relieved	turn	tremendous	slid
vaulted	crept	insignificant	watched
search	met	knifed	tremor
tore	miniscule	sparkling	peaceful

Rewrite with Slang

Students often have trouble distinguishing between "levels" of language, confusing formal and informal sentence structures or vocabulary. Help them learn to see the differences more clearly by having them rewrite examples of formal paragraphs, or selections from books, into slang. Slang, the casual speech used particularly by young people, is found mostly in young adult novels and doesn't usually occur in written prose, such as fairy tales. Students can make lists of their favorite slang expressions, or different ways of saying "That's good" or "That's bad." Then they can use these expressions to create new dialogue for storybook characters and rewrite descriptions of scenes. Discuss the effect this type of language has on the person reading the story. How does using slang change the impact of the passage? Challenge students to rewrite some of their slang examples into formal written English.

Anti-Cliché Writing

Students can learn to edit and revise their writing to eliminate the use of clichés, or stale, trite phrases. Have students start by generating a list of overused phrases or proverbs, such as:

> Don't put all your eggs in one basket.
> All's fair in love and war.

See if they can think of ways to rewrite these statements by changing the ending or by modifying the image.

> Don't put all your eggs . . . in the microwave.
> All's fair . . . in hockey.

Combined Revising and Peer Editing

Students can practice applying skills of sentence combining and peer editing to their writing. Have students fold a sheet of paper in thirds, horizontally. Hold the paper so they have three vertical columns. Give students a topic and have them write about it in the first column for two to three minutes. When the time is up, have students reread what they have written and use a marker to highlight sentences that could be improved by combining. In the middle column, students rewrite the sentences they have chosen. They can share some examples with the class. Now each student hands the paper to another student. That person reads the first column of text and again highlights sentences (using a different color) that can be improved or combined. He or she can also write questions about the content or comments on missing information. Hand each paper back to its original owner. The writer reviews the peer-editing comments and the newly highlighted sentences in order to rewrite sentences or add needed information in the third column. You can use these examples later in individual conferences as you review students' editing skills.

Penpals

An excellent motivation for children to practice expressing themselves in writing is a class penpal project. Students can write to classes in other parts of the country. Many English-speaking countries are good sources of penpals (for example, Australia, India, Scotland, Ireland, and some countries in Africa). Older students might be interested in corresponding with students who are studying English as a foreign language.

Classes with access to the Internet will have no trouble finding email penpals. This organization facilitates national and international connections:

> League of Friendship
> PO Box 509
> Mount Vernon, OH 43050

The first letters students write should include some basic information about themselves: name, age, school activities, interests, hobbies, and sports. Later letters can provide information about their city, state, and country. Some students will benefit from a structured framework to help them write, particularly for the first letter.

The class can discuss what they want to say in their letters and then write them individually. What do they think students in another region would want to know about their area? What do their penpals in other countries probably already know about this country?

Letter Writing Center

Set up a Letter Writing Center in the classroom, equipped with different kinds of paper, pencils, rubber stamps, notecards, stickers, and colored pens. Add a list of addresses of individuals and places that would interest students, such as Congressmen and Congress-women, local newspapers, and authors and their publishers.

Students can write to businesses for information or free materials. One source is *Free Stuff for Kids* (Meadowbrook, 1995). They can also write to their favorite authors about why they liked the books. Contact authors through their publishers or use the bio-graphical reference *Something about the Author* (Gale, updated regularly).

Thank You Notes

Students from primary to upper grades can write thank you notes to people who have come to speak to the class, visitors, helpers, or anyone involved with the school. The youngest students might dictate a class letter that they can all sign. Older students can discuss the structure of a letter (salutation, body, closing), the style for addressing the envelope, and examples of politeness formulas.

A book of hilarious letters to read aloud to all classes is *Dear Dragon* by Sesyle Joslin (Harcourt Brace, 1962).

Nice Notes

Students will benefit from establishing a connection with an older generation. A visit to a senior center, care facility, or convalescent home can lead to a regular correspondence as students exchange letters with the people they have met. Students can design special note-cards for this purpose, using the computer for graphics or using an art technique, such as printing or watercolor, to produce their own cover illustration. Talk about possible topics for these letters. Students can write about what they are doing in school, their favorite activities at home, or books they have read. They can also ask questions about their cor-respondents' lives and interests.

Letters across the Grades

Students in the elementary grades are often fearful about what awaits them the following year. Students in any grade can write letters to the students in the previous year, telling them about the year to come and reassuring them. For example, third-graders can recall and discuss the qualms they had before entering third grade. Invite conversations between the third-graders and second-graders about going into the next grade and have the third-graders take notes on the concerns expressed by the younger students. The "experienced" third-graders can then write letters to these second-graders, responding to their concerns and feelings. Several books to stimulate discussion of third-grade worries are:

> Paula Danziger. *Amber Brown Is not a Crayon.* Illustrated by Tony Ross. Putnam, 1994.

Betsy Duffey. *How to Be Cool in the Third Grade.* Illustrated by Janet Wilson. Viking, 1993.

Natalie Honeycutt. *Juliet Fisher and the Foolproof Plan.* Simon & Schuster, 1992.

Postcards

Students enjoy the simplicity of a postcard because the message can be short. Cut slips of paper or tagboard the size of postcards. Students can draw a picture on one side and on the other side write a note to a friend or relative. Why do people write postcards? What are typical things to say on a postcard? Perhaps the students could bring in stamps so that they can mail these cards. You can also laminate the cards to give them greater body for mailing. Discuss with students how writing a postcard differs from writing a letter. Point out examples of "telegraphic" writing from sample postcards and have students practice expanding the brief phrases orally or in writing.

Writing Scripts

After students have gained facility in different kinds of writing, offer them the challenge of turning a story into a *script*. They can select a favorite book or a story one of them has written. For a performance script, students will have to consider such topics as writing dialogue, using props to set the scene, and planning how to convey the theme. If a video camera is available, arrange for students to videotape the production. They can perform this dramatization or show the video to other classes in the school.

Getting to Know You

Especially at the beginning of the school year, consider planning a number of writing activities that allow students to express themselves and give you an opportunity to become acquainted with the class. The following examples are questions that you might pose; students can respond orally or in writing:

- If you were a food, what food would you be? Why?
- If you were an animal, what animal would you want to be? Why?
- If you could be any kind of machine, what machine would you be? Why?
- If you were a character from a book, which character would you be? Why?
- If you could be any age, what age would you choose? Why?
- If you were a haiku, what season would be your theme? Why?

Autobiographical Timelines

Most children have difficulty writing autobiographies. Start by asking them to list the five most important (happiest) things that ever happened to them. Each one can make a scroll that presents these happenings in order. They don't have to begin with being born. What do they want to begin with instead?

As children create this Scroll of Life, they are putting ideas in chronological order. They will naturally add events in sequence as they review their lives, and they will add

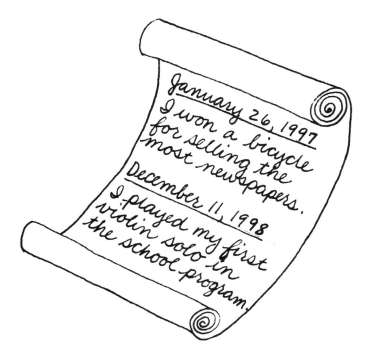

words to help explain the events depicted. Older students can write a more detailed auto-biography after making this concrete timeline of their lives. This activity also works well orally, especially for younger children.

Provide examples of autobiographies from children's literature for students to pass around as models, such as:

Betsy Byars. *The Moon and I: A Memoir.* Beech Tree, 1996.

Beverly Cleary. *A Girl from Yamhill: A Memoir.* Camelot, 1996.

David McPhail. *In Flight with David McPhail: A Creative Autobiography.* Heine-mann, 1996.

Bill Peet. *Bill Peet: An Autobiography.* Houghton Mifflin, 1994.

A Gift

Students often use writing to express their individuality. Ask students to write down one gift that they would give themselves if they could give themselves anything. Then have them write explanations of why they selected this gift. They can share this writing in small groups or with the class if they wish. Here are examples:

- I would give myself 10 pomegranate trees so I could eat them every day. I would also make them a different kind so they wouldn't make red spots everywhere and I wouldn't have to eat them on the front porch.

- I would give myself the power to play chess better than anyone else in the world. I would do this so I could beat my brother Ramon. Also I could probably become famous for beating those chess computers.

A variation on this activity is to ask students what they would give someone else. To whom would they give it? In their writing, students can justify or explain why they selected this person and what they would give this person, such as:

- I would give my Grampa one of those lawn-mowing machines that you can ride on because it hurts his back to use the pushing kind.
- I would give my mom a dishwasher because she is always too tired to wash the dishes and I break things sometimes. Then we wouldn't have to argue about the dishes all the time.

Talk about the spirit of giving and read books aloud for students to discuss. Here are some picturebooks that are suitable for all grade levels:

Demi. *The Greatest Treasure.* Scholastic, 1998. A Chinese folktale about happiness.
Katherine Paterson. *Marvin's Best Christmas Present Ever.* Illustrated by Jane Clark Brown. HarperCollins, 1997. Marvin is proud of the wreath he makes.
Benjamin Alire Sáenz. *A Gift from Papá Diego/Un regalo de Papá Diego.* Illustrated by Gerónimo García. Cinco Puntos Press, 1998. Diego's grandfather is far away in Mexico.

Drafting through Revising

The writing curriculum is based on two premises: students writing to enjoy language and make sense of the world (private) and students writing for an audience (public). In the first case, the emphasis is on self-expression. It is in primarily the second type of writing that students need practice with reworking and reseeing (revising) in order to present their ideas to a wider audience. Instead of the teacher correcting every paper, students should be placed in an active role as they learn to edit their own writing through activities such as writers workshop, peer conferences, and portfolio assessment (Atwell, 1987).

Revision as Reseeing

In the writing process model, students revise and edit their writing as part of the final stages. Because this can be a difficult task for many students, use a scaffolding activity to help students "resee" their work. Show selected student-written passages as examples on an overhead and model one *thinking aloud* strategy for the class, asking, "What information do I need to add?" Solicit student suggestions and try them out on the text. Then model the second *thinking aloud* strategy as you ask, "What information do I need to remove or delete?" As you make changes, write them in pen on and around the text. You are showing students how a writer questions and reviews his or her work. (Although revising is easier on the computer, it can be more difficult for students to follow what is going on.) You can help students learn to revise by breaking it into these two components.

Have students apply this model of revision to their own writing by (1) rereading their drafts, (2) checking whether to add anything, and (3) checking whether to delete anything. Post these strategies on the board so that students can refer to them as needed.

Comparing Patterns

When you give students a pattern for their writing (or a story skeleton, as on page 127), have them share what they have written with the class. Then have them revise their work. Hearing what others have written will stimulate new ideas and make them aware of different ways to make their stories stronger.

Selected Sentences

After you read a story aloud, select a sentence from it for students to analyze. Using this sentence as a base, how can they modify it? Encourage students to think of different kinds of revision, for example:

- Change a word.
- Add more information.
- Make the sentence shorter or longer.
- Reverse the order of the clauses.

Paragraph Revision

Provide additional practice in revision for the class by showing a paragraph (from a student paper) on the overhead. As you read the passage aloud, ask the students to concentrate on one feature only—for example, action verbs or descriptive language. This clearly defined task makes it easier for students to focus on possible changes.

Assigned Editors

After modeling various revision strategies with the class, students are ready to work in groups on revising their writing. For each student in the group, assign a specific editing task, such as:

check spelling
check sentence length
check focus
check organization
check word choice

As students switch roles, they will gain confidence in applying these strategies individually.

Individual Conferences

One means for guiding student development in writing is the individual conference that is held for a few minutes each week. Have students sit in the Author's Chair when they are ready to conference. You may choose to confer with each student about a specific piece of writing as the student analyzes strengths and weaknesses. Together, you decide on one or two suggestions for improving his or her work.

At this time you may note, for instance, that a child does not know how to use quotation marks, possessives, or the correct usage of *your* and *you're*. Take the time for a mini-lesson on this topic or refer the student to the relevant chart posted on the board.

You may focus a conference period on each student's writing folder, commenting on the variety of the writing, on the general types of errors that have been marked, and on improvements made. Make several suggestions for future work; you may, for instance, share an interesting word that might be particularly useful.

The personal conference shows each student that you are interested in what he or she is doing. It helps motivate student interest in improving, in trying different types of writing, and in telling you about plans for writing.

You're Great!

Remember that evaluation is more effective if you concentrate on emphasizing the positive aspects of student performance. Recognize student efforts and show them that you appreciate their work by presenting awards such as those shown on page 159.

Developing an Evaluation Rubric

When you assign a specific writing project to students—one that you expect them to revise and polish—you need to discuss beforehand how this writing will be evaluated. Have students brainstorm criteria for evaluation as a class, in order to model the process. Once they have experience, they can develop these lists in small groups. Use this rubric, or descriptive plan of criteria for evaluation, to provide feedback to students on their work as they go about revising it.

Dialogue Journal

Responding to student journals can be a rewarding way to assess student writing progress. Students hand in their journals at regular intervals for you to read and make comments on them. This material is not submitted for correction but for conversation (a dialogue between two people). Both of you can ask and answer questions, for example. At the same time, you have the opportunity to assess students' strengths and weaknesses and plan your curriculum accordingly. Students always have the option to keep some writing private.

A DOLPHIN SALUTE

FOR _____

SEAL OF APPROVAL

EARNED BY _____

Student Portfolios

Because students may be working simultaneously on writing projects that are at different stages, they need to keep their work in a folder that they have constant access to. However, their drafts are not going to be evaluated according to the same standard as their finished work. Students can prepare a *portfolio* of their writing that will be used to assess their progress. They select a few pieces of writing that they feel represent the best of their work, the range of their writing, or the growth they have made in writing. This portfolio, accompanied by a letter from the student explaining his or her selections, may be reviewed by the teacher and student for the final evaluation of the school year. The portfolio is also useful for parent-teacher conferences.

Collaborative Writing

Students can collaborate with their peers or students at another school to read each other's work and provide feedback for revision. With computer networking, it is easy for students to keep their drafts in folders that are available to other students. Each person who comments on their work or inserts a suggestion can use a different font to distinguish these ideas from the original.

Beyond Teacher Evaluation

Checking every paper of every student can be very time consuming. The following are some suggestions to help you reduce the paper load:

- Students read their papers to the class or a small group.
- Students write in journals and you read selected parts.
- Students choose which paper will be checked.
- Use symbols (✓, W.W., and E all signify error) in the margin of student papers to encourage self-editing. Allow students time to identify their errors before dividing into small groups to correct the mistakes.
- Experiment with peer editing. Students working together in small groups often catch mistakes more readily.

Writing Evaluation Policy

Many teachers feel obligated to read and correct every student paper because they think parents will insist on this. The following is an example of a letter you might send to parents explaining your writing evaluation policy and the reasons for it. If the parents are made aware of the procedures used in your class, they are less likely to misunderstand or complain.

Dear Parents:

In my writing program this year, I will be teaching and guiding your child as she or he writes. I have established a classroom environment where I hope students will be confident enough to try out new ideas. Because the goal of writing is communication, I am primarily interested in the content, not just the mechanics of expression. Therefore, I will be emphasizing only one or two mechanical skills at a time (periods, capitals, subject-verb agreement, etc.) and I will not be correcting every error on your child's paper. I will also be writing comments and reactions to the child's ideas. Recent research in writing has shown these teaching strategies to be most effective in developing fluency and competence in writing skills.

Your child's writing will be kept in a folder here at school. Although it is my goal to have students writing every day, they will not be perfecting or revising every paper. They will choose their best papers from the folder to revise. If you wish to see the folder, please send a note, and I will send the folder home for a night so you may look over the work.

Your encouragement and positive attitude towards your child's continued progress in writing will do much to hasten improvement.

Sincerely yours,

The I-Search Paper

Ken Macrorie is credited with setting up the structure for the I-Search paper. The key to writing an effective research paper is to have students begin by listing the questions that they want to answer. Students can generate a list of possible questions on a topic as a class and then develop more specific questions in small groups. Each student, or each group, chooses one of these questions to explore. This approach results in greater focus and clearer organization as students are less likely to accumulate a list of facts.

Inside the Magic Bus

In *On the Bus with Joanna Cole: A Creative Autobiography* (Heinemann, 1996), Joanna Cole, author of the Magic Bus series of informational books, explains how she does her research and prepares her books. She talks about how her books begin with a question that she is interested in exploring. Students can see how a real writer uses the writing process as she writes drafts and takes notes. Cole not only tells the inside story but she also provides specific instructions for students embarking on research reports or large projects. In addition, she describes the process of creating the book itself: the design, the text, and the illustrations.

Preparing the Report

Students can look at a variety of nonfiction books for models of how to prepare and organize the material that they want to present. Help them identify the features of a book that are designed to aid reader comprehension:

highlighted concepts
glossary or definitions

table of contents

summary

review questions

Which features would be appropriate to include in their report? How can they help the reader better understand the information that they want to share?

On the Bulletin Board

Quotations provide inspiring captions for displays of student writing. Use the following:

The world of reality has its limits; the world of imagination is boundless.
—Jean Jacques Rousseau
Anything one man can imagine, other men can make real.   —Jules Verne

You can also place this caption in the upper-left corner of the board. Display student stories of dragons and monsters.

```
TALES
E
R
R
I
F
Y
I
N
G
```

"Able Authors" or "Write On!" (see page 163) can be captions to feature student writing. Place each selection on a piece of brightly colored construction paper cut in an irregular shape.

Look for other public locations to display student writing, such as school hallways.

This Is Our Best

Students will enjoy compiling a book of their writing efforts. Even a simple book is an excellent type of material to distribute to parents at an open house. You may also consider a book of writings as an especially good gift for parents for holidays or birthdays. Place books of student writings in the school library for all students to read.

Our Tallest Tales

A natural follow-up for a lesson on tall tales, such as those about John Henry or Paul Bunyan, is to ask students to write some of their own. One teacher organizes what she calls the Liar's Club, and has certificates to give each child who completes a yarn or tall tale.

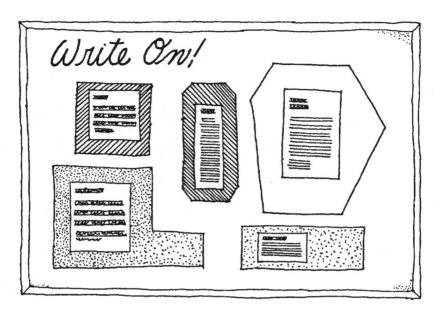

Write the tall tales on tall narrow paper, and put them in a tall narrow book. The Tall Tale Book can be a class project. Students can use this collection to read stories to children in the primary grades or to use for creative dramatization.

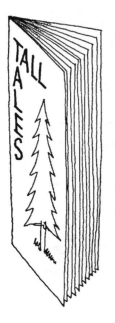

This certificate of appreciation is awarded to_____

on this day_____

for telling one of the biggest whoppers this side of the Rockies. Bearer must present this card as permanent identification.

Bookbinding

Here is an easy technique that students of all ages can use to produce neatly bound books. The only supplies required are yarn and a tapestry (large) needle.

1. Punch holes 1½" apart along the margin of the book cover and pages.
2. Measure and cut a length of yarn three times the size of the side of the book. If the yarn is thin, double it first.
3. Thread the needle with the yarn and pass the needle down through the first hole.
4. Bring the yarn up across the back and down through the first hole again.
5. Pull all the yarn through, leaving only a short piece hanging to tie later. Keep the binding loose.
6. Pass the yarn to the second hole and go up through the hole, bring the yarn across the back, and draw it up through the hole again.
7. Repeat step 6 until the yarn has passed twice through every hole. (See illustration #1.)
8. When you come out of the last hole, bring the yarn up and down alternating through the holes, so that a solid line is formed across the top and bottom. (See illustration #2.)
9. Tie the two ends together at the top in a knot or bow. (See illustration #3.)

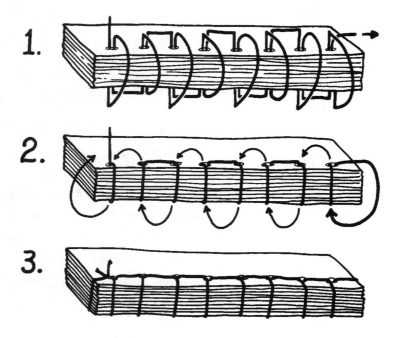

Book Covers

Older students can bind original stories for added interest and motivation as shown here:

Cut
- Cloth or contact paper 11" × 25"
- Child's story on 8" × 10" paper
- Colored paper 7" × 21" (2)
- Cardboard 8" × 10" (2)
- Cardboard for hinge 8" × 3/8" (1)

Fold
- Colored paper in half

Staple
- Sandwich style: one folded colored piece of paper on top, the stack of white paper in middle (the story), and one folded colored piece of paper on bottom
- Then fold colored piece on very top and very bottom, back ¼", then forward ¼"

Tape (vinyl)
- Hinge between covers to form back

Glue
- Cloth on covers plus hinge. Can add tape all around at hinge. Glue colored paper to inside covers. Trim colored paper to be even with first colored page.
- This makes a book that is 8" × 10".

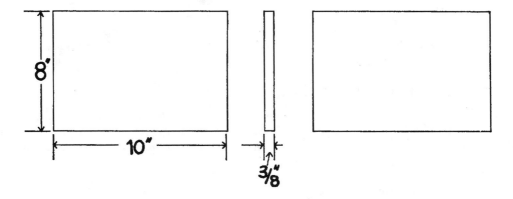

Sharing Writing

The following suggestions are designed to encourage students to write more and improve their skill at communicating ideas through writing:

- Invite older students to read their stories to other classes.
- Display stories on library and office bulletin boards where everyone can read and appreciate them.
- Hold bookbinding parties at regular intervals to encourage students to finish masterpieces.
- Collect the best of the class writing in a small three-ringed notebook. Students can easily revise and change their contributions. This collection can be bound at the end of the school year.

What's in a Book?

As students turn their writing into books that others will see, have them examine published books to understand the different components of a book and their purpose. Each student can look at a different sample book as the class generates possible features to incorporate into their own books. They might include:

information on book cover—
    title, author, publisher,
    illustration
	content divided into chapters

	information about the author, photograph
inside cover—summary of book	quotes from reviews of the book
title page	illustrations/diagrams/charts/maps
copyright information	appendices
table of contents	index
dedications	glossary
preface	

Discuss different categories of books and the features that would be typical of each, such as nonfiction versus fiction.

How Books Are Written

Pencil to Press (Lathrop, 1963) is a book about itself. Marjorie Spector follows a book from the time she first thought of writing it to the book being sold to the reader. She shows the different versions the text went through. *How a Book Is Made* by Aliki (Crowell, 1986) is suitable for primary students.

Performing Books

Many picture books—stories, folktales, or fables—are suitable for transformation into performance forms, such as plays or reader's theater. Students will have to study the story carefully in order to understand how to adapt it into the play format. Discuss with students the conventions of writing a play. How do plays differ from narrative fiction? Generate a comparison chart so that students can see what changes will need to be made.

Reader's theater requires less modification, as students rely more on the text to turn actions into spoken words. Students need to decide how many people they need to speak the dialogue they have written, plus one or more people for the narration. The performers can read from the scripts they have prepared. (See Chapter 2 for more information on using creative drama in the classroom.)

Students as Journalists

Students of all ages can learn and practice important writing skills by performing as journalists. Writing for a broad audience and preparing work to be published are the best motivators for students to revise and polish their work. A class or school newsletter is a great venue for publishing student writing. Older students, benefiting from computer technology, can create a magazine with regular issues to be carried by the public library and available to others by subscription. In a magazine, students can include a variety of genres, such as interviews, stories, letters to the editor, advice column, news items with photographs, poems, and reviews of books or current movies.

The following are books that introduce students to the world of journalism:

David Macaulay. *Black and White.* Houghton, 1990.
Norma Fox Mazer. *Bright Days, Stupid Nights.* Bantam, 1992. Teenagers are interns on newspaper.
Barbara Taylor. *Create Your Own Magazine.* Sterling, 1993.

Resource materials include:

Classroom Newspaper Workshop. Tom Snyder, 1995. CD-ROM, software lessons on newspaper publishing. For Mac.
Rookie Reporter. Meridian, 1995. CD-ROM newspaper publishing simulation, includes layout and copy editing. For Windows or Mac.
Write to Publish: Teaching Writing Skills through Classroom Magazine Publishing. Creative Teaching Press, 1996.

Submitting Student Work for Publication

There are many commercial magazines that publish students' writing, poetry, and drawings. Have students send for a sample copy, in order to determine what type of student work is published, or look for magazines in the library. For example, *Stone Soup* is one of several established literary magazines that publish only student writing. This magazine celebrated its 25th anniversary by releasing *The Stone Soup Book of Friendship Stories* (Tricycle Press, 1997).

Once students have investigated the possible sites and determined which ones are appropriate for their work, they can begin the submission process. Work with students to develop a cover letter to accompany their work. Talk about the concern of "plagiarism," borrowing from someone else's work without credit. Show them how to make sure their work is in the correct format (typed, double spaced). Make sure students understand that, just like adult writing, only a small portion of student work submitted to these magazines is actually published. A list of selected magazines is included in Chapter 10.

Discussion Questions

1. How can you plan opportunities for students to write every day?

2. What do you do with students who say they just don't like to write?

3. How would you explain your policy of not correcting every paper to concerned parents?

Exploring Further

Gisela Ernst and Kerri Richard. "Reading and Writing Pathways to Conversation in the ESL Classroom." *The Reader Teacher, 48* (1994/95).
Ralph Fletcher and Jo Ann Portalupi. *Craft Lessons.* Stenhouse, 1999.
The Oxford Dictionary of 20th Century Quotations. Oxford University Press, 1999.
Teachers and Writers Magazine. Published by the Teachers and Writer Collaborative. 5 Union Square West, New York NY 10003-3306.
Iris Tiedt. *Teaching with Picture Books in the Middle School.* IRA, 2001.

References

Nancy Atwell. *In the Middle: Writing, Reading, and Learning with Adolescents.* Boynton-Cook, 1987.
Ann Dyson. *Multiple Worlds of Child Writers.* Teachers College Press, 1989.
Donald Graves. *Writing: Teachers and Children at Work.* Heinemann, 1983.
Ken Macrorie. *Searching Writing.* Boynton-Cook, 1980.
Mina Shaughnessy. *Errors and Expectations.* Oxford University Press, 1977.

6 Putting Language to Work

You can't help respecting anybody who can spell TUESDAY, even if he doesn't spell it right.

—A. A. Milne, *The House at Pooh Corner*

In their ability to use their native languages, humans are extraordinarily creative. Any one of us can produce a (grammatical) sentence that has never been said (or written) before. There is no such thing as a "longest" sentence; a longer one can always be invented. In addition, languages themselves are extremely flexible. All languages change, despite people's efforts to keep their language "pure." Yet, English speakers can still read and understand the written words of Shakespeare, though his speech would be incomprehensible. And the languages of people who have never before seen modern technology have the capacity to take on new ways of speaking in order for people to be able to operate these new machines. To see the creativity and flexibility of language in use, you have only to look at a preschool child, for whom these discoveries are an endless source of delight and experimentation. Of course, we might like to regularize English spelling a little—after all, George Bernard Shaw invented the word *ghoti,* to be pronounced *fish,* according to the improbable rules of English spelling. On the other hand, we can only find language itself amazing, and the learning of language an incredible feat.

How *do* children pick up ("acquire") language, from the time they are babies? They seem to be able to learn whatever language is spoken around them and communicate more and more fluently, all without explicit instruction or even correction of grammatical "errors." In fact, children's language abilities seem to "unfold" instead of being taught. As children play with language, they are searching for patterns, making generalizations, and testing them. Children's use of such "regularized" forms as *foots* or *feets* for the plural of *foot* is evidence of this process in action. In addition, from a young age, they are able to speak differently to a familiar adult, a stranger, or a doll. Children show an early grasp of the way language is adapted to reflect social factors and the environment.

Compare this level of language *acquisition* to children's experiences with language *learning* when they reach school. Suddenly, they encounter an unfamiliar form of language: "school language" or classroom discourse (Cazden, 1988). Instead of *answering*

169

student questions, teachers are more likely to correct the *form* of the questions and then have students repeat the corrected form. Students are expected to put language to work, expanding their oral language abilities in controlled paths as well as learning to use written language for highly specific purposes. They are also evaluated on their "correct" performance in these activities rather than their ideas or playful inventions.

An effective language arts program must take into account aspects of both language acquisition and language learning. Teachers can provide increasingly varied and complex examples of language use as sources of data through which students can discover patterns. In addition, they can draw student attention to the many different factors involved in making meaning through language. Whether learning about spelling, grammar, or language study, students will actively participate in the analysis and interpretation of language forms. These subjects provide students with a significant arena in which to exercise their *metacognitive* abilities—their strategies for planning, self-monitoring, and evaluating language—in order to be able to use language appropriately and effectively.

Spelling English Words

Spelling poses special problems for English language users because the written forms preserve archaic pronunciations. For example, words with silent letters—such as *k*nife, ri*gh*t, and nam*e*—are spelled that way because at one time all of the letters were pronounced. Unfortunately, these "irregular" forms tend to be the ones we use most frequently and are therefore among the earliest words that children are taught to spell. However, memorizing a list of spelling words leaves students with the impression that English spelling is impossible and unpredictable. Instead, spelling instruction should show students the underlying patterns that do exist in words. An effective spelling program will include at least three categories of words:

Core words: The high-frequency words, often considered sight words

Personal words: Words from current lessons or words with which students have had problems

Pattern words: Words that illustrate a particular phonological (*-ear* or *-ate*) or morphological pattern (*-ize* or *-ify* used as verb suffixes)

Instruction needs to center on recognizing similarities and analyzing patterns in the composition of specific words, whether based on the sound system of English (phonology) or the system of prefixes and suffixes (morphology).

In the earliest stages of literacy learning, children already have a theory of how the sound system of their language works (Read, 1971), although they don't yet know formal spelling rules. Teachers need to encourage students' attempts to express this knowledge (*phonological* or *phonemic awareness*) through "invented spelling" as they begin to write (Chomsky, 1971). Building literacy instruction on young learners' phonological awareness may improve and accelerate their ability to make connections between sound and writing (Stanovich, 1986). Some controversy over the use of "invented spelling" in the classroom still exists. However, the National Research Council's exhaustive analysis of reading instruction (Burns et al., 1998) recommends the use of what they call "temporary" spelling in the primary grades. "Conventional" spelling will develop as students gain greater control over sound/symbol relations and are able to alter their focus from message *content* to message *form.*

Focusing on the Alphabet

Students need to know the letters of the alphabet and how these symbols relate to the spoken language. Particularly in primary grades, then, it is important to engage students in activities that support knowledge of the sound/symbol relationship. Personalize this activity by introducing the initial letters in children's names, for example:

- How many words can you name that begin like Tom?
- How many words can you name that begin like Samantha?

At first, just have the children say the words. Later, however, you could print the words on the board, pointing out the pertinent letter in each case, thus helping students relate the sound and the letter symbol.

Have children make posters featuring their individual names. They could cut pictures from magazines or draw pictures to illustrate items that begin with the same sound as their names.

Words around the Room

Long before they can read extended text, students should see words as expressing meaning. Therefore, display labels on objects in the classroom—door, window, keyboard, book, aquarium, and so on. Talk about these words, noting, for instance, that *door* is a short word compared to *window* and that *keyboard* is composed of two words, *key* and *board,* pointing to the two parts. Discuss how such a word might have evolved. Children can begin to understand something about words before they actually write them. For example, they learn that people can make up words when they need them. You can have students identify the letter symbols that are used to spell these words, noting that words that take longer to say may also require more letters to write.

Older students could create sentences to display around the room. A science display might bear the message: *We are learning about a praying mantis. Soon the eggs will hatch.* This practice is supportive for those who are learning English as an additional language as well as slower learners. It engages students in spelling for a purpose (e.g., "How do you spell 'praying mantis'? Look in a science book, try the dictionary, ask your teacher").

The Word Wall

Create a Word Wall using a long sheet of butcher paper. Use this to help students observe words in print and create word lists for current projects. If you plan a theme study on the circus, for example, you might ask students to name the animals, people, colors, and activities that they already associate with the circus. Sharing their prior experience and knowledge engages students in the topic and leads to better understanding. Through reading books and viewing filmed materials, students will add to their knowledge and provide more words for the class collection of Circus Words. Encourage students to refer to this Word Wall when they need to check their spelling and vocabulary in later writing activities. The Word Wall will grow as you include words from stories and group similar words together to illustrate spelling patterns.

Alphabetical Order

Provide a variety of activities to help children learn how to alphabetize, for example:

- Make sets of capital letters and small letters. Have students match the pairs and then put them in order.
- Place a set of alphabet cards in mixed order on a table, and have the students arrange them in correct order. Children can work in pairs as one shuffles the cards and the other puts them in order, with his or her partner doing the checking.
- Put letters on a flannel board and have students put them in the correct order.
- Have cut-out letters arranged on an overhead projector in a mixed-up manner. Students can put the letters in order as they are projected. This can be done in small groups, as all students will be eager to see their letters projected on the screen.

Letter Discrimination

To help students distinguish similar letters, prepare a worksheet with outline drawings of the letters *p, q, b,* and *d*. Ask students to color the vertical stems a light color and the curved parts a darker color. Students will then be able to see more clearly the direction the letters should be. Use the same colors to make large chalk letters on the board and ask the students questions, such as, "Who can point to the *p* that starts *pig?*" "Who can point to the letter that begins *baseball?*"

Word Family Chain

Children who are beginning to read and spell words will be intrigued by this kind of chain.

Notice that only one letter in the chain is changed each time in order to form a new word. Challenge children to create as long a chain as possible on the board as a group project, or start several chains at different places on the board at which children can work. This activity can also be developed into individual exercises that children can complete in a learning center. Good beginning sets of words are the following:

cat	slip	less
fat	ship	loss
far	shop	lost

Challenge more advanced students to create chains with longer words—for example, *short, shirt, shire, share.* The longer the words are, the harder the task.

Strange Sentences

Older students can enjoy playful alphabet activities as well, only on a more advanced level. Once they have become fluent readers and are less likely to confuse letter sounds with letter names, write this "sentence" on the board and challenge students to "read" it: "C D B!" Students may have to say the letters aloud several times before they can understand the cryptic sentence as "See the bee!" Once they have caught on to the method, they can challenge each other by inventing their own special sentences.

C D B! is also the title of a collection of more strange sentences for children and adults by cartoonist William Steig (Simon & Schuster, 2000). Fortunately, it includes an answer key at the back!

Alphabet Squares

Prepare 50 cardboard 1" squares on which the letters of the alphabet are printed. Make extra squares for vowels and the consonants that begin many English words—for example, *b, l, m, n, p, s,* and *t.* These squares can be used in many of the activities in this book. Encourage students to develop spelling games, such as drawing 10 squares and seeing if they can spell a word with the letters drawn.

If you glue the letter squares to magnets (using a thin magnetic sheet that you can cut up), students will be able to "write" favorite words on a metal board or rearrange letters to form new words.

Word Building

Students need experience in building words. Give them *u*-shaped blocks to fill in with three-lettered words that contain the short sound of *u.* Have the students fill in as many *u* blocks as they can. This activity can also be used in a learning center.

Mouse Maze

Letters can be connected in many different ways to spell different words. See how many words your students can spell from the mice below. Students must stay on the maze paths and cannot jump over a mouse.

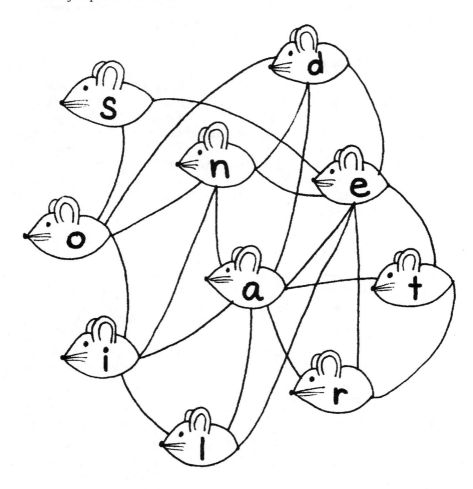

real   line   soil   dear

The Word Loop

Find as many words as possible in the word loop, going clockwise. All letters are to be used. Do not list any word more than once. Sometimes small words may be found within bigger words. There are more than 40 words in this loop. Note that a particular letter may be part of more than one word.

The size of the loop and the words used can be varied to suit any grade level. This game encourages students to use the dictionary to check words they think might be in the loop and to pay attention to spelling patterns.

Alphabetical Lists

A good first activity that stresses alphabetizing is to make ABC lists. Try making a list of alphabetical foods from *asparagus* to *zucchini*. Later, list all animals from *ant* to *zebra*. Another list could be names of people from *Alice* to *Zeb*. Many other lists can be developed from the alphabet. Students should have a chance to discuss their lists and to compare what they have come up with and what others have discovered. Display these lists where children can read them easily.

Spelling Race

Have each student write the letters *A* to *Z* down the left side of a piece of paper at the start of the race. The purpose of the game is to see how many words students can write for each of the alphabet letters. They must have a word for each of the letters; then they can go back and write a second word or a third word. What an incentive to learn *xylophone* and *zebra!*

You set a time limit for this activity. The first time the game is played, it might be necessary to allow more time so that each student can succeed at some level. After the game has been played several times, children can count the number of words they have written. Scoring by teams encourages improvement without focusing on failure.

Another modification of this activity is to say that each word has to be at least five letters long. The important thing, however, is that every student has an opportunity to write words at a personal level of proficiency. Sample lists look like this:

Easy List		*Advanced List*	
aim	now	aardvark	nuisance
black	open	bumpity	organized
care	pin	calendar	placid
dear	quit	destroying	quake
eagle	rat	equal	righteous
farm	soon	fantasy	shuffling
go	tame	ghostly	tedious
her	under	horrendous	understanding
ink	vase	irresistible	virile
jelly	wagon	journey	whimsy
kitten	x-ray	kitchen	xylophone
lame	yell	loosely	youth
meow	zoo	menacing	zipper

Use the following scoring chart as an example:

Length	*Value*
1–2 letters	0
3	1
4	1
5	3
6	4
7	6
8	7
9	7
10	10
11+	20

Spelling Who Am I?

Use the current spelling list for this game. Start the game by selecting a word from the list and asking the students to guess the word. Give identifying clues to help them figure out the word you have in mind. Examples are:

> *I have three syllables*
> *I contain a prefix*
> *I have a short vowel sound*
> *I can be used as an adverb*
> *One synonym for me is . . .*
> *One antonym for me might be . . .*
>   *Who am I?*

The student who guesses the word first can select the next word and prepare the clues. Help students by suggesting useful clues. Students can also play this game in teams. Each team vies with the other for the most interesting and difficult clues.

Scrambled Words

Challenge the more able students in your class by asking them to develop an activity sheet that the rest of the class can use. They can scramble 10 of the current spelling words and supply synonyms as clues, thus:

wroth	(toss)
thogs	(spook)
arhic	(seat)
soecl	(shut)
nayrg	(mad)
phapy	(glad)
kistc	(twig)
molob	(flower)
disel	(skid)
ghaul	(giggle)

Useful Spelling Patterns

This list of *rimes,* or common word endings, will be helpful in developing activities for students:

A		E	I	O		U
ab	ank	ead	ib	oad	oot	ub
ace	ant	eak	ibe	oat	ooth	uck
ack	ap	eal	ice	ob	op	uct
act	ape	eam	ick	obe	ope	ud
ad	ar	ean	id	ock	opt	ude
ade	ard	ear	ide	od	ord	udge
aff	are	ease	ie	ode	ore	uff
aft	ark	eat	ife	og	orm	ug
ag	arm	eave	iff	oll	orn	um
age	art	eck	ift	oin	ort	ump
ail	ash	ect	ig	oke	ose	un
ain	ast	ed	ight	old	oss	unch
air	aste	ee	ike	ole	ost	ung
ake	at	eed	ile	oil	ot	unk
ale	atch	eek	ill	olt	ote	unt
alk	ate	eel	ilt	olve	ouch	urch
all	ave	eem	im	ome	oud	ure
am	aw	een	ime	on	ought	url
ame	awl	eer	imp	ond	ounce	urn
amp	awn	eese	in	one	ound	urt
an	ax	eeze	ince	ong	ount	us
ance	ay	eet	inch	oo	our	use
and	aze	ell	ind	ood	ouse	ush
ang		em	ine	oof	out	ust
		en	ing	ook	ove	ut
		ence	ink	ool	ow	utch
		ench	int	oom	owl	ute
		end	ip	oon	own	
		ense	ipe	oop	ox	
		ent	ire	oose	oy	
		ept	irl			
		er	irm			
		erb	irt			
		erse	isk			
		ert	iss			
		erve	ist			
		esh	it			
		ess	itch			
		est	ite			
		et	ive			
		ew	ix			
			ize			

Give students a list of rimes and a beginning consonant or blend. Ask students to combine the consonant or blend with the word endings to make as many words as possible. For example, *b* + the A rimes would make words like *back, bat, bang, bail, bale,* and so on. Students may find this activity more exciting if you draw the beginning consonant or blend from a box or use a spinner to determine the rime list.

Key Letters

Students can become more aware of the internal structure of words through an activity focusing on letters in sequence. If you give them the letters *v* and *n,* they can supply words in which these two letters appear in that order, for example:

van	event
vane	evasion
vine	valentine
even	

Giving students three letters makes the task even more interesting as students search for words that fit patterns as shown here:

mbr: amber, lumber, member, jamboree

smn: jasmine, submarine, superman, smiling

ftr: feather, father, after, faster

rnd: rend, round, grind, rendition

Notice that three letters often appear on license plates, so this is a good game to play when traveling in a car.

Off to Washington!

Challenge students to see how many words they can find in the word *Washington.* The letters may be arranged in any order, but they may not be used more than the times they appear in this word. Examples include:

wash	as	tan
sing	ton	ant
wing	tin	want
ash	win	wag
sang	sin	sag
hang	hint	tag
tang	song	nag
saw	tongs	snag

Obviously, there are many words that can serve this purpose. As you do more of these, you might challenge students to list only words of at least four letters.

Riddle-Me-Ree

Students love riddles. Here, the riddle is used to teach students patterns of English spelling. The form of the riddle is a poem, with each line providing a clue for one letter of the answer.

> *My first is in* awl *but not in* all;
> *My second is in* car *but not in* bike;
> *My third is in* tea *but not in* coffee;
> *My fourth is in* pet *but not in* animal;
> *My fifth is in* air *but not in* sky;
> > *Riddle-me-ree;*
> > *What can it be?*

The clues tell us that the first letter is *w*. The second letter can be *c, a,* or *r,* and the third letter is *t* or *a*. The fourth is *p, e,* or *t* and the fifth is *a, i,* or *r*. Although the clues seem confusing as they are listed, the students can reason that since the word begins with *w,* it can't be followed by *c,* possibly might be *r,* but is most likely *a. Wa* can't be followed by another *a,* so the next letter must be *t*. The fourth letter then can't be *p,* but it can be *e* or *t*. Finally, the word can't end in *ea, ei, ta, ti,* or *tr* but only *er*. The answer is *water*.

This game can be used with younger students as well by making the examples easy. Here is a simpler example that would be good for slow readers:

> *My first is in* cave *but not in* brave;
> *My second is in* ask *but not in* question;
> *My third is in* take *but not in* give;
> > *Riddle-me-ree;*
> > *What can it be?*

The answer can only be *cat.*

Encourage students to prepare their own riddles to use in teams. Everyone will benefit from the vocabulary development and spelling practice.

Jumblies

Jumblies is a simple word game that students of any age can enjoy playing. Give the students a joke or a riddle and provide the answer, but with the letters scrambled. They will know when they have unscrambled the letters correctly because they will have the answer to the question.

You can use this technique on test questions or any time you are reviewing the students' knowledge. Knowing that they can discover the answer provides the motivation for working the puzzle. Riddle questions are excellent for this purpose, for example:

- *What is worse than raining cats and dogs?*
  giahinl xatabcsi
  (hailing taxicabs)

Rhyme Roots

You may wish to have a rhyming root of the week posted on the board. Ask students to contribute words to the list throughout the week. At the end of the first week, create a group poem using as many of the contributed words as possible. After practice with group poems, students may prefer to create small group or individual poems.

Students will also enjoy seeing who can come up with a "sensible" sentence using the most rhyming words, such as:

The sleek Greek mouse went once a week to take a meek peek at the creek and seek a leek and carry it away in her cheek before it began to reek.

Vowel Sounds

Using a chart is helpful in teaching the basic relationships between the vowel sounds. Display this chart prominently so that students can refer to it when they are confused. Be sure to explain that these sounds are not the only ones associated with these letters. Have students consult the dictionary to see what symbols are used to indicate vowel sounds.

	Long	Short	Followed by *r*
a	cake	bat	far
e	bee	net	her
i	nice	mitt	fir
o	so	mop	for
u	use	fun	purr

Use this chart to help students learn that one letter can represent three different sounds. From this base you can proceed to the study of other vowel sounds.

Working with Short Vowels

Encourage beginning spellers to become more aware of the simple vowel sounds in short words by developing a chart like this:

	a	e	i	o	u
hit					
pan					
ten					
him					
sang					
lock					
slip					

Children can fill in the chart as they test the vowel sounds to see if new words can be found. None of the words will work in all slots, so there will always be some empty spots. In the first list, for example, children can insert *hat, hit, hot,* and *hut.* (Someone may try to make a case for *het,* but you can always use the dictionary as the final test.)

Continue to refer to this chart as students encounter more examples of short words. The chart is also useful for a review or a warm-up activity.

Patterns of Vowel Spellings

You can help students become aware of different patterns by having them develop charts that record spelling variations like this one:

Spelling the phoneme /iy/ (*long* e)

eek	eak	eet	eat	eer	ear	eel	eal
leek	beak	beet	beat	deer	dear	feel	deal
meek	leak	feet	heat	beer	fear	heel	heal
peek	peak	meet	meat	jeer	gear	keel	steal
reek	teak	fleet	pleat	peer	hear	kneel	real
seek	weak	greet	seat	leer	near	peel	seal
week	sneak	sleet	peat	cheer	rear	wheel	peal
cheek	speak	sweet	neat	sneer	sear	reel	meal
creek	freak	street	treat	steer	year	steel	
Greek			bleat		smear		
sleek			wheat		spear		

Be sure that students generate these lists themselves rather than use reading lists you have prepared. Creating such rhyme lists helps students contrast the alternate spellings of common rimes. Students will find a number of *homonyms* across these lists. Talk about the spellings as students read the words they have listed.

Guess the *ie/ei* Word

Jointly brainstorm several lists of words designed to show patterns or spelling rules. You might create this list to demonstrate when to use the spelling *ie* or *ei:*

ie	*ei* (after *c*)	*ei* (long *a*)	*ei* (long *e*)	*ei* (long *i*)
chief	receive	eight	seize	height
genie	deceive	rein	weird	sleight
believe	conceive	neigh	caffeine	neither (variant)
babies		feign	neither (variant)	
relieve		neighbor		
niece		weight		
ladies				

Divide your class into two teams to review these words. One team begins by saying, "We are thinking of a word where *ie* sounds like long *e*." The other team has a certain number of guesses to discover the word—for example, "Does your word come out of a bottle and give three wishes?" You may wish to cover your class list after a few practice rounds.

Searching for Owls

The letters *owl* can be found in many words, and of course, these letters spell the name of a bird that hoots at night. Challenge students to see how many owls they can find, for example:

fowl
cowl
jowl

They can write their findings like this:

- An expression of displeasure   __ __ __ __ __
- A deep, threatening sound   __ __ __ __ __
- To cry loudly   __ __ __ __
- A baby owl   __ __ __ __ __ __

Students can search for cats and other animals, too.

Key Words

Show students a puzzle based on a key word like the one shown here. Then challenge them to create more puzzles based on key words they select, such as *happy, success,* or *create.*

1. __T__ ____ ____ ____
2. ____ __H__ ____ ____
3. ____ ____ __I__ ____ ____
4. ____ ____ ____ __N__ ____ ____
5. ____ ____ ____ ____ __K__

1. Used for camping
2. To demonstrate
3. To fool someone
4. Two times ten
5. A way of eating

Growing Words

Beginning with a one-lettered word, such as *i, a,* or *o,* make a word grow by adding one letter at a time. Each time, of course, a new word must be created, thus:

a	o
an	do
ant	nod
pant	node
paint	nodes
paints	

Challenge students to see how long a list they can make. One of the longest is the following:

I
in
sin
sing
swing
sewing
stewing
strewing
wrestling
sweltering

Add-a-Letter

This is a stimulating word game especially interesting for advanced students. Give the students a list of words that can be changed into new words by the addition of a single letter. Duplicate several lists of words and have answer sheets ready for the students to check themselves. Always leave room for the students to add new examples.

In this example, the Add-a-Letter is *e*. The student is to add an *e* anywhere in the word without changing the order of the letters.

far (fare, fear)	ban (bane, bean)
spar (spear, spare)	star (stare)
plan (plane)	brad (bread)
on (one, eon)	mad (made, mead)
man (mean, mane)	fast (feast)

Here are examples for the letter *i*:

run (ruin)	pad (paid)
plan (plain)	sad (said)
bran (brain)	pan (pain)

Students can challenge each other to discover new examples of words that can be changed by adding one letter:

even (event, seven)	sing (sling, sting)
tar (star, tear)	bed (bred, bead)

Hole in One!

To play Golf, open a textbook to a page of print. Place a slip of paper along the left side of the page so only three letters show, as in the illustration.

The student tries to make a word beginning with the letters given by adding as few letters as possible. The score equals the number of letters added. As in golf, the object is to get a low score. On a score sheet, record the data collected for each game of nine holes.

To encourage students to write longer words, play *Basketball*. The object then is to get a high score.

Hole		Play	Strokes
1	che	cheer	2
2	hea	head	1
3	don	donate	3
4	pas	pass	1
5	On	On	0
6	pro	problem	4
7	suc	such	1
8	tuc	tuck	1
9	hun	hunt	1
TOTAL			

To make the game more difficult for advanced students, specify that words must have at least four letters. Another variation would be that the words must contain three or four syllables.

Using a Code

Language is a kind of code. We can send and receive messages with people who know the same code: English. Part of the process of teaching children to read and to write is teaching them how to "encode" their knowledge of the spoken language into the written code, and how to "decode" written messages.

You can introduce the idea of encoding and decoding with a simple substitution code, such as:

A = 26	H = 19	O = 12	V = 5
B = 25	I = 18	P = 11	W = 4
C = 24	J = 17	Q = 10	X = 3
D = 23	K = 16	R = 9	Y = 2
E = 22	L = 15	S = 8	Z = 1
F = 21	M = 14	T = 7	
G = 20	N = 13	U = 6	

Using the key to this code (above), can you decode this message?

> "11-15-22-26-8-22, 14-26-8-7-22-9," 8-26-18-23/7-19-22/24-26-7, "4-18-15-15/
> 2-12-6/24-19-26-13-20-22/14-22/18-13-7-12/26/14-26-13?" 15-15-12-2-23/
> 26-15-22-3-26-13-23-22-9, *7-19-22/24-26-7/4-19-12/4-18-8-19-22-23/7-12/*
> *25-22/26/14-26-13.*

You should read:

> "Please, master," said the cat, "will you change me into a man?" Lloyd Alexander,
> *The Cat Who Wished to Be a Man.*

Code Variations

Once students have become familiar with the operation of a code, they can begin to construct more complex coding systems. There are many variations on the basic code that even slower students can use:

A = 1 + 3	A = Z
B = 2 + 3	B = Y
C = 3 + 3	C = X
D = 4 + 3	D = W

Students can also create codes in which nonletter symbols are used to represent letters, for example:

A = △ A = /\/
B = △ B = o—o
C = □ C = »→
D = ⊡ D = ᗡ

The relevance of using codes to teaching spelling and reading is that every time we use a code, we are encoding English spelling. To use the code properly, students must know how to spell the words correctly. Playing with codes, therefore, adds variety and interest to spelling lessons, while motivating students to pay close attention to spelling patterns.

You can also have a student write a message in code every day on the board. This could be a quote from a famous person, a favorite saying, or a passage from a book the class is reading. Provide keys to the code for everyone and let students work out the solution. Encourage students to develop their own codes.

A Code Wheel

A useful code device is based on the idea of a circle within a circle. The larger circle is mounted on heavy paper or cardboard. The smaller circle is attached to the larger by a brad or tack through the center of both circles so that the inside moves around freely. The band around the rim of both circles is divided into 26 spaces and the lines separating the spaces must extend evenly from the small to the larger circle. Write the 26 letters in alphabetical order counterclockwise around the edge of the larger circle.

Students can create a personal secret code by writing the letters of the alphabet around the smaller circle in any order. One way to do this is to select a key phrase or word with a variety of letters. A possible key phrase is the student's name. Arrange the key around the smaller circle in alternate spaces. Then fill in the empty spaces with the remaining letters in alphabetical order (see part 1).

To write in this cipher, first place the *A* in the outer circle against the *X* in the inner one (see part 2). After writing out the message in regular spelling, find each letter in the outer circle and write the corresponding letter in the inner circle.

To decipher the message, you use the same wheel, of course, as you reverse the process. Students can work in pairs for this activity. Round pizza boards make excellent wheels.

Cryptography

Cryptography, the science of writing secret messages, is a great word for students to learn as well as a subject that intrigues many students. Introduce the topic with a book such as *Secret Code Book: With Press Out Code Busters* by Helen Huckle (Dial, 1995), which explains the history of codes and includes cipher disks for student-created codes. Encour-

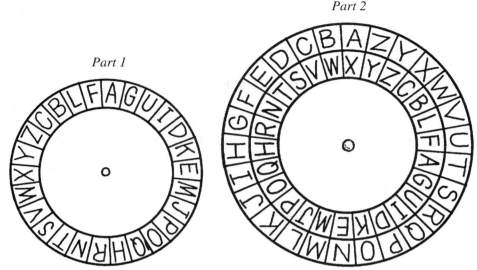

Part 2

Part 1

AHQG DQYYX BHTTJ MXPTG MT HFERUZ!
Translation: This pizza wheel makes me hungry!

age students to explore the subject further on their own. Other books you might share with them are:

Elvira Gamiello. *Secret Codes and Other Word Games.* KidBooks, 1998.
Jeffrey O'Hare. *Secret Codes and Hidden Messages.* BoydMills, 1997.

GHOST

In this game, you use squares with a letter of the alphabet on each one, turning the squares so the letters are visible. The first player chooses a letter to start a word. The players in turn add letters to continue spelling a word. The player forced to complete the word earns a letter from the word GHOST. A player who suspects the preceding player is bluffing can challenge the player to spell the entire word (V-A-L-L = ?). If the player was bluffing and cannot complete a word, or spells the word incorrectly (V-A-L-L-Y), he or she also earns a GHOST letter. If the player correctly completes the word (V-A-L-L-E-Y), the challenger earns a GHOST letter. A player earning all the letters in GHOST vanishes from the game. The dictionary may be used to settle challenges.

SUPERGHOST

In this version, letters may be added at either end (B, B-O, L-B-O, E-L-B-O, E-L-B-O-W). This variation is much more difficult. SUPERGHOST is a good review of affixes since strategy demands escaping into longer words (R-E-A, E-R-E-A, E-R-E-A-D, E-R-

E-A-D-I, . . . R-E-R-E-A-D-I-N-G). Challenges occur more often in this version, but players have five extra letters before becoming a SUPERGHOST and vanishing from the game.

Beginning and Ending Chain

Groups of children can play this game on sheets of paper or at the board. It also makes a good relay. The first person writes any word—for example, *ball.* The next person must begin the next word with the letter that ends the first, in this case, *l.* If that person writes *lark,* the next word must begin with *k,* and so on, thus:

ball—lark—kitchen—nice—easy—yes

For variety, chains can be printed in this form:

ballarkitcheniceasYesnowinter

Transformations

Another word game that fascinates students is to change one word into the opposite by changing only one letter at a time. Each time you must have a real word. The object is to reach the other word in as few steps as possible. See how you change *cold* into *heat* in these examples. Notice that there is more than one possible answer.

cold	cold
colt	hold
coat	held
boat	head
beat	heat
heat	

The longer the word, the more difficult the task is. Show students how to work the example and then challenge them to produce others. Have a student test pairs of words to make sure the transformation is possible before you challenge the rest of the class. Remember that there may be several different ways of reaching the end word.

work	work
pork	pork

perk	perk
peak	peak
beak	peat
beat	plat (surveyor's map)
seat	play
slat	
slay	
play	

Categories for Beginning Spellers

Choose several categories and write them on strips of tagboard. Some examples are *names in our class, animals, ice cream flavors, colors,* and so on. Give a category and a selection of squares with letters written on them, turned upside down, to each small group. Each player in turn draws a letter and gives a word beginning with that letter that belongs in the category. If the player cannot supply a word, the alphabet square is returned to the pile. Players get one point for correctly naming a word. To make the game more difficult, the player may be required to spell the word.

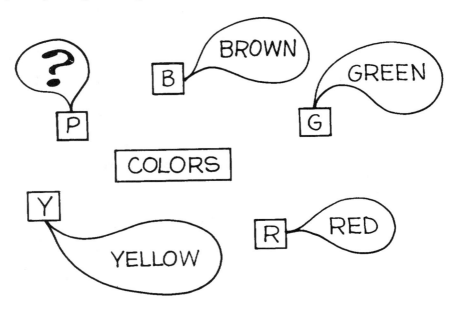

Categories for More Experienced Spellers

This game is played in groups of five. Each player will need a category chart. Each group will need a pile of alphabet squares from which to draw. Each player nominates one category, which all group members write on their charts (or you can provide five categories you wish to emphasize). Each player then draws one letter, which all write on their charts.

Then students compete to see who can fill in the most spaces on the chart. A kitchen timer can be used to set a time limit. One point is scored for each correctly spelled answer. (Pass charts to player on the left for scoring. Dictionaries and other references may be used to verify answers.) A scoring variation is to double the score of any category completely filled.

	Rivers	Countries	Mammals	Fruit	Insects
P					
A					
L					
T					
R					

Homonyms

Homonyms are words that sound the same but are spelled differently and have different meanings. The English language has many homonyms, and students are always intrigued to discover them. Have a contest to see who can list the most number of homonym pairs, for example:

hare-hair	blue-blew	stationery-stationary
bare-bear	deer-dear	stair-stare
bee-be	so-sew	son-sun
know-no	vane-vein	fair-fare
red-read	eye-I	principle-principal

There are even homonym triplets. Students probably know some of them:

pear-pair-pare	four-for-fore
to-too-two	aisle-I'll-isle
rain-reign-rein	carrot-caret-carat

Direct the students' attention to the spelling patterns shown by these homonyms. Many pairs end in *air/are, ea/ee, ail/ale.* Help students become more aware of homonyms and their spellings by writing sentences that contain both words:

- The bear that I found was completely bare.
- May I have a knife to pare this pair of pears?
- That last storm blew down the blue sign.

Dictate these sentences for spelling practice.

In discussing homonyms with the class, it is important to remember that people from some regions pronounce vowels differently and words that are homonyms for many students in the class may not be homonyms for everyone—for example, *Mary, merry,* and *marry.*

The Pair Tree

Create a large tree by anchoring a branch in a coffee can filled with gravel. Cover the can with colored paper and the words *The Pair Tree,* as shown on page 194. This tree will be used to display pears cut from yellow construction paper on which different pairs of homonyms are printed. The tree can also be used to emphasize other pairs of words, such as:

antonyms (full–empty; sharp–dull)
expressions (cats and dogs; beep and creep; Ps and Qs; ladies and gentlemen)
verbs and nouns (deceive–deception; explain–explanation)

Be sure to add a partridge to your pair tree!

Mnemonics

Children are intrigued by the concept and the word *mnemonics* (ways to help remember). Even though these memory devices don't work for everyone, they are fun to create. Talk about these aids to memory:

arithmetic: A *r*at *i*n *t*he *h*ouse *m*ay *e*at *t*he *i*ce *c*ream.
*almost, always: Al*most *al*ways spelled with one *l.*
balloon: A *ball*oon is like a *ball.*
parallel: All railroad tracks are par*all*el.
superintendent: There is a *dent* in superinten*dent.*
principal: The princi*pal* is a prince of a *pal.*
all right: All right is like *all* wrong.
chocolate: There is a second *o* in choc*o*late.
familiar: There is a *liar* in fami*liar.*

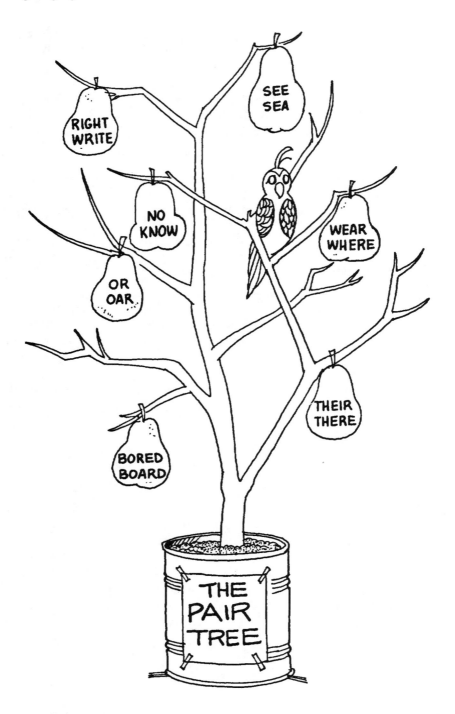

separate: There is *a rat* in sep*arat*e.

cemetery: Watch the *e*'s in c*e*m*e*t*e*ry.

Have students brainstorm suggestions for remembering how to spell the following words, or *spelling doozers.* Students can add their own words to the list.

accent, ascent, assent

dessert, desert

loose, lose, loss

accept, except

they're, there, their

you're, your

whose, who's

Encourage students to add *visualization* to their verbal mnemonic strategies. Sometimes students can remember a particular spelling more easily if they associate it with an unusual image. For example, if they picture the word *parallel* as 2 ("a pair" of) *Ls walking,* they may be more likely to remember the correct spelling has *ll* and then *l.*

Learning about Grammar

Like spelling, grammatical correctness has traditionally been confused with intelligence, moral fiber, superior culture, and a good education. Because this knowledge is so highly valued, we must take care to ensure that all students have full access to it (Delpit, 1995). And, like reading, grammar is more frequently tested (or corrected) than taught. Some students absorb the information they need from exposure; others benefit from explicit teaching. But teaching grammar is more than teaching names for the parts of speech or having students memorize types of sentences (interrogative, declarative, imperative, and so on). In fact, there is no evidence that teaching this kind of grammar improves student writing (Hillocks, 1986).

Knowing a language (language *competence*) requires coordinating a complex network of many different systems, such as the following:

Syntax: the organization of words in a sentence

Semantics: the meanings of words

Phonology: the sounds that make up different words

Morphology: separable elements of words that carry meaning

What we call grammar includes syntax but is really primarily *usage,* or the language conventions a particular group of people have agreed on that determine what words are appropriate in what circumstances.

Because everyone possesses language *competence,* grammar instruction can be thought of as helping students enlarge their competence in order to communicate better with others. In an effective language arts program, grammar instruction will aim at helping students identify the knowledge needed for access to a wider world.

Picturing Grammar

A series of distinctive books by Ruth Heller makes an excellent launching pad for grammar activities at all grade levels. Her books include:

> *Behind the Mask: A Book about Prepositions.* Paper Star, 1998.
> *Fantastic! Wow! and Unreal!: A Book about Interjections and Conjunctions.* Grosset & Dunlap, 1998.
> *Kites Fly High: A Book about Verbs.* Paper Star, 1998.
> *Many Luscious Lollipops: A Book about Adjectives.* Paper Star, 1998.
> *Merry-Go-Round: A Book about Nouns.* Paper Star, 1998.
> *Mine, All Mine: A Book about Pronouns.* Grosset & Dunlap, 1997.

The rhyming text and vibrant illustrations are especially effective for introducing grammar study in the primary grades, and each book provides simple, general definitions of grammatical terms, along with interesting new words that students can learn. The coverage of each topic, however, is sufficiently detailed that the books are helpful with students in the upper grades as well. For example, Hiller's book of nouns, *Merry-Go-Round,* includes discussion of such distinctions as types of nouns (common, proper, abstract), spelling rules for regular and irregular plurals, and different kinds of determiners, the parts of speech that precede nouns.

Word Classes

Rather than teach students definitions of classes of words that they must memorize, have the students discover on their own what characteristics can be used to group particular words together. Give the students five minutes to think of as many words as possible. You can do this as a group activity, writing the words on the board as the students think of them, or you can have them write their lists individually. Now divide the list by asking a series of questions:

- What words can be made plural?   *(tree, book, radio)*
- What words can be possessive?   *(girl, mother, cat)*
- What words can be changed from present to past tense?   *(ask, see, laugh)*
- What words can have *-ing* added to them?   *(listen, make, speak)*
- What words can follow *very?*   *(old, stupid, big)*
- What words can fall in several of these groups?   *(turn, head, paper)*
- What about the words left over?   *(the, never, quickly)*

• Are there any words we use commonly that were not on the list?   *(my, not, really)*

Once they have seen how the list can be divided, explain to the students that words are divided into classes, depending on how we can use them in a sentence. Help them to frame a generalization describing each grouping. They will remember the different word classes more readily if they use their own words for a definition.

Sentence Frames

Students can learn to test words to determine the word class they fit in by using such frames as these:

• *Noun*
   I need some _____.
   This is a _____.
• *Verb*
   Everyone _____ at home.
   What is he _____?
• *Adjective*
   It is very _____.
   The _____ children run.

Such exercises are useful in primary grades as children are developing "sentence sense." This simple framing test continues to serve older students as they work with grammar.

Parts of Speech Chart

Prepare a large chart to display in your room to aid students in recognizing different parts of speech. It is not necessary that students memorize such definitions, but using these terms makes it easier for them to talk about their writing. Use such terms as *noun* and *verb* in your speech, even in primary grades.

Language Terms
• *Noun:* A noun is a word that can be made plural or possessive and it may follow *the, a,* or *an.*   (flower, happiness)
• *Verb:* A verb is a word that can be changed from present to past, and *-ing* may be added to some verbs.   (speak, hear)
• *Adjective:* An adjective is a describing word that can follow the word *very* or a form of the verb *be* (is, are, was, were).   (easy, tired)
• *Adverb:* An adverb is a word that can follow a verb and tell how a thing is done.   (quickly, well)

- *Determiner:* A determiner signals that a noun follows. Included are articles, demonstratives, possessive adjectives, numbers, and so on.   (the, my)
- *Pronoun:* A pronoun substitutes for a noun but does not follow a determiner. (it, him)
- *Intensifier:* An intensifier precedes adjectives and adverbs.   (very, really)
- *Auxiliary:* An auxiliary signals that a verb follows. Some auxiliaries may also be verbs by themselves.   (is, has)
- *Subordinator:* A subordinator connects an independent clause with a subordinate clause.   (but)
- *Conjunction:* A conjunction joins equal groups of words.   (and)
- *Preposition:* A preposition usually introduces a phrase and signals that a noun follows.   (of, in)

Vocabulary Classes

Tell the students to write the word *vocabulary* down the left side of a piece of lined paper. Across the top of the page should go the words *adjective, noun, verb,* and *adverb.* They will head for the dictionary to find unusual words that fit the slots. Encourage them to work together on looking up the meaning, spelling, and parts of speech of these words. Some words can be nouns or verbs (for example, *ride* and *calm*). Discuss with students how they know what the word means when they see it in a sentence.

	Adjective	Noun	Verb	Adverb
V	vermilion		vilify	
O			open	
C		catamaran		casually
A	antique		ache	
B		byte		
U	unusual		unify	usefully
L	laborious	lift		
A		anemone	alight	abruptly
R	rambunctious			rudely
Y		yacht	yodel	

You can vary this activity by having students write their name down the left-hand side of a sheet of paper and try to fill in the boxes with words to make a sentence.

	Noun	Verb	Noun
B	Bob	builds	barns
A	Anna	ate	ants
R	Richard	robbed	Randy
B	Bill	borrowed	bolts

Lingo

This game, played like Bingo, will provide small groups of students with practice and review of the parts of speech. Prepare a set of large cards, marked off in squares, with LINGO written across the top. Fill in each square with different words that are nouns, verbs, adjectives, or adverbs. Make small squares for the caller that are labeled L—Adjective, G—Noun, G—Adverb, and so on. Also cut squares of paper for students to use to cover their cards. These should be labeled *adjective, adverb, noun,* and *verb.* Older students can prepare these materials on their own.

L	*I*	*N*	*G*	*O*
paint	quickly	game	purple	cast
create	dawn	forest	rocky	strange
volcano	bright	catch	surround	take
soft	fine	narrowly	candle	mineral
difficult	pencil	forget	short	slowly

As in Bingo, the caller shuffles the slips and calls them out, one at a time. The students look down the column to see if they have a word that belongs to the category called (noun, verb, adjective, or adverb). If they find a word that fits, they cover it with the corresponding marked square. The first person to cover a row, column, or diagonal can check to see if the words were identified correctly as a part of speech.

You can make the game more difficult by including words that can be different parts of speech—for example, *paint* or *fine.* Then the students must justify their answer by using the word correctly in a sentence.

Word Cubes

Students can construct Word Cubes (dice) by cutting this pattern from any stiff paper and folding it, as indicated in the illustration on page 200.

Ask students to work together in small groups to create four cubes on which they list (1) nouns, (2) verbs, (3) adjectives, and (4) adverbs. They can then use the cubes like dice to create sentences by rolling the four dice. They can add any structure words needed to

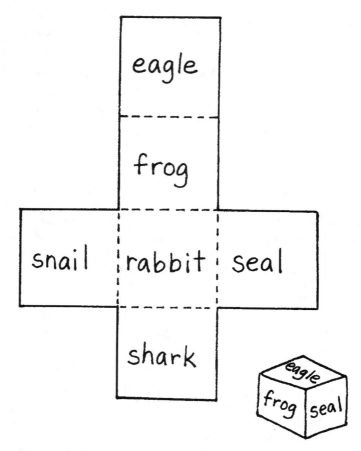

A "Nouns" word cube

create a sentence. If, for example, they rolled the words *eagle, flew, brave,* and *slowly,* they could create the sentence *The brave eagle flew slowly.*

If you want to encourage students to write long sentences, let them add as many words as possible to the four core words. Then the score is determined by the number of words written by each student. You might have such sentences as *The brave old eagle flew slowly over the small town, looking for the mountains in which he spent the happy days of his youth with brothers and sisters who loved to hide deep in the rocks so he couldn't find them.*

Adjective Story

Here is an activity that allows children to be as silly as they want, yet learn how to use adjectives creatively. Students can prepare a list of adjectives beforehand from which to choose or fill in whatever comes to mind as they read the story.

When Sally woke up this _____ morning, her _____ hair was in a _____ mess. She used a _____ brush to clean it up a bit, but it was still too _____ . She asked her _____ mother to help her out, but her _____ mother was _____ . Sally went across the _____ street to ask her _____ neighbor, but her _____ neighbor wasn't home. Sally sat on the _____ curb, wondering what to do next. Along came a _____ dog, who licked the _____ mess on Sally's _____ head. Hooray! The dog licked the _____ mess right out. Sally patted the _____ dog's _____ head, and the dog said, "I sure showed you a lick or two!"

Acrostic Adjectives

One version of acrostics is based on a person's name. Students can use their own first or last name or the name of a friend. The words chosen to fill in horizontally may be personal characteristics or adjectives that apply generally.

A	musing		R	ambunctious
M	ild		Y	oung
I	maginative		A	mbitious
R	owdy		N	oisy

Once students become accustomed to these acrostics, they can scramble the adjectives so that the others have to figure out whose name is being used.

Picture This!

Have students write a noun at the top of a sheet of paper. Then ask them to think of at least 10 words that could describe the noun. The result is a list of adjectives or adverbs. Have them create a picture outline of the noun using the descriptive words they have listed. A student who chose *tree,* for example, might create a picture from his or her list, as illustrated on page 202:

Tree

green	brown	graceful	tall	slippery
shady	hard	gnarled	cool	rough
leafy	scratchy	ancient	twisted	

Post the students' illustrations and point out imaginative choices of words.

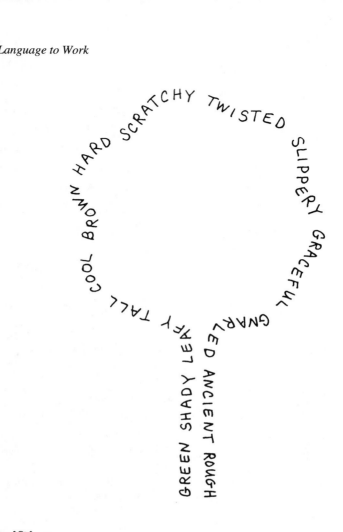

Tom Swifties

A favorite word game for children and adults, Tom Swifties are humorous sentences formed by matching a situation with an adverb to create a pun, such as:

- "I'm out of apples," Tom said fruitlessly.
- "What a pretty mirror," Tom said reflectively.

Challenge students to complete some of these sentences. There may be more than one possible answer. Examples are:

- "I'm waiting for the doctor," Tom said _____.   (patiently)
- "Who is fixing my car?" Tom asked _____.   (mechanically)

With more experience, students can make up their own examples to stump the class. (Hint: One strategy is to *start* with an interesting adverb.)

- "I think there are holes in my sweaters," he said _____.   (airily)
- "I've always wanted to go up in a balloon," he said _____.   (lightly)
- "I'm taking up medicine." he said _____.   (cuttingly)

Students can also work in teams, with one group supplying an adverb and challenging the other group to use it in a Tom Swifty. Notice that recording the examples also requires students to use quotation marks correctly.

Superlatives

Adjectives are the focus of attention in this activity. Ask students to brainstorm words that mean the "most" (or superlative adjectives), such as *slimiest, messiest,* and *funniest.* Have each student select one word from the class list and use it in a sentence according to the following form:

The _____ est thing in the world is _____.

Students can illustrate their sentences. Collect student examples in a book or post them on the board. Refer to these sentences as you talk about types and uses of adjectives. *Many Luscious Lollipops* by Ruth Heller will suggest different adjectives for students to use.

A variation of this activity is to have students write an adjective with *-est* on paper and pass them to another student to complete the sentence. Students will enjoy comparing their creations with the adjectives included in these books:

Judi Barrett. *Things That Are Most in the World.* Illustrated by John Nickle. Atheneum, 1998.
Brian Cleary. *Hairy, Scary, Ordinary: What Is an Adjective?* Illustrated by Jenya Prosmitsky. Carolrhoda, 2000. Part of the *Words Are Categorical* series.

Classifying Words

An engaging way to have students apply their knowledge of different word classes—such as verbs, adjectives, and nouns—is to give them a reading selection that contains many "nonsense" words. Younger students can use examples from authors such as Dr. Seuss, whereas older students will enjoy looking at passages such as the poem *Jabberwocky* by Lewis Carroll. Introduce the activity by providing examples in which you have highlighted nonsense words. Later, you can have students read through a selection individually or as a group and underline the words they think are made up. For example:

> *Twas* brillig *and the* slithy toves
> *Did* gyre *and* gimble *in the* wabe.
> *All* mimsy *were the* borogoves
> *And the* mome raths outgrabe.
> —Lewis Carroll, *Jabberwocky*

Give students a chart with columns for each part of speech that you have studied. Each group of students will have to decide where the nonsense words should be classified. Have students justify their choices. Note that some words may be appropriately classified in more than one column.

Punctuated Paragraphs

For a follow-up activity after discussing rules for punctuation, provide students with a paragraph from which you have removed all punctuation marks. Choose an excerpt from a book they have read in order to help them focus on form rather than comprehension. In the beginning, you may wish to include capital letters so students can identify which parts are sentences, or omit only a particular element, such as commas or quotation marks. Students can check their own work against the original text or hand the paragraph to another student to read aloud, testing that it makes sense. Remind students that there may be more than one "right" way to punctuate their paragraph.

Modified Stories

Give students opportunities to practice applying rules for grammatical agreement by having them rewrite familiar stories, making modifications, such as changing all first-person verbs to third-person, present-tense verbs to past-tense, or singular nouns to plural, for example. Another possibility is to have them change all of the dialogue in the story to reported speech, or descriptions of conversation into dialogue. Have them read the new version aloud in order to develop an ear for consistency and grammatical forms. This activity can also be used to provide students with extra individual practice in the learning center.

Sentence Wheel

Use a set of moveable disks to help students produce sentences as well as review parts of speech. You can use determiners, nouns, and verbs, or adjectives, nouns, and verbs. In the example on page 205, we have used nouns, verbs, and adverbs. Moving the different wheels to produce different sentences will help students see varied language patterns.

Understanding Syntax

Explain that everyone has a "sentence-making machine" in their brains that enables them to create new sentences any time they need them. Demonstrate this knowledge of English grammar by having students identify which of these groups of words is an English sentence and which is not:

- rode the boy park
- the boy the park
- the boy rode through the park

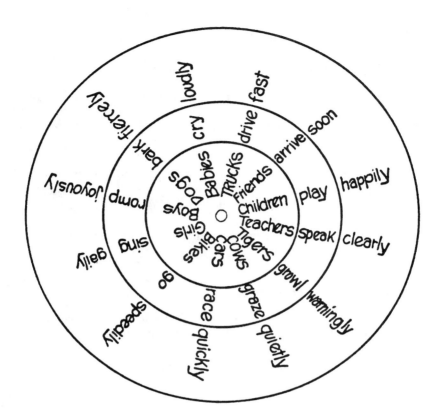

Almost every child will quickly identify the third group as a sentence. How do they know? Their sentence-making machines allow them to recognize something is missing in the first two examples, without knowing the proper names for word classes. Discuss how to turn these examples into sentences: What do you need to do? Change the order of the words, insert more words, eliminate words?

Original Sentences

Give students practice in producing new sentences. Print a word on the board and ask each student to suggest a sentence using that word. Don't try to record them, but point out that each sentence is an individual production and that each student can produce many different examples. Try these words for starters: *tiger, submarine, jump, wheels.*

After practicing sentences from one word, your students will enjoy the challenge of creating original sentences from two or more words: *sandwich–table, elephant–tree, school–fish, picture–red–dog, shark–cold–teeth.*

The Basic Sentence

Show students the simplest sentence pattern, which is only two words—a noun and a verb:

- Babies cry.
- Cars honk.
- People shiver.

Have the students write a number of two-word sentences. Then ask them to expand one of their two-word sentences. They can add words before or after the two words as they make the sentences as long as possible. This demonstration of how to add modifiers, clauses, and additional ideas shows students how easy it is to write longer sentences, such as:

> As I wait outside the door, I look up at the stars and wonder what I'm doing standing outside in the cold and dark while all around me <u>people shiver</u> in line so that they can buy tickets to the concert in the morning.

Underlining the original two-word sentence is an effective way of showing how the sentence was developed.

More Sentence Patterns

The most common pattern for sentences to follow is a noun *subject* followed by an active *verb* and an *object* (SVO). Have children generate sentences like these examples:

- Zvi asked a question.
- The girl raised her hand.
- Raychelle studied gymnastics.

Discuss with the students the need for an appropriate determiner *(the, a, an)* with subjects and objects. Note what happens when there are two objects (direct and indirect).

Mount a large picture on the bulletin board. Have everyone write a sentence in the SVO pattern to display with this picture. Everyone will be pleased to see and read the sentences displayed.

To Be a Sentence . . .

Another common pattern is the sentence with a form of *to be,* followed by an adjective or a noun, thus:

- Pablo has been sick.
- Alex is a student.
- We were late.
- Mrs. Okawa is our teacher.

Have students generate a number of sentences using *am, is, are, was, will be, shall be, were, has been, have been,* or *had been.* Notice that such forms as *is playing* or *was going* are aspects of the verbs *play* and *go,* not the verb *to be; be* can be used as an auxiliary to make progressive forms of other verbs.

Suspect Sentences

More advanced students will appreciate the challenge involved in this activity. Give students several paragraphs of fiction or nonfiction writing and tell them that the word processor has developed a bug in the *Cut* and *Paste* commands. As a result, some of the paragraphs have a sentence in them that belongs in another paragraph. Can they find the sentences that don't belong in that paragraph? Provide examples from student reading material in which you have moved some sentences into other paragraphs but perhaps not in all of them. You can also insert "forged" (wrong) sentences into the text for students to uncover. Students will be able to create these challenges for each other.

Formula Sentences

Print sentence formulas on strips of paper that students can pull from a sentence dispenser made from a paper towel tube, a box that held long fireplace matches, or a painted coffee can. Use sentence formulas like this:

Adj & N & V & Adv = S
D & Adj & N & V & Obj = S
N & V & I & Adv = S

Appropriate sentences that students might write for the formulas above include:

- Young children smile gracefully.
  New babies wail loudly.
- The inexperienced waiter spilled the drinks.
  A black dog chased a squirrel.
- Teachers work quite hard.
  Birds chirp very often.

Abbreviations for formulas are:

D—Determiner
Adj—Adjective
Adv—Adverb
N—Noun
V—Verb
I—Intensifier
Obj—Object
S—Sentence

Build-a-Sentence

Prepare a chart listing words in different categories that students can use in sentences, as shown here:

Determiner	Adjective	Noun	Verb	Adverb
The	ravishing	chefs	growled	stupidly
Several	confused	flowers	screeched	ferociously
These	scrumptious	princes	gobbled	hastily
Three	gallant	typewriters	burned	slowly
Those	humorous	ropes	scurried	happily
Six	realistic	tigers	examined	hopefully
Forty	delighted	ostriches	slid	heartily
Several	dilapidated	racers	gasped	mournfully
Nine	handsome	tables	exploded	menacingly
Many	strong	owls	floundered	helplessly

For example, students might use the chart to create these sentences:

- Several ravishing princes floundered slowly.
- Forty gallant tigers gobbled heartily.

Sentences created can be used as Story Starters. Students might also illustrate their sentences.

Silly Sentences

Give students sentences that contain words that do not fit the meaning of the sentence. Have the students cross out the "silly" word and make a written or oral substitution. Allow for individual differences and accept any substitution that makes sense. Students will enjoy creating their own silly sentences to share.

- The baby slept on the roof.
- The moon was very square last night.
- Isabel played the banana after school.
- The dog had brown and blue fur.
- The rock floated in the air.
- Jesse drank the chocolate cake.

Word Order

Merely including all the right words is not enough to make a sentence. Show the students how important word order *(syntax)* is in English by having them compare these two sentences:

- The girl sat on the friendly horse.
- The horse sat on the friendly girl.

Ask the students if the two sentences mean the same thing. What's the difference?

Can students understand the following sentences? Each includes all the words necessary to make a sentence. What else is necessary to make these sentences comprehensible?

- Maria to each speak Luis and often other.
- sick the today are teachers all.
- radio from music the comes.

Note that one group of words may make several possible sentences.

Scrambled Sentences

Ask the children to unscramble these examples to make sentences:

- spaghetti supper Marty for made
- dove waves The the under seal
- broken the mended She vase
- planted a Mike garden vegetable
- Cassie two younger has sisters

Occasionally, include an extra word so students really have to think about their sentences, such as:

- the Gail in bowl radio oranges the put
- from picked garden his newspaper Walt squash ten
- pictures Jennie pretty cooked draw can
- her to wrote a Nancy letter car friend
- on sandcastle built they a beach wave the

Any school text is a good source for the construction of more examples. The ability to make these groups of words into sentences illustrates a student's language competence.

Grammar Review

The best way to learn a subject is to teach it to another. For an effective review of grammar studies, ask students to create an informational book that explains grammar to younger students. They will have to consider what topics to include and how to present them in a way that is interesting and comprehensible to second-graders, for example. A model for this presentation might be *The Amazing Pop-Up Grammar Book* by Jennie Maizels (Dutton, 1996).

A variation is to have students make up their own song about grammar, similar to the popular *Grammar Rock* program on television. How can they use words and music to communicate grammar concepts to their classmates? Or perhaps clarify aspects of grammar for students who are learning English as an additional language? *Grammar Rock* is available in several formats: CD-ROM, software, and audiocassette.

Focusing on Problem Areas

As students use language, you will find that different students need help in particular areas. Don't drill the whole class on the uses of *their* and *there* if most of them already know how to use these words correctly. If, however, you note that one student or a small group of students needs this information, teach it to those students in an individualized approach.

Obtain a set of 10 language workbooks. Take the books apart and reassemble into little booklets covering related skills. Color code the covers and key the booklets to student needs, so that you can refer a student to the green set, for example, to practice verb forms. Or students can work on these booklets in small groups. If some of the students continue to make errors, have other booklets of lessons available for additional practice. Students can also correct each other's work, which reinforces the skills learned.

Studying Our Language

What should be included in the teaching of English, besides spelling and grammar? In this section, the concept of *phonemic* awareness is extended to language in general, through playing with language and expanding *language* awareness. The purpose of language as a subject of study is to develop in students a sense that language is vibrant and vital, including the voices of many different people, reflecting traditional and modern influences, systematic but always changing. *Language awareness* means that students can use language for their own purposes, rather than letting language use them. The following section addresses topics such as standard English, language history, and dictionaries, in order for students to ask the questions: "Who determines what counts as a language?" and "Whose language is represented here?" (Labov, 1972).

New Ways of Walking

As students become aware of the importance of language, they will enjoy making a class *thesaurus,* a dictionary of synonyms. Talk with the group about words that have been so overworked that they are no longer meaningful—for example, *walk*. Create a Word Wall on which to list synonyms for *walk*. Begin by brainstorming all the words students can think of at the time, such as:

> sneak
> stride
> stumble
> march
> tramp
> waddle

Then, have students add words as they discover additional synonyms. Students can demonstrate how each kind of walking is done, so everyone has a clear idea of the meaning of each word.

Class Synonym File

Have each student choose one word—for instance, *big, good, dog,* or *beautiful*—and make a card for a Synonym File. Over the period of a week, they are responsible for gathering 10 synonyms to record on each card and place in a file box for all students to consult. This file can be used during many class activities, such as when students are searching for a more interesting word to use in writing. Encourage students to add to the class thesaurus that they have created rather than copy words they don't know from a published thesaurus.

Add these books to your class library to provide students with more examples of interesting word usage:

> Jon Agee. *Who Ordered the Jumbo Shrimp? And Other Oxymorons.* HarperCollins, 1998.
> Norton Juster. *As Silly As Bee's Knees, As Busy As Bees: An Astounding Assortment of Similes.* Beech Tree, 1998.

Word Connotations

Synonyms are words with the same meaning, but remind students that no words mean precisely the same thing. Synonyms are used differently depending on their different *connotations*. In certain circumstances, some words are more appropriate than others, because they have a positive or negative connotation. For example, when you agree with people, you might say they have "the courage of their convictions." If you disagree, you might call them "stubborn." Ask your students, "Which of these terms would you call yourself? A friend? An enemy?"

> Pig-headed
> Obstinate
> Strong-minded

Discuss with the students the different shades of meaning, or connotation, for each word.

"Polite" Words

Have students brainstorm different ways to ask someone to close the window, such as:

- It's cold in here.
- Shut the window!
- Would you please close the window?
- Aren't you cold?
- If you don't close that window right now . . .

Note with students the various forms that this "request" can take, from *imperative* to *declarative* or *interrogative*. Discuss the differences between the examples. When might you use each one? Working in small groups, have students put these items in order of politeness, from most polite to least polite. Student groups can share their decisions with the class and justify their choices.

Other requests that can be phrased in many different ways include:

- Answer the phone.
- Take out the garbage.
- Clean your room.

It's Not What You Say, It's the Way You Say It!

Give students the opportunity to experience the change in meaning created by different ways of saying the same word or the same sentence *(intonation)*. For example, give a sentence to your class and have the students say it happily, sadly, or angrily. Let them experiment with the sentence: *What have you been doing?*

How many ways can the students think of to say "no"? Can saying "no" ever really mean "yes"? For example, ask different students to demonstrate how they would say "yes" if they meant:

- I would love to go to the party.
- I have finished my carrots.
- I am ready to go to the dentist.
- I would like some ice cream.
- The baby is asleep.

Body Language

We also use body language to communicate meaning. Have students work in pairs to plan and act out a "conversation," using no words or sounds, only body language. Afterwards, discuss with the class the skit they have just watched. What did they think was happening? What was each person trying to communicate? How did the actors use their bodies to show what they meant?

Heteronyms

Heteronyms are words that are spelled alike, but a slight change, usually a shift in pronunciation or word stress, signals a change in meaning, for example:

- She likes to keep the papers *separate.*
- I will *separate* the correct words from the incorrect.

Many heteronyms are noun-verb pairs, such as:

- The administration will not *permít* this behavior to continue.
- He got the *pérmit* for the car today.
- I would like to *addréss* the conference next month.
- I never write because I don't have your *áddress.*

Examples of heteronyms are the following:

content	record	entrance
desert	subject	rebel
object	present	produce
project	reject	bow
tear	refuse	use

Have students write sentences including pairs of heteronyms like these. They can practice listening for heteronyms and add them to the class collection of interesting words.

A Spelling Poem

Share this humorous poem with students. Let them follow along on paper as you read the poem aloud.

A Strange Language
When the English tongue we speak,
Why is "break" not rhymed with "freak"?
Will you tell me why it's true
We say "sew" but likewise "few";
And the maker of a verse
Cannot cap his "horse" with "worse"?
"Beard" sounds not the same as "heard";
"Cord" is different from "word";

> *Cow is "cow" but low is "low";*
> *"Shoe" is never rhymed with "foe."*
> *Think of "hose" and "dose" and "lose";*
> *And think of "goose" and yet of "choose."*
> *Think of "comb" and "tomb" and "bomb";*
> *"Doll" and "roll" and "home" and "some."*
> *And since "pay" is rhymed with "say,"*
> *Why not "paid" with "said," I pray?*
> *We have "blood" and "food" and "good";*
> *"Mould" is not pronounced like "could."*
> *Wherefore "done" but "gone" and "lone"?*
> *Is there any reason known?*
>
> *And, in short, it seems to me*
> *Sounds and letters disagree.*
>
> —Anonymous

Discuss the poem. Do students agree that the unpredictable relationship between sound and spelling in English is a problem? Students can research the history of English words in order to have a better understanding of the language as we know it today. Provide resources for students to investigate, such as:

Donna Brook. *The Journey of English.* Illustrated by Jean Day Zallinger: Prentice-Hall, 1998.
Charles Funk. *Thereby Hangs a Tale.* Harper, 1985.
Adrien Room. *The Fascinating Origins of Everyday Words.* NTC Publishing, 1997.

Older students can prepare pro and con arguments for a debate—*Resolved: English spelling should be modified to match English pronunciation.*

Important Words

Ask the students, "What are the 10 most important words in our language? What are the 10 most crucial words—words that we cannot do without?" List all the words suggested. Then have students vote on the 10 most crucial or important words. How did they define *important* or *crucial?*

Encourage students to argue for or against the inclusion of certain words before voting takes place. This list can be displayed as a chart: The Ten Most Important Words in English, Selected by Room 27. Incorporate these words regularly in your language arts activities.

Word Treasures

Have each student keep a small book of words based on his or her interests. These are words that they have heard in class or found while reading. Pages can be allocated for:

Words I Need to Write
My Favorite Words
Interesting Words I Found
Strange Animals

Hidden Homonyms

Increase students' awareness of homonyms (or homophones) by playing this language game. Give them a sheet of sentences in which words have been left out. The missing words in each sentence are homonyms. The goal is to determine which homonyms are suitable and fill them in, including spelling them correctly. Of course, once the student has guessed one of the words, the other should be obvious. Here are some sentences (with answers indicated) to start with:

- Have you _____ the book with the _____ cover?
  (read)   (red)
- The _____ people in the hospital all _____ from the same dish.
  (eight)   (ate)
- They were surprised to _____ that the ship was already at _____.
  (see)   (sea)
- I can't _____ the way everybody goes _____ foot in summer.
  (bear)   (bare)
- Would you like to _____ the author of *700 Ways to Cook Snake* _____?
  (meet)   (*Meat*)
- When they arrived at the camping _____, they found an unforgettable _____.
  (site)   (sight)

Have duplicated sheets of these sentences available for students to work on when they choose. Students will also enjoy thinking up examples to try on the class.

Homonyms

Here is a practical list of less common homonyms to use with many different language activities:

metal, mettle	cast, caste	write, right, wright, rite
horse, hoarse	waive, wave	carrot, carat, caret
aloud, allowed	dough, doe	cite, site, sight
knew, gnu, new	mete, meet, meat	censor, censer
raze, raise	colonel, kernel	climb, clime
knight, night	mane, main, Maine	complement, compliment
dew, due, do	you, ewe	stationery, stationary
feint, faint	all, awl	council, counsel
mist, missed	flair, flare	baron, barren

hew, hue	paced, paste	roe, row
gage, gauge	barer, bearer	great, grate
core, corps	pier, peer	cede, seed
whet, wet	sold, soled, souled	wile, while
wails, whales, Wales	pique, peek, peak	tear, tare
suite, sweet	foul, fowl	sloe, slow
assent, ascent	sign, sine	knave, nave
sty, stye	idle, idyl, idol	wind, whined, wined
faun, fawn	so, sow, sew	seine, sane
choir, quire	bald, bawled, balled	not, knot
magnet, magnate	heroine, heroin	

Looking at Dialect Differences

Encourage students to talk about differences in the way people pronounce certain words. In your discussion of interesting aspects of language, draw these examples to their attention. You might present the students with a list of words such as these so they can listen for different pronunciations:

pin/pen	cot/caught
car	greasy
merry/Mary/marry	roof
aunt/ant	vase

Can students find any patterns in the differences? Sometimes people from one part of the country will pronounce the same word differently from people in other regions. These ways of speaking are called *dialects.*

Recognition of these differences will lead to many questions: Why do these differences exist? When we move to a different part of the country, what happens to our speech? How do we learn these differences? Do some dialects sound better to us and why? Students at every grade level can engage in these discussions, because all students are fascinated by language.

British English

We say that the British and Americans speak the same language, but do they? Students reading books by British authors often notice differences in vocabulary. Explore these differences with students by researching forms of British vocabulary, pronunciation, and spelling. Here are some examples to get you started:

British English	*American English*
underground	subway
sweet	dessert

biscuits	cookies
petrol	gasoline
wireless	radio
lift	elevator
dustbin	garbage can
geyser	hot water heater
vest	undershirt

Students may have encountered some of the British words in context, without knowing the American equivalent. Obviously, one form cannot be considered more correct than the other.

Children will also notice differences in spelling, for instance, *colour* and *color*. Upper-grade students will enjoy looking for more of these examples in books by British authors. For instance, in the popular *Harry Potter* series, by J. K. Rowling, they might find unfamiliar words for food (such as a dessert called *knickerbocker glory*), or clothing (such as school uniform hats called *boaters*), in addition to words from the world of magic (such as *quidditch*). Discuss strategies for understanding the meaning of these unfamiliar words when students read them in books.

Language Reflects Society

Children become more aware of how language reveals values when they compare and discuss such words as the following:

mailman
policeman
mankind
businessman
chairman

Why would people prefer not to use some of these words? Contrast the previous words with alternatives such as *letter carrier* and *police officer*. Can a woman be a *businessman?* Can a man be a *secretary?* Or a *stewardess?* (Note that both men and women are now called *flight attendants.*)

Students might also want to consider which adjectives are traditionally applied to women and which to men, such as:

sweet
delicate
strong
sensitive
pretty
handsome

How and why are these words used? Are there more precise or descriptive words we could use? Do we need to have different words for boys and girls, men and women?

In Black and White

Older students can investigate other examples of word use, such as the different meanings for *black* and *white.* Have students list expressions or phrases that include the words *black* or *white,* such as the following:

blackmail
in the black
White House
black death
whiter than white
blacken a reputation

After they have a number of examples, ask them to sort these expressions by positive, neutral, or negative associations. Are they surprised to find that most of the examples of *black* are in the negative column and most of the ones that include *white* are listed as positive? Discuss the results with students. What does this mean? What can we, as speakers of this language, do about these findings?

Cataloguing Idioms

Every language has colorful expressions that are part of everyday speech. These expressions, called *idioms,* would not make sense, however, if translated into another language. Some of the most familiar are:

- It's raining cats and dogs.
- He was hot under the collar.
- That's the last straw!
- I could eat a horse!

Have your students begin a study of idioms. You may want to spread this activity over several days, so that the students can enlist their parents' help in providing less familiar examples and unique regional idioms. Students will enjoy discovering idioms they have never heard before. Some idioms on your list may be:

- To have a finger in the pie
- To jump out of one's skin
- To pull another's leg

Collect these idioms in a book for the class to share. Students can add to this compilation as they find more unusual idioms.

Ask your students to practice using some of these idioms in their descriptive writing. Encourage them to develop their use of figurative language by using idioms from their list and by making up new expressions.

Students can also investigate the origins of idioms. Look for resources such as:

Daniel Porter. *Cat Got Your Tongue: The Real Meaning Behind Everyday Sayings.* Illustrated by Donna Reynolds. Troll, 1999.
Marvin Terban. *Punching the Clock: Funny Action Idioms.* Clarion, 1990.

Translating Idioms

Challenge students to translate English idioms for a person who is just learning to speak English. Give students sentences like these which they are to explain:

- The family had a hard time *keeping the wolf from the door.*
- Joe was always *barking up the wrong tree.*
- Bess advised her friend not to *burn the candle at both ends.*
- Don't *get your feathers ruffled* if you aren't chosen first.
- The detective suspected the butler mainly because he looked like the *cat that swallowed the canary.*
- Ralph decided to *butter up* his parents before showing his report card.

Students can also provide examples of other idioms from different languages translated into English.

Literal Idioms

Share a book from the series about Amelia Bedelia, by Peggy Parish, with students, such as *Amelia 4 Mayor.* Amelia is always in trouble because she insists on taking idioms *literally.* Have students illustrate Amelia's impressions of some of their favorite idioms.

To rake up the past	To fly into a rage
To have something up your sleeve	To have bats in the belfry
To get down to brass tacks	To be completely in the dark
To weigh your words	To know which way the wind is blowing
To turn the tables	To be all wrapped up in your work
To be a stick in the mud	To be up the creek without a paddle
To be on the tip of the tongue	To be caught red-handed
To steal one's thunder	To lean over backwards

Teaching Orthography

Most students will not be familiar with *orthography,* the scholarly word for spelling. Teach orthography for a change in your classroom. Begin by discussing the meaning of this word, "the art of spelling words according to accepted usage."

Show students how to analyze this word into two parts, *ortho* and *graphy,* that come from the Greek language. *Ortho* means "straight, upright, correct." This root appears in many other English words, for example:

orthodontist	orthodox
orthopedics	orthogenesis

Graphy is used to describe some form of "drawing, writing, or recording." This root word is used widely in words that students may know, for example:

geography	biography
photography	autobiography
choreography	lithography

Other related words that use the root *graph* include:

graphics	grapheme
graphite	graphic

How does knowing the meaning of each root help you understand the meaning of the whole word?

Dictionary of Slanguage

Because slang is a major part of everyday speech, students can learn about language by studying slang. Have students list as many slang words as they can to be defined, categorized into word classes, used in sentence patterns, and compiled by "lexicographers" into a class *Dictionary of Slanguage.*

> *hacker* (haḱ ẽr), n. 1. an expert computer programmer. 2. a person with little sense of right and wrong; as, having the morals of a hacker.
> *tight* (tīt), adj. 1. very strict. 2. unfair.

Who would use a dictionary of slang? Will the words in this dictionary go out of date? Discuss with students what words they would include in a dictionary.

Dictionary Scavenger Hunt

Use the following activity to help students become familiar with the dictionary. Provide a list of 10 questions for them to answer using the dictionary, such as these:

- What word follows *tomorrow* in the dictionary?
- Is a *limerick* gregarious?
- What are two *kinds of birds?*
- Does a lion eat *oxymorons?*

Students can work on this project in class if there are enough dictionaries for everyone or they can complete the exercise for homework.

What Words Really Mean

Read the following passage, from *Through the Looking Glass* by Lewis Carroll, to students:

> ". . . There's glory for you!"
>
> "I don't know what you mean by 'glory,'" Alice said.
>
> Humpty Dumpty smiled contemptuously, "Of course you don't—till I tell you. I meant, 'There's a nice knock-down argument for you!'"
>
> "But 'glory' doesn't mean 'a nice knock-down argument,'" Alice objected.
>
> "When I use a word," Humpty-Dumpty said in rather a scornful tone, "it means just what I choose it to mean, neither more nor less."
>
> "The question is," said Alice, "whether you *can* make words mean so many different things."
>
> "The question is," said Humpty-Dumpty, "which is to be Master—that's all."

What are Alice and Humpty Dumpty arguing about? Discuss the difference between the two points of view. Humpty Dumpty claims that he can choose to use a word in whatever way he wants. Alice is concerned that people wouldn't understand each other if a word could mean anything. What do students think about this argument? How do we know what words mean?

Advanced students can research how words get in dictionaries and the debates over which words should be included.

Bilingual Books

Many books are available with the text in English and a second language, such as Spanish or Vietnamese. Having bilingual books in the classroom supports students who speak another language. Reading these stories aloud also helps other students learn more about a culture and language that may be unfamiliar to them. Encourage your students to learn some vocabulary from another language.

Several books in Spanish and English demonstrate the range of bilingual books to use with students. *This House Is Made of Mud/Esta Casa Está Hecha de Lodo,* written by Ken Buchanan and illustrated by Libba Tracy (Rising Moon, 1991), tells a simple story about living in the southwestern desert. *Gathering the Sun,* written by Alma Flor Ada and illustrated by Simón Silva (Lothrop, 1997), honors César Chávez and the Latino farm workers by using an ABC framework to present powerful poems. Students can learn more about the Spanish language with *Say Hola to Spanish,* by Susan Middleton Elya and illustrated by Loretta Lopez (Lothrop & Low, 1998).

Other books are useful to expand student awareness of the many different languages in the world. Some suggestions are: *If I Had a Paka,* a book of poetry by Charlotte Pomerantz and illustrated by Nancy Tafuri (Mulberry, 1998), which includes examples of words from languages such as Swahili, Vietnamese, Samoan, and Spanish; *Come Sign with Us: Sign Language Activities for Children,* by Jan C. Hafer (Gallaudet, 1996); and *Secret Code,* by Dana M. Rau and illustrated by Bari Weissman (Children's Press, 1998), a story about a blind boy who reads Braille.

Discussion Questions

1. How can you best assess the knowledge base about language that the child has when he or she enters a new classroom?

2. What strategies will help you build on the knowledge base of each child about grammatical concepts?

3. How can you develop a thematic study about the English language and about other languages of the world?

Exploring Further

T. Augarde. *A to Z of Word Games.* Oxford University Press, 1994.

W. Bean and C. Bouffler. *Spell by Writing.* Heinemann, 1991.

Faye Bolton and Diane Snowball. *Ideas for Spelling.* Heinemann, 1993.

Lita Ericson and Moira Fraser Juliebo. *The Phonological Awareness Handbook for Kindergarten and Primary Teachers.* International Reading Association, 1998.

Grammar Rock: Schoolhouse Rock. CD-ROM for Mac/Windows. Creative Wonders, 1995.

Grammar Rock: Schoolhouse Rock. Videocassette. Scholastic Rock/ABC-TV, 1998.

Michael Opitz. *Rhymes and Reasons: Literature and Language Play for Phonological Awareness.* Heinemann, 2000.

Gladys Rosencrans. *Teaching Children How to Spell, Not What to Spell.* International Reading Association, 1998.

C. Smith and E. Reade. *Word History: A Resource Book for the Teacher.* ERIC Clearinghouse on Reading and Communication Skills, 1994.

Hallie K. Yopp and Ruth H. Yopp. *Oo-pples and Boo-noo-noos: Songs and Activities for Phonemic Awareness.* Harcourt, 1996.

References

R. A. Allred. *Spelling Trends, Content, and Methods.* National Education Association, 1987.

A. C. Baugh and T. Cable. *A History of the English Language, 4th ed.* Prentice-Hall, 1993.

William Bryson. *The Mother Tongue: English and How It Got That Way.* Morrow, 1990.

Marilyn Burns, Peg Griffin, and Catherine Snow. *Preventing Reading Difficulties in Young Children.* National Academy Press, 1998.

Courtney Cazden. *Classroom Discourse: The Language of Teaching and Learning.* Heinemann, 1988.

Carol Chomsky. "Approaching Reading through Invented Spelling." In Lauren Resnick and P. Weaver (Eds.), *Theory and Practice of Early Reading Vol. II.* Erlbaum, 1971.

Lisa Delpit. *Other People's Children: Cultural Conflict in the Classroom.* The New Press, 1995.

J. R. Gentry and J. W. Gillet. *Teaching Kids to Spell.* Heinemann, 1993.

Shirley Brice Heath. *Ways with Words: Language, Life, and Work in Communities and Classrooms.* Cambridge University Press, 1984.

Shirley Brice Heath and Leslie Mangiola. *Children of Promise: Literate Activity in Linguistically and Culturally Diverse Classrooms.* National Education Association, 1991.

E. Henderson. *Teaching Spelling.* Houghton Mifflin, 1985.

George Hillocks. *Research on Written Composition.* National Council of Teachers of English, 1986.

William Labov. *Sociolinguistic Patterns.* University of Pennsylvania Press, 1972.

Richard McCrum, William Cran, and Robert MacNeil. *The Story of English.* Viking, 1986. Also available as a video series, *The Story of English,* PBS.

Charles Read. "Preschool Children's Knowledge of English Phonology." *Harvard Educational Review, 41* (1971): 1–34.

T. Samoyault. *Alphabetical Order: How the Alphabet Began.* Viking, 1998.

John S. Simmons and Lawrence Baines (Eds.). *Language Study in Middle School, High School, and Beyond.* International Reading Association, 1998.

Keith Stanovich. "Matthew Effects in Reading: Some Consequences of Individual Differences in the Acquisition of Literacy." *Reading Research Quarterly, 21* (1986): 360–407.

Hallie K. Yopp. "Read-Aloud Books for Developing Phonemic Awareness." In Richard Allington (Ed.), *Teaching Struggling Readers.* International Reading Association, 1998.

7 Learning through Literature

Make believe was so real to Peter Pan that during a meal of it you could see him getting rounder.

—James Barrie, *Peter Pan*

Literature has become a major component of the reading/language arts program. Children's literature, in the form of fiction and nonfiction, shows up in basal readers and has even replaced textbooks in some classrooms. Not only does literature provide a rich base for instruction but it also appeals to teachers because it has the power to spark a child's imagination and open up a new world of experience. In addition, children's talk about books and other similar literacy activities are fundamental to language acquisition. This early exposure to book reading continues to have a significant long-term impact on children, both in learning to read and later school achievement.

The way we teach literature has also changed. Research has shown that the perspective a reader brings to the text affects the reader's interpretation of that text (Stein & Glenn, 1982). This influence that *schema* (prior knowledge and experience) has on comprehension implies that the "meaning" of what one reads is located in the reader's head rather than in the words on the page. In other words, because every reader brings a different set of expectations to a story, the story will not have a single, fixed meaning but will be interpreted in a variety of ways, depending on the reader, the context, and the purpose for reading. As a result, instead of having students write summaries for book reports, the literature program will focus on having readers respond to what they read and share their responses with others. In Rosenblatt's influential work (1978), she describes the act of reading as a kind of *transaction* between reader and author, in which each has an important part to contribute.

Teachers want students to develop a love of reading that will last a lifetime. But the primary reason for using literature in the language arts program is the fact that, through fiction and nonfiction, children can learn about themselves and others. The best of children's literature provides *windows* through which students can explore the world and *mirrors* in which they can see themselves more clearly.

Motivating Reading through Literature

The earliest form of literature that engages students is probably the story. As students listen to find out what happens next, they are learning "story grammar"—a base on which they will build later literature understandings. Children are intrigued by nonfiction as well, highly motivated to search complex texts—such as *The Guinness Book of World Records,* instruction manuals, and articles evaluating video games—in order to obtain information they need. Instead of having students "report" on the books they have read, teachers encourage increased peer-led discussion with book clubs and literature circles. As a result, the teacher's role changes from *directing* group discussion to *facilitating* students' own interpretation of text, through *scaffolding* and *coaching* (O'Flavahan, 1995).

Reading in the Classroom

Plan along with students as you tell them that reading is the top priority for the classroom you all share. Let them suggest ways to promote reading and to help every student become a better reader.

Maintain a classroom environment that stimulates student interest in reading. Use the following activities to promote a positive attitude toward student reading:

- Talk to the class about what you are reading.
- Give parents a list of suggested gift books.
- Join a book club.
- Have an author or illustrator come and talk to the class.
- Distribute a list of suggestions for summer reading.

Story Time

Share books with your students by reading aloud to the class. Not only will you model reading as a pleasurable activity but you will also arouse student interest. Choose a picturebook such as *Tiny and Bigman* by Phyllis Gershator (Marshall Cavendish, 1999) for younger students, *Spider Sparrow* by Dick King-Smith (Crown, 2000) for older students, or keep a book such as *The Horribly Haunted School* by Margaret Mahy (Viking, 1997) going, reading a chapter a day, as students eagerly await the outcome.

As you read, pause at significant points to ask students questions such as: What do you think will happen next? Why did the characters do that? How did one of the characters feel? You are introducing students to vocabulary that they will use in discussing literature and modeling the questions that readers ask themselves as they read.

Read, Read, Read Aloud

Reading aloud is not just for the primary grades. Always have a good book going in your classroom. Sharing a book together establishes a healthy rapport among students and a sense of community. It also cements a warm relationship between you and the children you are teaching. For middle and upper-grade students, choose novels by reputable authors, for example:

Laurence Yep	Mildred Taylor
Virginia Hamilton	Lloyd Alexander
Yoshiko Uchida	Cynthia Rylant
Katherine Paterson	Gary Paulsen

You might make a point of choosing books that offer multicultural perspectives—for instance, Scott O'Dell's fascinating survival story about a young Native American girl, *Island of the Blue Dolphins,* or Mary Lyons's sensitive historical fiction, *Letters from a Slave Girl: The Story of Harriet Jacobs.*

When you read to students, they can concentrate on enjoying the story without struggling to read every word. In addition, they are absorbing examples of what book language sounds like, from conversational intonation patterns to new grammatical structures.

Reading Challenges

Provide a variety of reading challenges for students to stimulate them to read more:

- Read an easy book from back page to front.
- Read as many books as you can in a week by the same author.
- Read a book out loud to a younger sibling every day for a week.
- Read five nonfiction books about something you know nothing about.
- Read a book your parent read when he or she was your age.
- Bring in three favorite stories to read to a friend.

Quotations on Display

Prepare a Gallery Walk by displaying 5 to 10 quotations from literature on the wall around the room. Use some of the quotations at the beginning of each chapter in this book or select from the examples that follow. You might choose lines that follow a theme or express a controversial idea. Beside each quotation, attach a large piece of newsprint on which students can write their responses—questions, comments, pictures, and so forth. Then everyone circles the room, reading the quotations and the comments. Each person chooses one idea that especially intrigues him or her and writes about that idea. Writings can then be shared in small groups. Note that just moving around the room provides a change of pace for students who have been sitting quietly for some time. These literature quotations will perhaps motivate students to read the book from which the quotation is taken.

- It won't do you a bit of good to know everything if you don't do anything about it.
  —Louise Fitzhugh, in *Harriet the Spy*
- Can't keep still all day—I like adventures, and I'm going to find one.
  —Louisa May Alcott, in *Little Women*

- Do you want an adventure now, or would you like to have your tea first?
  —J. M. Barrie, in *Peter Pan*
- Expect everything, I always say, and the unexpected never happens.
  —Norton Juster, in *The Phantom Toll Booth*
- Squirrels must pass messages along to each other—messages that tell what kinds of nuts and where the trees are.
  —Jean Craighead George, in *My Side of the Mountain*
- If it had grown up it would have made a dreadfully ugly child; but it makes rather a handsome pig.
  — Lewis Carroll, in *Alice's Adventures in Wonderland*
- Generally, by the time you are Real, most of your hair has been loved off, and your eyes drop out and you get loose in the joints and very shabby. But these things don't matter at all, because once you are Real, you can't be ugly, except to people who don't understand.
  —Margery Williams, in *The Velveteen Rabbit*
- What is the use of a book without pictures or conversation?
  —Lewis Carroll, in *Alice's Adventures in Wonderland*
- Mongoose just sat there [in the library], like he was hypnotized by the book in front of him. Other books were spread across the table, like he was taking a bath in books.
  —Jerry Spinelli, in "Mongoose," from *The Library Card*

Fractured Titles

Students can have fun rewriting the titles of familiar books, which is a good way to encourage and maintain interest in reading. Give the students a list of book titles that are familiar names in disguise, as shown here. Have them match the "improved" titles with the original versions. Once they have completed this list, students can make up their own examples to enjoy with the rest of the class.

Familiar Titles	*Fractured Titles*
1. *Wind in the Willows*	__Trip to the Middle of the World
2. *The Red Balloon*	__Ice Crystals and Flatfish Skeletons
3. *Hailstones and Halibut Bones*	__Breeze in the Trees
4. *Journey to the Center of the Earth*	__Into the Mirror
5. *Kidnapped*	__The Happy Exploits of Bird Hat
6. *Through the Looking Glass*	__Cry of the Untamed
7. *Call of the Wild*	__Abducted
8. *The Merry Adventures of Robin Hood*	__The Ruby Inflatable

As a variation, write one or two fractured titles on the board for a warm-up during roll call. Students may wish to sign up for the responsibility of providing the next day's title.

The Classroom Library

A library can be created in any corner of the classroom. Perhaps an old carpet will be available to make the corner attractive and comfortable. Encourage students to enhance the library by constructing bookshelves, painting chairs, or making pillows to sit on.

Students can also serve as "librarians" to check books out for reading at home. They can make book covers for older books and mend those that become torn. Often, students can contribute reading material for the library, such as paperback books or magazines.

Using the Library

Talk with students about libraries and how they are used. Do any students have a library card? They can explain how to check out books. Provide information on obtaining a library card for students who don't have one. Students will learn more about libraries from *Let's Go to the Library* by Lisl Weil (Holiday House, 1990).

Making Books

As students "publish" their writings in book form, add them to the class library. Students will enjoy making a variety of books, following the directions in *Making Books That Fly, Fold, Wrap, Hide, Pop-Up, Twist, and Turn* by Gwen Diehn (Lark, 1998).

Literature Learning Center

You can also set up a learning center at which individuals or small groups of students can work. Make cards that describe a project that students can work on related to reading. A sample card is included here that tells students how to make interesting bookmarks to share with other students.

Choose Your Favorite Kind of Book

Dog stories	Adventure
Mysteries	Biographies
Science fiction	Sports
Folktales	Humor

Make a list of 5 to 10 books you would like to recommend to your friends. Cut a strip of colored construction paper 3" × 12" to make a bookmark. Draw a picture to decorate the bookmark, then print your list of books neatly below.

Exchange your bookmark with someone else so you can enjoy reading each other's favorite books. Make more than one copy of your list to exchange if you would like to have more than one list yourself.

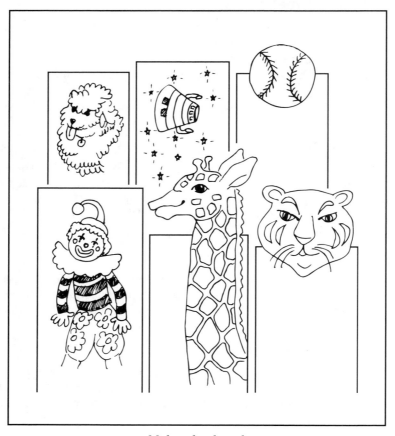

Make a bookmark

Extend Student Reading

To encourage students to broaden their reading, provide each student with a list of differ-ent *genres* (categories) to complete. Leave space to write the name of the book next to the category. Sample categories might include:

science fiction   historical fiction
informational   fantasy
mystery   biography
humor   adventure

Students who complete the first category chart by reading one book of each type may move on to the bonus chart, which could include:

poetry
mythology/folktales
sports

The Genre Tree

Cut out a tree shape from brown paper and mount it on the board. Label each limb with a different genre, such as *historical fiction* or *biography*. As students read a book in each category, they write the titles and their names on a piece of green paper and attach it to the tree, like a leaf. Students who are looking for ideas of what to read in a different genre can consult the tree for suggestions.

Beyond the Book Report

Throw out the traditional single-page book report form that quickly becomes meaningless for your students. Instead, brainstorm with students about how they can share a book that they have read with others who might enjoy reading the book. Let students know that they all have different kinds of strengths *(multiple intelligences)* and that you want them to have a chance to share their abilities. Keep the list of suggestions in a visible place to remind students of choices they can make, for example:

a poster that illustrates some of the events
an overhead transparency with interesting questions to introduce a booktalk
reading aloud several pages that describe an exciting moment
writing a letter to the author (and really mail it!)
a woodcarving
a small quilt
a multimedia presentation using the computer

Keeping a Reading Journal

Remember too not to penalize good readers by making them "report" on every book they read. Just recording each book on a special page in their Reading Journals is enough information for you and them to talk about during an individual conference.

Literature Circles

Students can read and discuss books in small groups or *literature circles*. The books they read can be chosen based on a topic or theme, such as social studies, author, or genre. "Booktalk" selected titles to the class and have students break into groups, one for each book. Work with students to design an outline or guide on which to record their discussions. Because many books are available on audiocassette to assist students reading at a lower level, even poor readers are able to benefit from the comprehension practice. Liter-

ature circles also have the advantage of mixing students of different levels or from different classes.

Book Notes

As students read, encourage them to take note of interesting passages, unusual words, or
unfamiliar sentence structures that they can talk about later in their literature circle. To
avoid interrupting the flow of reading or writing in the book, have them mark the place
with "sticky notes." Students who have read the same book can present it to the class by
selecting favorite passages and reading them aloud, in turn, to create an "impression" of
the book rather than summarize the plot.

A Readers' Theater Presentation

Divide the class into cooperative learning groups (CLGs) and have each group read a
selected novel. After reading and discussing the book, have each group plan a readers'
theater presentation to share with your class or perhaps students in another room. Guide
students through the process of preparing their presentations:

1. *Planning:* Tell the class what a readers' theater presentation is—for example, they
   will read from a prepared text, sitting on chairs in front of the room. Based on the
   novels they have read, each group can choose a theme to develop related to what
   they want to share. They can search anywhere for suitable poetry, documents, quotations, excerpts from their book, and so on. They can write a script they want to
   read—for instance, an introduction to the topic.
2. *Searching for Material:* Plan at least one class trip to the library so that you and the
   librarian can assist students in finding what they need.
3. *Preparing the Script:* Duplicate copies of material students select from a book to
   use so they can mark the material, as needed. Encourage students to be inventive—
   for example, using rap or dialogue, if they like. They should split up longer seg-
   ments among several readers to provide variety.
4. *Rehearsing:* One student can be assigned the role of director, who signals the group
   to stand or sit. This person should also see that each person reads clearly and loudly
   enough so the audience can hear.
5. *The Presentation:* Each group may perform before the rest of the class. This provides a kind of "dress rehearsal." Then, one group may be chosen to present before
   another class.

Advertising Posters

Interest other students in reading by selling a book through a poster. Display book advertising posters on the bulletin board to catch students' attention. Include catchy slogans and
attention-getting artwork and lettering on these posters, as well as the author and title of
the book (see page 233).

WHY MOSQUITOS BUZZ IN PEOPLE'S EARS

BY VERNA AARDEMA

PICTURES BY LEO AND DIANE DILLON

Why was the owl too sad to wake the sun?

Why is everyone mad at the mosquito?

Why does the iguana have sticks in his ears?

Why did the python dive into the rabbits hole?

Make a Mobile

A mobile provides a particularly striking visual display of a book. Students can make mobiles illustrating events or showing characters from a book they have read. Each mobile can be hung from the ceiling, to stimulate interest in the book on the part of other students.

Almost any art technique could be used for the mobile. Be sure to have the students include the title and author of the book. The simplest way to hang the mobile is with thread and sticks of wood. The heavier the pieces used by the students, the easier it will be to balance the mobile properly.

Book Jacket

Have students make book jackets for the books they read. They can draw a picture for the cover that says something about the story and is designed to get people to read the book. They should also make a jacket *blurb* that summarizes the book and gives information about the author and illustrator.

These book jackets can be displayed on the bulletin board or they can actually be put on the book. They are effective in motivating other students to read the books.

Read Me a Story

When students enjoy books, they also enjoy telling others about the books and sharing the stories. For older students, arrange with teachers of lower grades to have your students visit their classes and read stories to the younger students. Students should pick a story that they are enthusiastic about. Have them practice in front of their own class, a small group, or with a tape recorder, before they go to the other class. Small groups of younger students can be brought into your classroom at first if reading in front of another class is too frightening. Telling a story is great practice in oral language skills, with the added bonus of near-guaranteed audience appreciation.

If your class is younger, explore the idea of having older students tell stories to your class.

Group Reading

A small group of children who are interested in reading the same book may choose to share the story by reading aloud together. Let them decide how the reading will be done. Perhaps each one will take a turn reading a page as the book is passed from person to person. Or the group may decide to let people who like to read aloud volunteer to do the reading while others listen. After the story is completed, this group can share the story with the class by dramatizing a portion, painting a small mural, or some other interesting method that seems appropriate.

Sharing Books

Give students a choice of alternative ways to respond and react to books they have read. Some activities may be more appropriate for particular books. Here are some suggestions:

- Write a new ending for your book.
- Compare this book with another book on the same topic or by the same author.
- Read a selection from the book to a lower grade class.
- Tell a friend or write about your favorite part of the book.
- Write down some new or unusual words from your book.
- Illustrate a scene from the book.
- Prepare a selection from the book for dramatic presentation. Enlist the help of a friend or two to act out the scene.
- Write an incident from the book as a newspaper article. Include an eye-catching headline.
- Write an epitaph or obituary for one of the characters.
- Create a map of the area where the story takes place.
- Make a model of the house or dwelling where the characters live.

Successful Oral Presentations

In order to sell other students on books, oral book reviews need to be stimulating. Presentations should be short and should employ varied approaches. The following tips will liven up the traditional report:

- Show the class the book cover. How does it relate to the story?
- Read an especially interesting or vivid passage to the class. Be sure to tell the audience what has led up to this scene.
- Talk about the author. What other books has he or she written? Is the story based on something that happened to the author?
- Talk about a suspenseful part of the book. Ask the class what they think will happen next.

Puppet Talk

Students can produce a puppet show version of their favorite book. Have the puppets enact an interesting incident from the book or use the puppets to introduce several of the characters. Whether you have a puppet stage ready or not, you can always have simple hand puppets for the students to use while standing up.

Puppets are an effective means of presentation even when only one student is presenting the book. The student can use one puppet to tell the story from that character's point of view. (See Chapter 2 for examples of easily made puppets.)

Interpreting Literature on Tape

Students can select attractive picturebooks to interpret orally and to record on tape for use in a listening center. This will provide them with the much needed practice in pronouncing words correctly and enunciating clearly. Recorded tapes can be purchased, but students benefit from creating original ones.

These recordings would be useful in primary-grade classrooms to support emergent reading. Young readers can follow the text in the book, assisted by the spoken words on the tape. Using a listening center in this way is a recommended method of helping children learn to read. Illustrations in picturebooks also help learners understand the text presented as they visualize what is happening in the story.

Such recordings are also helpful for students learning English as a second language. They, too, can listen/read a picturebook through hearing the words of a native speaker of English on tape as they observe the printed words in the book.

Studying Literary Concepts

As teachers introduce literature to students and share books with them, they are also providing a structure for later independent reading. Teachers model attending to literary concepts such as *characterization, plot, setting, use of dialogue,* and *imagery* to organize the student's interpretation of the text. Student practice with these concepts, in the context of group discussions, will enable them to incorporate and internalize these understandings into their own approach to reading.

Questions for Summarizing Stories

Students need experience in summarizing information and connecting details. After reading a selection, have the students practice retelling the story or text. Make sure they include all the important information by writing the elements of the story on the board. Then help them organize this information as the class puts events in order and selects the main idea. Guide the students by asking questions, such as the following:

- Who were the important characters in the story?
- Where and when did the story take place?

- What happened at the beginning of the story?
- What did the characters do?
- Why did they do that?
- What happened at the end of the story?
- How did the characters feel?

Flannel Board Stories

Have students work in pairs to present a story on the flannel board. One student can tell the story to the class while the other student moves the characters on the board. This method helps students visualize the sequence of events.

In order to develop an effective flannel board presentation, students will need to make a list of characters and other plot elements. Then they can outline the events of the story. They must also decide how to illustrate these events so that the class will be able to follow the story action.

Students will want to rehearse their presentation at least once before going in front of the class. A successful flannel board presentation can go "on tour" to other classes or grades.

Mapping a Story

After reading any story, students will benefit from *mapping* the components that make up the story. You might introduce this technique after rereading a familiar nursery tale, perhaps "Little Red Riding Hood." Have students map the parts of this story following this framework:

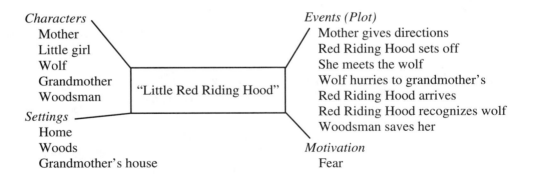

Characters
Mother
Little girl
Wolf
Grandmother
Woodsman

Settings
Home
Woods
Grandmother's house

"Little Red Riding Hood"

Events (Plot)
Mother gives directions
Red Riding Hood sets off
She meets the wolf
Wolf hurries to grandmother's
Red Riding Hood arrives
Red Riding Hood recognizes wolf
Woodsman saves her

Motivation
Fear

By analyzing a story in this manner, students see what the author had to construct in order to write or tell the story. Such an analysis will help them write stories. It will also help them in retelling such stories to younger children—a wonderful activity for older students.

Using Suspense

When reading a book to the class, use high points in the book to create suspense. Choose an exciting moment or decision point, stop reading, and ask the students to predict what will happen next. Have them discuss various possibilities and what clues affected their choice. Then continue reading. Pause again for students to check their predictions.

Fables

Fables are teaching stories with a long history. A book that all ages can enjoy is Arnold Lobel's *Fables* (Harper and Row, 1981), with its beautiful illustrations. Discuss the stories with the students. What is the story about? How can they apply the story to their own experience? Students will learn as well as laugh after reading these fables. Other fables to stimulate discussion include:

> Anne Gatli. *Aesop's Fables.* Harcourt, 1992.
> Isaac Bashevis Singer. *The Fools of Chelm and Their History.* Illustrated by Uri Shulevitz. Farrar, 1973.

After reading fables, children can write their own. Provide a list of endings (or moral sayings) to start students thinking.

- Curiosity killed the cat.
- A stitch in time saves nine.
- Too many cooks spoil the broth.
- A bird in the hand is worth two in the bush.
- Every cloud has a silver lining.

Older students will be interested in collecting and comparing proverbs from different countries, such as:

- *Germany:* Speech is silver; silence is golden.
- *Greece:* Before you can score, you must have a goal.
- *China:* It is the great tree that tempts the wind.
- *Scotland:* It is far better to bend than to break.
- *Spain:* To change one's mind is a sign of prudence rather than ignorance.

Personification in Literature

Personification, giving characteristics of animacy to inanimate objects, often appears in poetry written for children, as in "The fog creeps in on little cat feet" (Carl Sandburg). However, personification appears in children's prose, as well, providing an interesting opportunity to show students how this literary device works. An example of personification comes from Holling C. Hollings's picturebook, *Tree in the Trail.* This historical fiction tells about a tree that stands at a juncture of the Santa Fe Trail and observes Native Americans and pioneers who pass by on their way West. Students can also write imaginative stories that include personification—for example, a story about the Empire State Building in New York City and what it has seen through the years.

Graphics That Support Student Analysis

Graphic diagrams help students collect their thoughts about literature so that they gain a better understanding. Try these and make up others to meet your needs. In the first example on page 240, students can use circles (a Venn diagram) to list similarities and differences. In the second example, students benefit from a closer look at how characterization operates in a story.

Interpreting Motives

Introduce the concept of motive through a discussion of a book you are reading. Use the following questions with students:

- How did the main character feel at the beginning of the story? Why? Did the main character feel differently at the end of the story? How can you tell? What caused the change?
- Choose an important thing the main character did in the story. Tell what you think the reasons were for his or her action.
- Why did the main character choose that way of solving his or her problem? Do you think it was a good solution? Would the same solution have worked for you, or for a character in another book?

Features of a Character

As you read and discuss books, talk about the *characters* in a story. List some of the features that distinguish characters from each other and tell us who they are:

- Appearance
- Personality
- Motivation
- Personal history
- Relations with others
- Problem to solve
- Change over time?

Have students practice applying this list with familiar characters such as Peter Rabbit, Yoda *(Star Wars),* or the Three Little Pigs. Older students can extend the study of characterization by comparing what a character *says* with what the character *does*.

Venn Diagram – Comparison

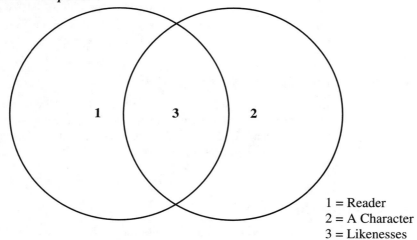

1 = Reader
2 = A Character
3 = Likenesses

Describing a Character – Analysis

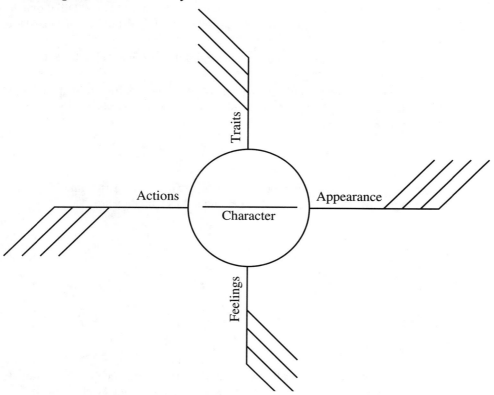

Expressing Character

After reading several stories, students can explore different activities to express the authors' use of characterization. The following are some suggestions:

- Pantomime a character.
- Tell what might be in the character's pocket.
- Predict what the character might be doing in 10 years.
- Bring together characters from different stories and have them talk to each other.
- Give characters an award for Most Popular, Worst Friend, Craziest Family, and so on.
- Put the character on trial and call witnesses.
- Imagine the character's favorite food, color, or clothing.

Books Are by People

When students read books, encourage them to think about the person on the other side of the book—the author (or illustrator). Challenge students to find out more about favorite authors or illustrators. Give them a list of questions to answer and some suggested sources to research, and then post the results on a bulletin board. You might ask the following questions:

- Can you find a picture of the author?
- When was he or she born? (When did he or she die?)
- Where does the author come from?
- Why did the author write this book (or these books)?
- When was the book written?

Sources that students can investigate for more information include:

- Biographical information and a photo are often found on the book jacket.
- Students can write to the publisher or to the author in care of the publisher.
- Reference books are available in the library (such as *Contemporary Authors* and *Current Biography*).
- Look for collections of author autobiographies such as: Amy Ehrlich (Ed.). *When I Was Your Age: Original Stories about Growing Up* (2 volumes). Candlewick, 1999.

Pseudonyms

Pseudonym means *false name* but it does not always mean a hidden identity. Pseudonyms used to be popular among writers, not necessarily because they were ashamed of their works. The most familiar pseudonym or pen name is Mark Twain (Samuel Clemens). Clemens chose his name from the riverboat custom of marking off the depth of the Mississippi River.

Early women writers commonly used male names for their books because they were afraid that books by women would not be published or taken seriously. Examples of pseudonyms that may be familiar to some students are:

O. Henry—William Sidney Porter
Saki—H. H. Munro
Andre Norton—Mary Alice Norton
Dr. Seuss—Theodor Geisel
Lewis Carroll—Charles Dodgson

Children may enjoy making up their own pseudonyms to use on their writing. Some may choose a name that refers to an interest or a physical characteristic. Others may choose a nickname or a name they've always wanted to be called. Encourage the children to share their names with the class and explain why they chose them.

Students will find other pseudonyms as they read more. Have them present these to the class when they discover the author's real name.

Focus on the Author

Students need to be reminded to pay attention to the person behind the book they are reading. Select an author such as Katherine Paterson as the subject of a thematic study that crosses the curriculum and incorporates all the language arts. Have students read several books by this author and then discuss what they have learned about her from her books. Do her books seem to be based on personal experience? Does she write in one genre or in more than one category? Students can develop a list of questions that they would like to have answered and use these as a base for further research about Paterson's life and work or write a letter to the author. *Newbery on the Net* by Ru Story Huffman offers background information on many Newbery Award–winning authors such as Katherine Paterson.

An Illustrator's Style

Students can also select an illustrator whose work they like to be the subject of a study. Consult references such as the list of Caldecott Award winners in Chapter 10 to start them off with some suggestions. Trina Schart Hyman, Jerry Pinkney, Maurice Sendak, and Chris Van Allsburg would be interesting choices. Collect as many examples of the illustrator's work as you can find, using libraries for out-of-print materials. Then talk about the artist's medium, use of color and form, and choice of subject matter. Does this artist have a distinctive style that students can recognize if they see it again? Students can also explore some of the artistic techniques used by these illustrators, as outlined in Chapter 9.

Author-Title Dominoes

Construct this game by cutting out 30 cardboard rectangles. Use a colored pen to draw a line dividing each rectangle in half. On each half write the author or title of a book. Use about 10 different authors with matching titles from books in your class library. Dominoes is an easy game for students to play on their own and is motivation for further reading. Encourage students to add dominoes to the set.

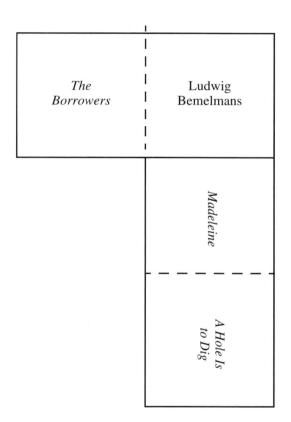

BOOKO

Small groups of students can play BOOKO and learn about authors and titles of books at the same time. Prepare five or six large bingo cards marked off into squares.

Write the title or author of a book in each square. Make a card for each title and author to use for calling. Make slips for covering the bingo card. After you have taught the students to play the game, you can leave the cards in a learning center for small groups of students to play.

Bud, Not Buddy	Louis Sachar	*The Dark Frigate*	Rachel Field	*Jacob Have I Loved*
Onion John	Ellen Raskin	*Holes*	*...And Now Miguel*	*Rabbit Hill*
Esther Forbes	*A Gathering of Days*	Lois Lenski	*Miss Hickory*	*Call It Courage*
Scott O'Dell	*The High King*	Betsy Byars	Free	*Westing Game*
Sounder	Joan Blos	*The 21 Balloons*	Katherine Paterson	E. L. Konigsburg

Newbery Award winners

You can make separate games for titles, authors, and author-titles. Encourage reading by using books from the school library. Students will be curious about books that they have not heard of, and you can take advantage of their interest by taking them to the library. You might make a set of cards featuring the Newbery Award winners.

Word Crossings

In this game, a puzzle is constructed by crossing an author's name, running vertically, with related words. The students are given clues to help them figure out the words and fill in the blanks.

```
                        T
   _ _ _ _              H              _ _ _ _ _ _
                        E
                        O
   _ _ _               D              _ _ _ _
                        O
             _          R              _ _ _ _
                        
   _ _ _ _ _ _          G              _ _ _ _ _ _ _
                        E
   _ _ _ _ _            I              _ _ _ _ _ _ _
                        S
   _ _ _                E              _ _ _
                        L
```

Clues:	Answers:
1. The first name of the boy who had lots of hats.	1. Bartholomew
2. The name of the kind-hearted moose.	2. Thidwick
3. Who stole a holiday from the children?	3. Grinch
4. The title of a book about breakfast.	4. *Green Eggs and Ham*
5. Who came back?	5. The Cat in the Hat
6. Theodor Geisel's pseudonym.	6. Dr. Seuss

Students will enjoy thinking up Word Crossings to stump their friends. They may choose this as a way of sharing a book they have read or describing the life of a favorite author.

Check with the children's librarian at your local library to see if there are any authors who live locally. Invite one of them to speak to the class, perhaps during Book Week in November.

All Kinds of Literature

Students need to become aware of the varied forms that literature can take. It can, for example, be true or not true, fiction or nonfiction. Books can be written in poetry or prose. And the writer can express ideas in the form of a fable, a letter, or a personal journal, among others. Introduce children to these forms through selected literature. (Poetry is featured in Chapter 8; nonfiction is presented in Chapter 9; other ideas about literary forms are discussed in Chapters 3 and 5.) Here are additional ideas:

- *Letters:* Beverly Cleary. *Dear Mr. Henshaw.* Morrow, 1989. This story is told through a boy's letters to a well-known author. The book won the Newbery Award.
- *Diary or Personal Journal:* Marissa Moss. *The All-New Amelia Series.* Pleasant, 1999. Amelia records happenings in school in an entertaining journal. Students can discover more about this character by connecting with <www.americangirl.com>.

- *Fable:* Leo Lionni. *Fables.* HarperCollins, 1980. Author/illustrator Leo Lionni, who has written many picturebooks, presents contemporary versions of fables that students can compare with the classic ones by Aesop.
- *Autobiography:* Bill Peet. *Bill Peet: An Autobiography.* Houghton Mifflin, 1986. The personal story of a Disney animator and the author of humorous books for children.
- *Fictionalized Biography:* Alan Schroeder. *Minty: A Story of Harriet Tubman.* Dial, 1996. Illustrated by Jerry Pinkney. Imagined story of Tubman's girlhood based on research.
- *Riddles:* John Bierhorst (Ed.). *Lightning Inside You: Native American Riddles.* Morrow, 1992.
- *ABC Books:* Martin and Tanis Jordan. *Amazon Alphabet.* Kingfisher, 1996. Through spectacular illustrations, this book introduces information about the animals that live in the Amazon.

Developing Esteem and Empathy

Planning an inclusive, multicultural program is an important consideration when planning the literature curriculum. Teachers must *teach multiculturally*—that is, choose methods and activities that allow students to bring in their diverse experiences and incorporate multiple perspectives. In addition, teachers must *teach with multicultural materials,* which means selecting books and other resources that reflect classroom diversity as well as represent the diversity found in the U.S. population. In a multicultural literature program, students will:

- Develop self-esteem
- Value diversity
- Work effectively with others
- Learn about themselves and others
- Employ global perspectives

Self-Esteem Poster

Children need to know that each one of them is important and that their different feelings are respected. Introduce the topic of *esteem* in the primary grades by reading *ABC I Like Me!* by Nancy Carlson (Viking, 1997) to the class. In a humorous fashion, this book presents the idea that everyone is someone special. Bring in materials for drawing and painting and provide pictures to cut up. Using a large piece of poster board as a base, students can make an "I Like Me" poster, including pictures, information about themselves, hobbies, and so on. You may want to brainstorm with the class and discuss what kinds of ideas they want to include to get them started thinking about how to portray themselves. This poster activity is also a good way for students to get acquainted with each other.

Feelings

Children may feel sad, unhappy, or lonely but feelings are rarely discussed in a classroom. Provide students with the time and vocabulary they need to cope with strong emotions. Begin by asking if students have ever been really, really, angry. Most students will identify with Sophie in *When Sophie Gets Angry—Really, Really, Angry* by Molly Bang (Scholastic, 1999) or Alexander in *Alexander and the Horrible, No-Good, Very Bad Day* by Judith Viorst, illustrated by Ray Cruz (Aladdin, 1987). Read one of these stories aloud and discuss with students how these children felt and what they did about it. Connect the discussion to students' own lives by asking students what they might do to help themselves when they get angry. Students can draw pictures to illustrate how they feel. What colors would they use for *angry?* For *sad?*

Another book about emotions is *Today I Feel Silly and Other Moods That Make My Day* by Jamie Lee Curtis, illustrated by Laura Cornell (HarperCollins, 1998).

For Older Students, Too

Students in the upper grades will also benefit from learning to recognize their own feelings in others. Read a story, such as the classic picturebook *Crow Boy,* by Taro Yashima (Viking, 1976), to students and discuss how the boy feels (lonely) and why (he's going far away to a strange school). Have students ever been in similar situations or had similar feelings? Help students relate this story about a young boy in Japan to their own lives. Do they know students who are new to the school or anyone new in the neighborhood that might be feeling as the Crow Boy does? How can they reach out to these other people? Encourage the class to share ideas for helping others who might be lonely.

The Value of Giving

Many "simple" stories can inspire deeper thinking and extended discussions in class. An excellent example to use is Shel Silverstein's modern *parable* (teaching story) *The Giving Tree* (HarperCollins, 1986), which tells of a tree that gives everything it can to a boy until it is only a stump. And even then, it provides a resting place for the child grown up. As is true of the best in literature, this story of their relationship touches on many philosophical issues, from the meaning of giving and receiving to the value of one's connection with nature.

Understanding People Who Are "Different"

When people look different from those around them—because of physical or mental disability, for example—they are often treated as if they were not fully human. Help students learn to accept these differences and empathize with others, by sharing books about people like themselves who may be blind or retarded, or who have a disabling physical condition. Such books as Paula Fox's *Radiance Descending* (DK Ink) will help students understand how it feels to have a brother with Down syndrome.

Children are curious about differences, as well, even if they pretend to ignore them. Ask the students if they know people—perhaps friends, family members, or neighbors—who have a disability, visible or invisible. Bring in nonfiction such as P. McMahon's *Listen for the Bus: David's Story* (BoydMills, 1995), which describes the first day of kindergarten for a boy who is blind and deaf. Discuss with students how they would feel if they were David.

Give students the opportunity to experience a Blind Walk. Bring in scarves or strips of cloth for half the class. Students work in pairs. One student blindfolds the other and guides him or her around the room (or any safe environment) for about three minutes. Then have them exchange positions. Following this activity, discuss with students how it felt to trust someone to guide them and to keep them safe. Are there similarities between their brief experience with the blindfold and actually being blind? Students can write about their Blind Walk in their response journals.

Heroes and Sheroes

Literature can offer students a sense of who they are and where they belong. Provide students with literature about people of all nationalities, races, and ethnic groups in order to recognize the contributions made by many different people from "parallel cultures" (a more accurate term than *minorities*). African American students, for example, will be pleased to see books about well-known African Americans such as Colin Powell, Maya Angelou, Duke Ellington, and Spike Lee. But all students, not just the African American ones, need to read stories about African Americans who have been honored, in order to counteract the negative images everyone receives from the media, for example.

Picturebook biographies are especially effective with students of all ages because they focus on "stories," lending a personal slant not always found in factual accounts. Look for examples to read aloud, such as the following books about important African Americans:

> Eloise Greenfield. *Mary McLeod Bethune*. Illustrated by Jerry Pinkney. HarperCollins, 1994. Life of the great educator.
> Reeve Lindbergh. *Nobody Owns the Sky*. Illustrated by Pamela Paparone. Candlewick, 1996. Biography of Bessie Coleman, first African American to win a pilot's license even though she had to move to France to do it.
> Andrea Davis Pinkney. *Dear Benjamin Banneker*. Illustrated by Brian Pinkney. Harcourt Brace, 1994. Noted early astronomer.
> Alan Schroeder. *Satchmo's Blues*. Illustrated by Floyd Cooper. Doubleday, 1996. Based on the childhood of musician Louis Armstrong.

Students who want more information about a person will be able to find it in the excellent biographies available for young people, such as:

> Philip Hart. *Up in the Air: The Story of Bessie Coleman*. Carolrhoda, 1996.

Patricia McKissack and Frederick McKissack. *Red-Tail Angels.* Walker, 1995. The Tuskegee airmen, African American flyers, persevered against racism in World War II and proved their heroism.

Poster Quotes

Students can work in small groups to prepare a poster featuring a quotation on the significance of literature, for example:

- "There is more treasure in books than in all the pirates' loot on Treasure Island . . . and best of all, you can enjoy these riches every day of your life."
  —Walt Disney
- "This is one of the pleasures of reading—you may make any pictures out of the words you can and will; and a poem may have as many different meanings as there are different minds."
  —Walter de la Mare

If students have access to a computer, they can test different fonts to find the most suitable lettering to use for their quote. They can also illustrate the quote they have chosen.

Reading Opens Doors

Many people who have achieved a lot despite early obstacles give credit to others who have helped them along the way, particularly ones who opened the doors to reading. Do students agree that it is difficult to succeed without being able to read? Share and discuss a few true stories with the class:

William R. Miller. *Richard Wright and the Library Card.* Illustrated by Gregory Christie. Lee & Low, 1999. The African American writer couldn't have a library card as a young man because he was black, so he had to borrow a card from his boss and pretend he was checking books out for a white man.

Pat Mora. *Tomás and the Library Lady.* Illustrated by Raúl Colón. Dragonfly, 2000. The child of farmworkers, Tomás moved so often he never had the opportunity to read until a librarian noticed his interest in books and helped him. Tomás Rivera became the head of a university.

Patricia Polacco. *Thank You, Mr. Falker.* Philomel, 1998. The noted children's author couldn't read and others teased her, until her fifth-grade teacher paid attention and provided extra instruction.

After discussing what reading meant to the people in these books, talk about reading, what it is and why we do it. Give students the following prompt to respond to in their journals:

Reading is _____.

Selecting Multicultural and Anti-Bias Materials

In order to create an inclusive curriculum, teachers must make special efforts to choose literature that:

- Reflects the heritage of the children in the classroom
- Represents the parallel cultures of this country's diverse population
- Includes different perspectives, such as those of marginalized groups (women, disabled, elderly, poor people)
- Connects individual experience with larger social and historical forces
- Actively counters pervasive stereotypes and prejudice

The following are some of the considerations necessary in evaluating materials for appropriateness:

1. What is the literary quality of this literature? Is the story well written and interesting to students from a broad range of backgrounds? Are the illustrations appealing and consistent with the story?
2. Is this literature culturally authentic? Do both the storyline and illustrations represent a specific culture accurately and in detail, without resorting to stereotypes?
3. Where does the information about the culture come from? If a folktale, does the author include information about the source of this version?
4. Are the words included from different languages representative of this particular region or culture and incorporated into the text in a natural way?*

All Kinds of Families

Ask students what *family* means. Who do they think belongs in a family? List some of the possible relationships on the board:

> mother, father, 2 boys
> grandmother, mother, 1 girl
> mother, adopted girl
> mother and stepfather, stepmother and father, children

In your discussion, point out that there are many types of families. The stereotype of the nuclear family—consisting of a mother, a father, a girl, and a boy—may not apply to many of the children in your class. Encourage the class to develop a definition of *family* that includes all of them. You can also show students the video *That's a Family* (Debra Chasnoff and Helen Cohen, Women's Educational Media, 2000), a half-hour presentation in which children talk about their different family arrangements.

Consciously select books for your library that represent a variety of family arrangements, such as:

*List adapted from Smolen and Ortiz-Castro, 2000.

Charlotte Anker. *Last Night I Saw Andromeda.* Walck, 1975. Eleven-year-old girl and mother; father visits.

Candy Dawson Boyd. *Chevrolet Saturdays.* Macmillan, 1993. Joey, a fifth grader, can't accept his mother's remarriage, but his family understands him.

Lucille Clifton. *Everett Andersen's Nine Months Long.* Holt, 1987. Everett's mother, a widow, has remarried and is going to have a baby. Look for other stories about Everett, an African American boy.

Allen Say. *Allison.* Houghton Mifflin, 1997. Allison is angry because she looks like her Asian doll, not like her Caucasian parents.

Zilpha K. Snyder. *The Witches of Worm.* Atheneum, 1972. Twelve-year-old girl and divorced mother.

Johnny Valentine. *One Dad, Two Dads, Brown Dad, Blue Dads.* Illustrated by Melody Sarecky. Alyson Publishers, 1994. Lou has to answer questions about his dads. His friends discover that blue dads are like other dads.

Jacqueline Woodson. *From the Notebooks of Melanin Sun.* Scholastic, 1995. Thirteen-year-old African American boy is upset when he finds out his mother is in love with a white woman.

Developing Empathy

Literature can help students develop an awareness that we are not alone in the world by putting them in another's place. Display this poem in your classroom for students to think about. Students can discuss it and write a paragraph applying this thought to their own lives.

> *If I am not*
> *for myself, then*
> *who will be*
> *for me?*
> > *And if*
> > *I am only*
> > *for myself,*
> > *then*
> > *what am I*
> > > *And*
> > > *if*
> > > *not now,*
> > > *when?*
> > > —Rabbi Hillel, in the Mishnah, c. 100 C.E.

Getting Along with Others

Sometimes literature can help students understand themselves by illuminating conflicts with others. Jean Craighead George tells how people take sides and can't see the other's point of view in her chapter book *There's an Owl in My Shower* (HarperCollins, 1995), about loggers versus conservationists. Pose these questions to students: Can people on opposing sides talk to each other? What might you do to reduce the conflict? Then read this book to find out.

Look for other books about facing problems that students can read independently.

Breaking Down Stereotypes

Because literature can take us into other people's minds, ways of thinking, and experiences, it is often used for dispelling stereotypes. An effective way to introduce students to the concept of *stereotype*—defined as a fixed preconception about an idea or a group, or applying false generalizations to every individual—is to look at cultural ideas about animals. For example, wolves are the villains of many western European tales, so students who have been exposed to this traditional folklore—"Little Red Riding Hood" and "The Three Little Pigs," especially—are more likely to have stereotyped ideas about wolves as a group.

Have students write *Wolf* in the center of a piece of paper and then add adjectives and phrases that they associate with the word to create a personal concept web. Put this web away. Then read a variety of literature, such as:

- *Fiction:* Folktales, unconventional or "revised" versions of popular tales, and positive stories of wolves

    Becky Bloom. *Wolf!* Illustrated by Pascal Biet. Orchard, 1999.
    Jean Craighead George. *Julie of the Wolves.* Dell, 1996.
    Peter Nickl. *The Story of the Kind Wolf.* Illustrated by Józef Wilkón. North-South Books, 1985.
    Jon Scieszka. *The True Story of the Three Little Pigs.* Viking, 1995.
    David Vozar. *Yo, Hungry Wolf.* Illustrated by Betsy Lewin. Delacorte, 1995.

- *Nonfiction:* Information about how wolves live and efforts to fight prejudice and reintroduce wolves in the wild

    Jean Craighead George. *Look to the North: A Wolf Pup Diary.* Illustrated by Lucia Washburn. HarperCollins, 1997.
    Stephen Swinburne. *Once a Wolf: How Wildlife Biologists Fought to Bring Back the Gray Wolf.* Houghton Mifflin, 1999.

For more facts about wolves, check out this website: <www.gorp.com/gorp/resource/us_national_park/wy/wild_yell.htm>.

Talk with students about the different points of view represented in these books. Does any of this information conflict with what they thought about wolves? Does knowing more about how wolves live in the natural world change their image of wolves? Afterwards, ask students to complete another web about wolves, then pull out the first version, and compare. How have their webs changed?

Help students extend the idea of breaking down stereotypes to examples closer to home. What stereotypes might be affecting their thinking right now? Do they hold stereotyped images of boys and girls?

Building Bridges

Students today live in an increasingly diverse world. They have the opportunity to encounter people of many different cultures, languages, beliefs, and abilities. Through literature, students will learn that everyone is connected and interdependent in this global society. Children's literature builds bridges to people who are *like* your students as well as people who are *different* from them.

Haemi Balgassi. *Peacebound Trains.* Clarion, 1996.

Barbara Bash. *In the Heart of the Village: The World of the Indian Banyan Tree.* Sierra Club, 1996.

Rosemary Breckler. *Sweet Dried Apples: A Vietnamese Wartime Childhood.* Houghton, 1996.

Susan Fletcher. *Shadow Spinner.* Atheneum, 1998. Set in the Arab world.

Minfong Ho. *Maples in the Mist: Children's Poems from the Tang Dynasty.* Lothrop, 1996.

Ted Lewin. *The Storytellers.* Lothrop, Lee & Shephard, 1998. A boy and his grandfather in Fez, Morocco.

Nancy Luenn. *A Gift for Abuelita: Celebrating the Day of the Dead/Un Regalo para Abuelita: En Celebración del Día de los Muertos.* Rising Moon/Northland, 1998. Bilingual book, set in Mexico.

Paul Morin. *Animal Dreaming: An Aboriginal Dreamtime Story.* Harcourt Brace, 1998. Australian aborigine stories.

Elinor Batezat Sisulu. *The Day Gogo Went to Vote: South Africa, 1994.* Little, 1996.

Cinderella in Other Lands

The story of the valiant, loyal girl who is mistreated by her (step) sisters, but whose worth is finally recognized, is found in different versions in many cultures. To introduce this tale to children, first read aloud a version of Charles Perrault's *Cinderella* that may be familiar to some of them. (See Chapter 3 for examples.) Follow up by reading aloud at least one other version of this tale from another culture. Discuss and compare the different versions with students. What features define this as a Cinderella story? How is the text different from other versions? How do the illustrations differ? What choices have the storyteller and illustrator made to emphasize certain points or to create different effects? Have students develop a list of the key elements that make up a "Cinderella" story. There are numerous versions from which to choose. Students can work in small groups and select one example to analyze, such as:

Shirley Climo. *The Egyptian Cinderella.* Illustrated by Ruth Heller. HarperCollins, 1989.

Shirley Climo. *The Irish Cinderlad.* Illustrated by Loretta Krupinski. HarperCollins, 1996.

Ai-Ling Louie. *Yeh-Shen: A Cinderella Story from China.* Philomel, 1982.

Penny Pollock. *The Turkey Girl.* Illustrated by Ed Young. Little, 1996. A Zuni tale.

Robert San Souci. *Sootface: An Ojibwa Cinderella.* Doubleday, 1994.

Robert San Souci and David San Souci. *Cendrillon: A Caribbean Cinderella.* Illustrated by Brian Pinkney. Simon & Schuster, 1998.

Alan Schroeder. *Smoky Mountain Rose: An Appalachian Cinderella.* Illustrated by Brad Sneed. Dial, 1997.

Students can report their findings using the following three-part Venn diagram to compare several versions of Cinderella. In the large portion of each circle, print the title of one version, such as John Steptoe's African-based tale, *Mufaro's Beautiful Daughter* (Lothrop, 1987). In the areas that overlap, have students write phrases that describe key elements that are similar in each story. In the part where all three story circles overlap, they will write descriptions of the features that are common to all three stories.

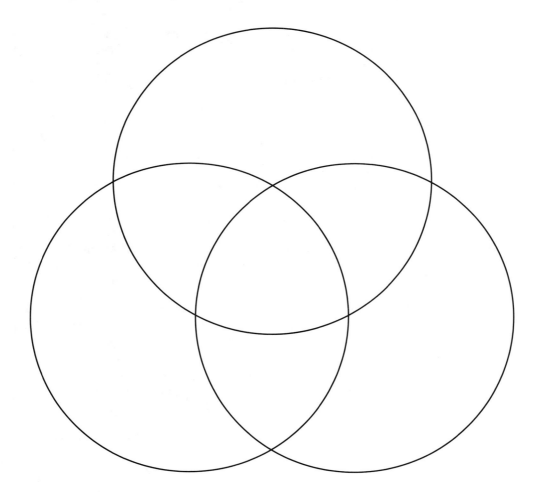

Students can use the diagrams that they have prepared individually or in small groups as a basis for writing a paper comparing and analyzing several Cinderella tales.

Developing a Thematic Unit

Picturebooks are particularly suited to serving as core books for a theme around which you and your students can plan a more extensive unit of study. Try these examples:

> Ryan Collay and Joanne Dubrow. *Stuartship*. Illustrated by Sydney Roark. Flower Press, 1998. Uses a story to introduce concepts of *stewardship* and *relations with nature*.
>
> Margy Burns Knight. *Talking Walls*. Illustrated by Anne Sibley O'Brien. Tilbury, 1992. *Talking Walls: The Stories Continue*. Tilbury, 1996. These innovative books use the *wall* as a metaphor for different cultures that are divided or unified by the partitions they live with. Also available on audiocassette with the authors reading excerpts from both volumes (Audio Bookshelf, 1998).
>
> Faith Ringgold. *Tar Beach*. Crown, 1991. This vibrant description of New York City and children lying on rooftops in the hot summer would make an excellent centerpiece for a study of *cities* and *urban life*.

Quilts: A Metaphor for Life in the United States

A quilt offers a different way of looking at the United States. An alternative to the image of the "melting pot," a quilt is made up of many tiny pieces that are assembled into a larger pattern without losing their individual identities. Use Patricia Polacco's *The Keeping Quilt* (Simon & Schuster, 1998) as the center for a thematic study, such as a unit on the U.S. "multiculture." Polacco traces her family's Jewish heritage through a quilt made from relatives' clothing and passed down through generations to celebrate births, marriages, and deaths. In each shape she can see the stories she's been told of her family.

Students can read about quilting traditions in different regions, reflecting diverse cultures.

> Doris Faber. *The Amish*. Illustrated by Michael Erkel. Doubleday, 1991. Nonfiction.
>
> Georgia Guback. *Luka's Quilt*. Greenwillow, 1994. Luka wants to make her own pattern, not the traditional Hawaiian one.
>
> Ann Whitford Paul. *Eight Hands Round: A Patchwork Alphabet*. Illustrated by Jeanette Winter. HarperCollins, 1991. Stories of the different patterns and their names.

Students can combine art, math, and reading as they recreate patterns—such as "Rocky Road to Kansas" or "Jacob's Ladder"—by cutting out and assembling squares and triangles.

> Jane Bolton. *My Grandmother's Patchwork Quilt: A Book and Portfolio of Patchwork Pieces*. Doubleday, 1994.
>
> Mary Cobb. *The Quilt Block History of Pioneer Days*. Millbrook, 1995. Projects for children using paper and cut magazines.
>
> Ann Whitford Paul. *The Seasons Sewn: A Year in Patchwork*. Harcourt, 1996.

They can also use the concept of quilting to explore the roots of their own cultural heritage.

Valerie Flournoy. *The Patchwork Quilt.* Illustrated by Jerry Pinkney. Dial, 1985. When Tanya's grandmother gets too sick to work on her quilt and tell stories about family history, Tanya decides to finish the quilt herself.

Deborah Hopkinson. *Sweet Clara and the Freedom Quilt.* Illustrated by James Ransome. Knopf, 1993. As a slave, Clara is not allowed to read or write, so she carefully stitches into her quilt the information she needs for her escape.

Quilts often are intended to be "read" as a story of a person or group of people, preserving their story in stitchery.

Dia Cha. *Dia's Story Cloth: The Hmong People's Journey of Freedom.* Lee & Low, 1996. The cloth in this book, stitched by the author's aunt and uncle, chronicles Hmong life, past and present.

Mary Lyons. *Stitching the Stars: The Story Quilts of Harriet Powers.* Scribner's, 1993. Nineteenth-century African American artist made Bible-based quilts.

Faith Ringgold. *Aunt Harriet's Underground Railroad in the Sky.* Crown, 1995. Noted African American artist creates immense painted quilts that she has turned into picturebooks, framed by her quilts.

Quilts also represent a pioneer tradition of making do, creating warmth and beauty out of old scraps, and working cooperatively in quilting bees to help each other.

Raymond Bial. *With Needle and Thread: A Book about Quilts.* Houghton Mifflin, 1996. A social history of quilting.

Eleanor Coerr. *The Josefina Story Quilt.* Harper, 1989. On the road to California in 1850, Faith's old hen Josefina saves the family from danger. Later, Faith sews a quilt to commemorate Josefina and the trip.

Ellen Howard. *The Log Cabin Quilt.* Holiday, 1996. Quilt scraps warm a family by providing chinking for their new cabin in Michigan.

Friendship Quilts*

Many modern quilts, called *friendship quilts,* are composed of different blocks, each created by a different person. Students at all grade levels can participate in making these group quilts. They may be motivated to make quilts to express their creativity, to distribute to the homeless, or to raise money. For example, they can select one of the many attractive Amish designs to cut out and sew, using solid colors. The drafting of the patterns for cutting will involve use of basic geometric shapes. Students in fourth grade and up can handle a sewing machine or a needle and thread with some adult assistance. Students can also make a crazy quilt, using donated scraps of fabric. Have each student assemble the

*From *Multicultural Teaching: A Handbook of Activities, Information, and Resources,* 5/e by Pamela Tiedt and Iris Tiedt, Copyright © 1999 Allyn & Bacon. Reprinted by permission.

odd-sized pieces on a foundation block of a fixed size so that the quilt can be assembled easily. Another popular theme for student quilts is "Our Neighborhood." Each student can make a block representing a house, embellishing each house differently with trim and buttons. Or they can make individual blocks for particular features of the community—special buildings, sights, people. Students can also make an international quilt, showing children from many different countries and different backgrounds.

Primary students can draw on fabric with fabric crayons that become permanent after ironing. One kindergarten class made an alphabet quilt. For students who were unable to draw a letter, the teacher outlined large letters and the students colored them in. Students tied knots with yarn to hold the quilt together.

Discussion Questions

1. How can you promote and develop your school library in a time when funds are not readily available?

2. What is the best way of developing theme studies that engage students of different abilities with a large amount of literature?

3. How can you handle the concerns of parents who object to the use of specific books in the classroom?

Exploring Further

Rudine Sims Bishop (Ed.). *Kaleidoscope: A Multicultural Booklist for Grades K–8.* NCTE, 1994.

Gloria Blatt. *Once Upon a Folktale: Capturing the Folklore Process with Children.* Teachers College Press, 1993.

The BookWorm Student Library. Grolier Interactive, 1999. CD-ROM for Windows/Macintosh. Multimedia approach to literature.

Robert W. Cole. *Educating Everybody's Children: Diverse Teaching Strategies for Diverse Learners.* Association of Supervision and Curriculum Development, 1995.

Kendall Haven. "Good to the Last Drop: Making the Most of Stories to Enhance Language Arts Learning." *California Reading, 32,* no. 2 (Winter 1999).

Ru Story Huffman. *Newbery on the Net: Reading and Internet Activities.* Highsmith Press, 1999. Updated regularly on the Highsmith Press website.

Carol Brennan Jenkins. *The Allure of Authors: Author Studies in the Elementary Classroom.* Heinemann, 1999.

Valerie V. Lewis and Walter M. Mayes. *Valerie & Walter's Best Books for Children.* Avon, 1998.

Hughes Moir et al. *Collected Perspectives: Choosing and Using Books for the Classroom.* Christopher-Gordon, 1990.

Vivian Paley. *The Kindness of Children.* Harvard University Press, 1999.

Nancy L. Roser and Miriam Martinez (Eds.). *Book Talk and Beyond: Children and Teachers Respond to Literature.* IRA, 1995.

Beverly Slapin and Doris Seale (Eds.). *Through Indian Eyes: The Native Experience in Books for Children.* OYATE, 1998.

Iris McClellan Tiedt. *Teaching with Picture Books in the Middle School.* International Reading Association, 2001.

References

R. A. Bamford and J. V. Kristo (Eds.). *Making Facts Come Alive: Choosing Quality Nonfiction Literature K–8.* Christopher-Gordon, 1998.

Bernice Cullinan and Lee Galda. *Literature and the Child* (3rd ed.). Harcourt Brace, 1994.

Marilyn J. Eisenwine and Diane A. Hunt. "Using a Computer in Literacy Groups with Emergent Readers." *Reading Teacher, 53,* no. 6 (2000): 456–458.

E. B. Freeman and D. G. Person (Eds.). *Using Nonfiction Tradebooks in the Elementary Classroom: From Ants to Zeppelins.* NCTE, 1998.

Violet Harris (Ed.). *Using Multiethnic Literature in the K–8 Classroom.* Christopher-Gordon, 1997.

Jerome Harste, Vivian Woodward, and Caroline Burke. *Language Stories and Literacy Lessons.* Heinemann, 1984.

Frances E. Kendall. *Diversity in the Classroom: New Approaches to the Education of Young Children* (2nd ed.). Teachers College Press, 1996.

Lindo Labbo. "Twelve Things Young Children Can Do with a Talking Book in a Classroom Computer Center." *Reading Teacher, 53,* no. 7 (2000): 542–546.

Judith Langer. *Envisioning Literature: Literary Understanding and Instruction.* Teachers College Press, 1995.

Susan Lehr. "The Politics of Children's Literature in the Elementary Classroom." *Teaching and Learning Literature, 97,* no. 6 (1994).

Donald J. Leu, Jr. "Our Children's Future: Changing the Focus of Literacy and Literacy Instruction." *Reading Teacher, 53,* no. 5 (2000): 424–429.

James Moffett and Betty Jean Wagner. *Student-Centered Language Arts and Reading, K–13* (3rd ed.). Houghton Mifflin, 1996.

B. Moss, S. Leone, and M. L. Dipillo. "Exploring the Literature of Fact: Linking Reading and Writing through Trade Books." *Language Arts, 74* (1997): 418–429.

John O' Flavahan. "Teacher Role Options in Peer Discussions about Literature." *Reading Teacher, 48,* no. 4 (1995): 354–356.

Michael Opitz (Ed.). *Literacy Instruction for Culturally and Linguistically Diverse Students.* IRA, 1998.

Louise Rosenblatt. *The Reader, the Text, the Poem.* Southern Illinois Press, 1978.

Timothy Shanahan and Susan Shanahan. "Character Perspective Charting: Helping Children to Develop a More Complete Conception of Story." *Reading Teacher, 50* (1997): 668–677.

Lynn Atkinson Smolen and Victoria Ortiz-Castro. "Dissolving Borders and Broadening Perspectives through Latino Traditional Literature." *Reading Teacher, 53,* no. 7 (2000): 566–578.

Nancy Stein and C. G. Glenn. "An Analysis of Story Comprehension in Elementary School Children." In R. O. Freedle (Ed.), *New Directions in Discourse Processing, Vol 2.* Ablex, 1982.

Pamela Tiedt and Iris Tiedt. *Multicultural Teaching: A Handbook of Activities, Information, and Resources* (5th ed.). Allyn and Bacon, 1999.

Hallie Kay Yopp and Ruth Helen Yopp. *Literature-Based Reading Activites* (2nd ed.). Allyn and Bacon, 1996.

8 Promoting Poetry

Suddenly everybody was happy. It was like seeing a rainbow when it was still raining.
—Walter Dean Myers, *Fast Sam, Cool Clyde, and Stuff*

In an assessment-driven curriculum, poetry is not typically given a large place. The few poems that are taught, by classic authors, tend to be analyzed to death and torn apart looking for symbolism and the authors' intent. Not surprisingly, many students come to believe that poetry is boring. Yet, poetry has a power to reach people, to communicate experience and emotion, and create a bridge between people in a different way than prose. Unlike writing narrative or expository prose, with its focus on clarity and organization, poetry can open up students' imaginations as they play with the twists and turns of language, and it can bring an unusual level of personal engagement to the classroom experience.

Kenneth Koch has pioneered teaching poetry in the elementary classroom, introducing great poets to the students in *Rose, Where Did You Get That Red?* (1990) and teaching students to write poetry in *Wishes, Lies, and Dreams* (2000). Teachers participating in Poets in the Schools programs have discovered that good poetry can be written in the language of the streets, and subjects for poetry can come from students' own lives. Poetry deserves a larger place in the language arts program, and thus an entire chapter of this book is devoted to it.

Enjoying Poetry

Poetry speaks directly to our senses and shows us what makes us human. When you read to students, select poems that bring a positive and enthusiastic response, such as poems with strong rhyme or rhythm, humorous poems, or story poems. Through pleasure, students learn to attend to language and how it can make them feel. They learn that different people can have different responses to a poem and that a poem concentrates rich ideas and emotions in a small space.

Jump Rope Rhymes

Have the children collect the rhymes they chant as they jump rope. Make a book of Rhymes for Jumping Rope. Boys and girls can join in compiling this book as the children all interview friends and family to learn new rhymes. Here are a few examples:

> *Teddy Bear, Teddy Bear, I am sick*
> *Send for the doctor, quick, quick, quick.*
> *Teddy Bear, Teddy Bear, turn around,*
> *Teddy Bear, Teddy Bear, touch the ground,*
> *Teddy Bear, Teddy Bear, are you lame?*
> *Teddy Bear, Teddy Bear, spell your name.*
> *Teddy Bear, Teddy Bear, has much to do.*
> *Teddy Bear, Teddy Bear, you are through.*

> *Monkey, monkey in the tree*
> *How many monkeys do I see?*
> *1, 2, 3, 4, 5, 6, etc.*

> *Down by the meadow where the green grass grows,*
> *There sat _____, sweet as a rose.*
> *She sang, and she sang, she sang so sweet,*
> *Along came _____ and*
> *kissed her on the cheek.*
> *How many kisses did she get?*
> *1, 2, 3, 4, 5, 6, etc.*

Students may know other counting rhymes for different games. Encourage them to share examples with the class.

The Rhythm of Poetry

Students will become aware of the rhythms of poetry by singing rounds. Each group must sing the same rhythm or the round won't come out right. The following are songs that some students may already know and that are enjoyable at all ages: "Row, Row, Row Your Boat," "Three Blind Mice," and "Are You Sleeping?"

White Coral Bells

Children who have had experience with rounds will be able to sing the lovely song, "White Coral Bells." More examples of rhymes and poems that can be adapted are in:

> Joanna Cole and Stephanie Calmenson. *Give the Dog a Bone: Stories, Poems, Jokes, and Riddles about Dogs.* Doubleday, 1996.
> Alvin Schwartz. *And the Green Grass Grew All Around.* Harper, 1992.

White Coral Bells

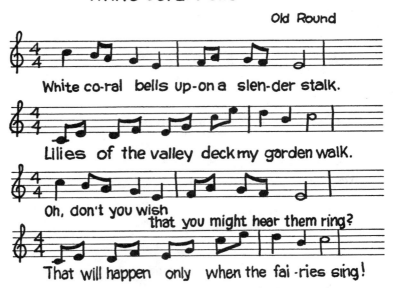

Old Round

White co-ral bells up-on a slen-der stalk.

Lilies of the valley deck my garden walk.

Oh, don't you wish that you might hear them ring?

That will happen only when the fai-ries sing!

Discovering Couplets

Studies have shown that students enjoy hearing rhymed verse. One of the simplest types is the couplet. This rhyming form is used in play, in jump rope games, and in jingles. Encourage students to find examples of couplets such as these:

> *January brings the snow,*
> *Makes our feet and fingers glow.*
> —Mother Goose

> *Star Light; star bright;*
> *First star I see tonight.*
> —Old Saying

Have students illustrate a favorite couplet and post the examples on the board. Point to the printed lines to have all students say the couplet aloud.

Collections of nursery rhymes to investigate with students are:

Lucy Cousins. *Jack and Jill and Other Nursery Rhymes.* Dutton, 1996.
Shari Halpern. *Old MacDonald Had a Farm.* North-South, 1997.
Iona Opie (Ed.). *My Very First Mother Goose.* Illustrated by Rosemary Wells. Candlewick, 1996.
Simms Taback. *There Was an Old Lady Who Swallowed a Fly.* Illustrated by Pam Adams. Child's Play, 1999.

Learning Limericks

Children love the playful rhyming pattern of limericks. Here are two they can learn quickly:

> *There once was a lady from Niger*
> *Who smiled as she rode on a tiger*
>   *They came back from the ride*
>   *With the lady inside*
> *And the smile on the face of the tiger.*
>   —Cosmo Monkhouse

> *There was an old man of Blackheath,*
> *Who sat on his set of false teeth.*
>   *Said he, with a start,*
>   *"Oh, Lord, bless my heart!*
> *I've bitten myself underneath."*
>   —Unknown

Once they have seen some examples, ask them to look at the rhyme pattern. What are the rhyming lines in a limerick?

Quatrains

One of the most commonly used poetry forms is the quatrain, a four-line poem. Children can find many examples of quatrains in Mother Goose poems—for example:

> *Simple Simon met a pieman*
> *Going to the fair.*
> *Said Simple Simon to the pieman,*
> *"Let me taste your ware."*

Students of all ages enjoy reciting these verses as a group. Other Mother Goose verses are quatrains with different rhyming patterns:

> *There was a crooked man, and he went a crooked mile;*
> *He found a crooked sixpence against a crooked stile;*
> *He bought a crooked cat, which caught a crooked mouse,*
> *And all lived together in a little crooked house.*

> *Pat-a-cake, pat-a-cake, baker's man,*
> *Bake me a cake as fast as you can;*
> *Pat it and prick it, and mark it with a T,*
> *Put it in the oven for Tommy and me.*

As students identify quatrains, have them examine the rhyme scheme to see how many different arrangements they can find. Demonstrate how to identify the rhyming pattern of *Simple Simon* as *abab,* whereas *The Crooked Man* is *aabb.*

Combining Quatrains

The quatrain is often used in combinations to form longer poems. Present examples like "A Bird" to the children. Check the rhyme scheme in this quatrain:

> *A Bird**
> *A bird came down the walk,*
> *He did not know I saw;*
> *He bit an angleworm in halves*
> *And ate the fellow, raw.*
> *And then he drank a dew*
> *From a convenient grass,*
> *And then hopped sidewise to the wall*
> *To let a beetle pass*
> —Emily Dickinson

Have the students close their eyes while you say the poem. They can visualize the image described in this poem. Afterwards, discuss the different pictures they saw in their minds.

Poetry Doesn't Have to Rhyme

Show the children examples of poetry that doesn't rhyme to dispel the idea that rhyming is a necessary aspect of poetry. Well-known poets who write "free verse" (unrhymed poetry) include Hilda Conkling, Carl Sandburg, e. e. cummings, and Walt Whitman.

Also look for examples of free verse among winners of the prestigious Caldecott Awards such as *A Visit to William Blake's Inn: Poems for Innocent and Experienced Travelers* by Nancy Willard (Harcourt, 1982), illustrated by Alice and Martin Provensen.

Favorite Poems to Read Aloud

Keep a poetry book on your desk so that you always have a poem handy for a spare moment. Mark some of your favorites or any poems that tickle your imagination. Students of all ages will enjoy the following poem:

Eletelephony*
Once there was an elephant,
Who tried to use the telephant—
No! No! I mean an elephone
Who tried to use the telephone—
(Dear me! I am not certain quite
That even now I've got that right.)

Howe'er it was, he got his trunk
Entangled in the tetephunk;
The more he tried to get it free,
The louder buzzed the telephee—
(I fear I'd better drop the song
Of elephop and telephong!)
                                        —Laura E. Richards

One excellent collection to keep close by for frequent reference is Jack Prelutsky's *The 20th Century Children's Poetry Treasury,* in which poems are indexed by theme.

Poetry Festival

The Children's Book Council has designated a week in April for Young People's Poetry Week. This week is an opportunity to bring poetry from the margins of the curriculum into the center of school life. Invite your class to participate by learning poems, writing poetry, and displaying pictures of poets and their poetry throughout the classroom. Check the Children's Book Council website for more information <www.cbcbooks.org> or write:

CBC
568 Broadway
Suite 404
New York, NY 10012

The CBC has also published poetry from the past forty years: *Book Poems: Poems from National Children's Book Week 1959–1998.*

Folk Songs Are Poetry, Too

Provide the printed words of songs that children sing to show them that a song is also a poem. They will be interested in reading the words they sing. One good example is the folk song "The Erie Canal."

The Erie Canal

First Verse

I've got a mule, her name is Sal,
Fifteen miles on the Erie Canal.
She's a good old worker and a good old pal,
Fifteen miles on the Erie Canal.

We've haul'd some barges in our day,
Fill'd with lumber, coal and hay,
And we know ev'ry inch of the way
From Albany to Buffalo.

Refrain

Low Bridge, ev'rybody down!
Low bridge, for we're going through a town,
And you'll always know your neighbor,
You'll always know your pal,
If you ever navigated on the Erie Canal.

Second Verse

We better get along on our way, old gal,
Fifteen miles on the Erie Canal,
Cause you bet your life I'd never part with Sal,
Fifteen miles on the Erie Canal.

Git up there, mule, here comes a lock,
We'll make Rome 'bout six o'clock
One more trip and back we'll go
Right back home to Buffalo.

Many traditional songs are available in picturebook format, with outstanding illustrations. See, for example, *This Land Is Your Land,* words and music by Woody Guthrie and paintings by Kathy Jakobsen (Little, Brown, 1998).

Story Poems

Make poetry a part of your classroom as you read students a dramatic epic poem such as "Casey at the Bat." Older students can also learn this poem to recite to the class, as its rhyming structure makes it easy to memorize. Other enjoyable narrative poems found in many anthologies include:

"Antonio, Antonio" by Laura E. Richards
"The Shooting of Dan McGrew" by Robert Service
"Paul Revere's Ride" by Henry Wadsworth Longfellow

Also look for picturebook versions, such as "The Cremation of Sam McGee" by Robert Service, with paintings by noted Canadian artist Ted Harrison (Kids Can Press, 1986).

How to Teach a Poem

As you talk about a poem with children, you want them to experience the texture of the poem and respond to its rich associations. After discussion of how students felt, reread the poem to focus their attention not only on the surface but also on the inferences and implications important to a deeper comprehension of the poem.

> ### The Wind
> *I saw you toss the kites on high*
> *And blow the birds about the sky;*
> *And all around I heard you pass,*
> *Like ladies' skirts across the grass—*
> > *O wind, a-blowing all day long,*
> > *O wind, that sings so loud a song!*
>
> *I saw the different things you did,*
> *But always you yourself you hid.*
> *I felt you push, I heard you call,*
> *I could not see yourself at all—*
> > *O wind, a-blowing all day long,*
> > *O wind, that sings so loud a song!*
>
> *O you that are so strong and cold,*
> *O blower, are you young or old?*
> *Are you a beast of field and tree,*
> *Or just a stronger child than me?*
> > *O wind, a-blowing all day long,*
> > *O wind, that sings so loud a song!*
> > > —Robert Louis Stevenson

Questions can lead students from the literal to the inferential level and beyond.

Literal Level
- What is the rhyme scheme?
- Tell one thing the wind did.

Inferential Level
- What is the poet saying in this poem?
- In what different ways does the poet picture the wind?

Creative Level

- Write a poem on how you feel about the wind.
- Do you enjoy being outdoors? What is it that makes you feel good?
- Look for other poems about the wind.

Poets Are People, Too

The Teachers and Writers Collaborative organizes a people's poetry gathering to illustrate the diverse cultural traditions of the people who write poetry. They include cowboy poets, griots (West African rememberers/storytellers), hobo poets, traditional blues singers, and poets representing traditions from Mexico to Japan. Have students select a favorite poem and learn more about the author of that poem. With each student representing a different poet, you can discuss the diverse community of poets and their poetry.

For more information about this gathering, check the website <www.peoplespoetry.org>.

Meet the Poets

Find out if your district has a Poet in the Schools program. You may be able to invite a poet to speak to your class, read poetry, and stimulate students to write poetry. You can also use video to show poets in action. *The Power of the Word* and *The Language of Life*, two videos from PBS, feature Bill Moyers talking with and listening to poets who write poetry as if their lives depended on it.

Poetry for Students to Read

Include in your classroom library books of poetry that students can explore on their own or use to prepare poetry for public performance. Here are some suggestions:

Simon James. (Sel.). *Days Like This: A Collection of Small Poems.* Candlewick, 1999.
Shel Silverstein. *Falling Up.* HarperCollins, 1996.
Jane Yolen (Comp.). *Sky Scrape/City Scape: Poems of City Life.* Illustrated by Ken Condon. Wordsong, 1996.

Particularly suited to reading aloud are the following:

Arnold Adoff (Ed.). *I Am the Darker Brother: An Anthology of Modern Poems by African Americans.* Simon & Schuster, 1997.
Lori M. Carlson (Ed.). *Cool Salsa: Bilingual Poems on Growing Up in the United States.* Holt, 1994.
Joyce Armstrong Carroll and Edward E. Wilson (Eds.). *Poetry after Lunch: Poems to Read Aloud.* Absey, 1997.
Catherine Clinton. *I, Too, Sing America: Three Centuries of African American Poetry.* Houghton, 1998.

Lillian Morrison (Comp.). *Slam Dunk: Basketball Poems.* Illustrated by Bill James. Hyperion, 1995.

Naomi Shihab Nye (Sel.). *The Tree Is Older than You Are: A Bilingual Gathering of Poems and Stories from Mexico with Paintings by Mexican Artists.* Simon & Schuster, 1995.

Students in the primary grades will especially enjoy these books:

Sandra De Coteau Orie. *Did You Hear Wind Sing Your Name? An Oneida Song of Spring.* Illustrated by Christopher Canyon. Walker, 1995.

Nikki Giovanni. *The Sun Is So Quiet.* Illustrated by Ashley Bryan. Holt, 1996.

Pat Mora. *Confetti: Poems for Children.* Illustrated by Enrique O. Sanchez. Lee & Low, 1996.

Jack Prelutsky (Sel.). *The Beauty of the Beast: Poems from the Animal Kingdom.* Illustrated by Meilo So. Knopf, 1997.

Looking at Patterns in Language

Poetry achieves much of its impact through the pleasure the poet communicates to the reader in playing with sound and meaning. As students respond to the depth of meaning carried by poetic language, they can begin to look more closely at the strategies poets use to achieve these effects. Looking at the language of poetry helps them develop better writing skills and motivates them to read more attentively, as they incorporate alliteration and onomatopoeia, for example, into their own work.

Alliteration

Alliteration, the repetition of initial consonants, contributes to the musical quality of poetry. Encourage your students to identify examples in word play and poetry. Notice how alliteration (and *assonance,* the repetition of vowel sounds) is used in the following tongue twister poems to provide rhythm and humor:

Betty Botter bought some butter,
But, she said, the butter's bitter;
If I put it in my batter
It will make my batter bitter,
But a bit of better butter
Will make my batter better.
So she bought a bit of butter
Better than her bitter butter,
And she put it in her batter
And the batter was not bitter.
So 'twas better Betty Botter bought a bit of better butter.

How much wood would a woodchuck chuck
If a woodchuck could chuck wood?
A woodchuck would chuck as much as he would chuck
If a woodchuck could chuck wood.

Alliterative Phrases

Students will enjoy writing phrases that contain words beginning with the same sounds, for example:

fancy fringed feathers
reasonably red raspberries
lithe leaping lizards

Some students will be motivated to write whole sentences in this manner. This is a good small-group activity.

Black-browed bears bowled briskly before breakfast.
Aunt Agatha asked angrily and agile Abraham answered anonymously.

Composing such sentences will lead students to the dictionary as they pore over words listed under one letter. They will encounter new vocabulary in this way, too.

Onomatopoeia

Savor with students examples of words that sound like what they mean *(onomatopoeia)*. Children will be able to list a number of familiar words such as:

slush	sizzle
sneeze	roar
crackle	splash
meow	beep
hiss	chomp

As you read poetry together, encourage students to note other examples of such words. Help children observe how this effect adds to the music of language. Even the word *onomatopoeia* is fun to say aloud.

An excellent poem to use with students is "Galoshes" by Rhoda Bacmeister, which describes the sounds of mud and slush.

Rhyming List

Words that rhyme usually have the same ending—*rain, stain, gain*—but it is good to remember that rhymes are sounds and that words don't need the same written ending to rhyme, for example, *said, head.*

Here are examples of words that are easy to rhyme. Challenge students to find five rhymes for each word:

mean

sat

pan

cup

Each student can make a rhyme list for several words, such as *bend, light, round.* Older students can find rhymes for multisyllabic words, such as *butterfly* and *composition.* The class can assemble a rhyme dictionary to help each other when they write poetry.

Featuring Funny Poems

Many poems that feature rhymes and onomatopoeia are also very funny. These poems appeal especially to primary students because of their humor. Older students will appreciate the special uses of language for effect. Use these poems with students for the following:

choral reading (groups of students read different lines)

chanting lines

playing with language

models for writing

reciting words and phrases

Some examples are:

P. D. Eastman. *Go, Dog, Go! P. D. Eastman's Book of Things that Go.* Random, 1997.

Bruce Goldstone. *The Beastly Feast.* Illustrated by Blair Lent. Holt, 1998.

Lee Bennett Hopkins. *Good Rhymes, Good Times.* Illustrated by Frane Lessac. HarperCollins, 1995.

Anne Isaacs. *Cat up a Tree: A Story in Poems.* Illustrated by Stephen Mackey. Dutton, 1998.

Jack Prelutsky. *The Gargoyle on the Roof.* Illustrated by Peter Sis. Greenwillow, 1999.

Nancy Shaw. *Sheep in a Jeep.* Illustrated by Margot Apple. Houghton, 1986.
Rosemary Wells. *Noisy Nora.* Dial, 1997.

Riddle Poems

Many old poems set up riddles to be answered. Answering correctly usually depends on unraveling the metaphor. Can your students follow the riddling metaphor in these examples?

> *Little Nancy Etticoat,*
> *With a white petticoat,*
> *And a red nose;*
> *She has no feet or hands,*
> *The longer she stands*
> *The shorter she grows.*
>
> > *(a candle)*

> *As I was going to St. Ives,*
> *I met a man with seven wives;*
> *Each wife had seven sacks,*
> *Each sack had seven cats,*
> *Each cat had seven kits:*
> *Each cat had seven kits:*
> *Kits, cats, sacks, and wives,*
> *How many were there going to St. Ives?*
>
> > *(one)*

Printing Poems

Let children select one poem they especially like and have them print it on a Poetry Poster. They can use manuscript printing or try other styles of calligraphy to create an artful presentation, such as the illustration of "Morning" on page 272 by Emily Dickinson. Simple drawings enhance the poem and suggest its content.

Younger students can explore the different fonts on the computer and printer to print up posters of their favorites.

Speaking Poetry Together

All poetry was originally oral. Children can learn to speak a poem together. Mother Goose books are a good source of poems that children enjoy speaking. They can sing the verses, too, of poems like this one:

MORNING

by Emily Dickinson

Will there really be a morning?
Is there such a thing as day?
Could I see it from the mountains
If I were tall as they?

Has it feet like water lilies?
Has it feathers like a bird?
Is it brought from famous countries
Of which I've never heard?

Calligraphy by Pat

Sing a Song of Sixpence
Sing a song of sixpence,
A pocket full of rye,
Four and twenty blackbirds
baked in a pie.
When the pie was opened,
The birds began to sing.
Wasn't that a dainty dish
To set before the King?

The King was in his counting house
Counting out his money;
The Queen was in her parlor,
Eating bread and honey;
The maid was in the garden,
Hanging out the clothes;
Down came a blackbird
And snipped off her nose.
—Mother Goose

Acting Out Poems

Poems with pronounced rhythms, such as the following, are good choices for oral performance:

The Pirate Don Durk of Dowdee*

Ho, for the Pirate Don Durk of Dowdee!
He was as wicked as wicked could be,
But oh, he was perfectly gorgeous to see!
  The Pirate Don Durk of Dowdee.

His conscience, of course, was as black as a bat,
But he had a floppety plume on his hat
And when he went walking it jiggled—like that!
  The plume of the Pirate Dowdee.

His coat it was crimson and cut with a slash,
And often as ever he twirled his mustache
Deep down in the ocean the mermaids went splash,
  Because of Don Durk of Dowdee.

Moreover, Dowdee had a purple tattoo,
And stuck in his belt where he buckled it through
Were a dagger, a dirk, and a squizzamaroo,
  For fierce was the Pirate Dowdee.

So fearful he was he would shoot at a puff,
And always at sea when the weather grew rough
He drank from a bottle and wrote on his cuff,
  Did Pirate Don Durk of Dowdee.

Oh, he had a cutlass that swung at his thigh
And he had a parrot called Pepperkin Pye,
And a zigzaggy scar at the end of his eye,
  Had Pirate Don Durk of Dowdee.

He kept in a cavern, this buccaneer bold,
A curious chest that was covered with mold,
And all of his pockets were jingly with gold!
  Oh jing! went the gold of Dowdee.

*By Mildred Plew Merryman from *Child Life Magazine*. Copyright 1923, 1951 by Rand McNally & Company.

His conscience, of course, it was crook'd like a squash,
But both of his boots made a slickery slosh,
And he went through the world with a wonderful swash,
> *Did Pirate Don Durk of Dowdee.*

It's true he was wicked as wicked could be,
His sins they outnumbered a hundred and three,
But oh, he was perfectly gorgeous to see,
> *The Pirate Don Durk of Dowdee.*
> > —Mildred Plew Merryman

Group Reading

In this activity, every student in the class begins with the same collection of reading material—for example, a book, a story, an article, or a newspaper. Each student chooses a phrase or line to underline. Then a leader selects students to read their individual lines, one at a time. The order in which students read is random, and more than one student may have chosen the same line. Some students may speak more than once. As they read aloud, students are participating in the creation of poetry. Record the session so students can hear the effect of their poem.

Found Poetry

Another unusual approach to poetry is called *found poetry*. Students begin by selecting a passage from one of the books they are reading. As they copy the passage, they decide where to break the lines to create a poem. Then they share their "poem" with the class. In this way, students learn that many kinds of language can be poetry.

Similes and Metaphors

Introduce students to *similes* and *metaphors* with examples from the poems they are reading. Help them understand the difference: Both similes and metaphors compare two dissimilar objects, but similes include the words *like* or *as*. Many similes have even become cliches, such as "busy as a bee," "wise as an owl," and "big as a house." However, fresh comparisons create colorful poetry and open up the mind to new ways of looking at the world. Provide students with examples of stale comparisons and invite them to replace the tired image with one that will make you wake up.

- As quiet as a _____
- As soft as a _____

As you read poems to students, talk about the comparisons that are being made. What effect do the metaphors and similes have on the listener?

Other Comparisons

Personification is another kind of comparison—one in which something that is not human is described in human terms. It is often used in poems about objects and abstract ideas. Many poets use personification to make their images more vivid. Read "Dandelion," in *Poems by a Little Girl* by Hilda Conkling and discuss how the personification creates a strong impression. Tell the students that the poet was a little girl when she wrote this and other poems.

Developing Sensory Awareness

Take a poetry field trip or display colorful pictures that appeal to each of the five senses for this discussion. Pose these questions, followed by the experiential activities suggested here:

- What do you taste when you think yellow?
  Pass around pieces of lemon to taste.
- What do you see when you think red?
  Take a walk around the school. Come back to class and share all the things that you saw that were red
- What do you smell when you think purple?
  Provide things that have different fragrances for students to experience—lavender, ripe purple grapes, grape juice.
- What do you feel when you think?
  Include discussion of emotional feelings as well as touch. Bring objects for tactile sensations.
- What do you hear when you think blue?
  Provide a tape of ocean sounds, birds, or anything else you feel would be appropriate.

Green Is . . .

Give students an opportunity to discuss some of their favorite colors. Ask the students what their favorite color is and have them break up into small groups by color. Each student in the group can describe something that is his or her favorite color or discuss why a specific color is his or her favorite. The group can prepare a color collage featuring clippings of pictures and words that depict, for example, the color green. They can also write a poem about the color, beginning "Green Is . . ."

A model for writing color poems is *Hailstones and Halibut Bones,* poems by Mary O'Neill (Doubleday, 1989) and illustrated by John Wallner, which explore colors in nature.

Composing Poetry

Students can be poets, too. Students who might have difficulty articulating ideas and emotions in prose may find their voice in poetry. Writing poetry encourages students to use their imaginations and look at the familiar world in new ways, offering an opportunity to make meaning in which everyone can participate. When students look at poems as writers, they understand that they are not limited by conventional formats and topics but they cannot create their own world.

First Poems

After you explore a variety of poems with students, select a topic and use this theme to create couplets about a month, a season, a holiday, an event, or the weather. Then discuss what possibilities this exercise offers. Provide the first line for a poem, and then have the class suggest the next line. Some examples of first lines are:

- What do you do in the spring?
- I woke up early one day.
- Across my face came a smile.
- We ran on the sand.

Limerick

The limerick consists of a triplet and a couplet. The triplet is lines 1, 2, and 5; the couplet is lines 3 and 4. Limericks can be written about anything: people in the classroom, famous people, or people from literature. This is a simple poetic structure with which everyone can experience success. Give students a series of beginning lines that they can use as starters, for example:

- There once was a doggy named Rover...
- There was a young bookworm called Booky...
- There once was a girl dressed in pink...

Use one of these lines to compose a group poem like this:

> *There once was a doggy named Rover*
> *Who rolled in a patch of green clover.*
> *His master came out;*
> *Said he with a shout,*
> *"Look! Rover's got clover all over!"*

Number Poem

Numbers form the structure for interesting poems that students can write, thus:

> *One is the only, the most, the best;*
> *One is lonely, rejected, alone;*
> *One is a baby's first birthday party;*
> *One is the power atop the throne.*

Alliteration Number Poems

More advanced students might enjoy the challenge of creating alliterative lines for an unrhymed number poem. Notice that alliteration is based on sound, not spelling.

> *One whistling wild warbler winged westward.*
> *Two trembling timid turtles tiptoed to town.*
> *Three throbbing thrushes threaded through thrillingly.*

Terse Verse

Just two words can form a poem that has meaning, for instance:

> *Go*   *Hot*   *Snack*
> *Slow*   *Shot*   *Pack*

Students can discover many such pairs as they play with rhyming words. They can illustrate such poems for display.

Two-Word Lines

Another simple, but effective, poetry pattern consists of just two words on each line. No rhyming is required although it could be included in different ways.

> ***Fun***
> *Bikes racing;*
> *Balls batting;*
> *Skateboards swishing;*
> *Hoops twirling.*
>
> ***Noise***
> *Bells, yells;*
> *Waves, raves;*
> *Sports, snorts;*
> *Clouts, shouts.*

Free Verse

Free verse is a style of poetry that children can write very successfully. There are few restrictions in the writing of free verse; there is no set pattern of rhyme, no set length of line or content, and any topic can be used. Free verse can even consist of 1 line or 20 lines. One way of helping students create free verse is to show them a group of pictures or photographs on a theme. Then have them describe this idea with one, two, three, or four words. Having the whole class participate in this beginning experience of writing free verse is an excellent strategy for introducing this form.

Another method is to present a familiar concept. For example, have students list all things that are hard. Begin a group poem, thus:

> *What is hard?*
> *Hardness is a baseball.*
> *Hardness is doing homework.*

Other useful topics include: "Summer Is . . . " or "A friend Is. . . . " Students might suggest lines like this:

> *Vacation Is . . .*
>   *swimming in the pool,*
>   *going camping.*

Poetry Takes Shape

Help students think of poetry in concrete terms. Have them draw a large shape on a sheet of colored construction paper—an animal, an object, or an imaginary shape—and cut it out. Ask them to tell the class about the shape by writing a poem on the paper. Encour-

age them to perceive this shape with all their senses. They can write their poems on the shape they have cut. Mount the picture poems on the bulletin board for everyone to enjoy.

Wake Up House/Rooms Full of Poems, by Dee Lillegard and illustrated by Don Carter (Knopf, 1999), includes poems in the shape of stars and a stegosaurus.

The Five "Ws"

Journalists know the rule: A good story can be written by answering the five "Ws" in the first paragraph. Older students can use this same formula to write striking poems. Each line must answer one of the *W* questions: *Who, What, When, Where, Why.* Students can answer these questions in their poem in any order. Their lines will range from one-word responses to longer sentences, using the techniques of poetry such as metaphor and rhyme to express their ideas. Because these poems often have dramatic effect, let the students share what they have written by reading the poems aloud to the class. Student poets will be gratified by the response of their classmates.

Acrostic Poem

The acrostic is another simple structure for a poem. It might be only a couplet, or a group of words, and it can vary in rhyme scheme and in length. The special characteristic of the acrostic poem is that the first letters of each line are part of a word that can be read vertically. Poems like this can be used to honor a famous person, spell a subject, or celebrate a season, as in this example:

> *Sleepy blue lake*
> *Unveiled by disappearing mist;*
> *Memories of summers past*
> *Make permanent the*
> *Etchings; while I sit here*
> *Reclined before a warm winter fire.*

The possibilities for a poem like this are endless. Develop a class poem around a word. Print the letters at the left first, and then fill in the poem. Students can develop individual acrostic poems in the poetry learning center.

A Listing Poem

An easy kind of poem for children to write is a list of related words. The topic could be animals, automobiles, or favorite things. This poet describes "swift things":

Swift Things Are Beautiful*
Swift things are beautiful:
Swallows and deer,
And lightning that falls
Bright-veined and clear,
Rivers and meteors,
Wind in the wheat,
The strong-withered horse,
The runner's sure feet.
—Elizabeth Coatsworth

Sensible Remembering

Smell is one of the most important senses for awakening memories. Ask students to think of a special food, perhaps from the past, that they associate with their families. Can they remember how it smelled? Talk about ways to describe these smells, using techniques such as onomatopoeia and imagery. Have students write poems describing these smells and the memories they evoke. How can they make someone else experience the same smell?

Ancestral Voices

Have students talk about the ties that link them to their ancestors—people in the past they have never met. What connects them with these people so long ago? What would those ancestors want to say to them today? What gift or gifts would the ancestors want to give their descendants? Students can identify feelings, such as a desire to belong somewhere and to be part of a community, that they would like to communicate. After this discussion, students will be stimulated to write a poem taking on the voice of their ancestors and explaining what they wish to leave behind.

Praise Poem

In the West African tradition, poets, called "griots," often create poems in praise of someone. Students can write praise poems, as well. These poems can be about a person they know, someone in history, or someone they admire, for example. Their choice of subject will influence their use of language and rhythm in the poem. A praise poem about a grandmother will sound and read differently from a poem about a favorite rap artist. For original African examples, see John Williams Johnson, Thomas A. Hale, and Stephen Belcher's *Oral Epics from Africa: Vibrant Epics from a Vast Continent* (African Epics Series) (Indiana University Press, 1997).

The Blues

Lyrics from the songs known as the blues can also provide useful models for writing poetry. Play examples of traditional blues for students to listen to, such as:

> *Before the Blues, Hard Times Come Again* (Shanachie Records)
> *The Roots of Rap* (Shanachie Records)

Invite students to describe the structure used in these lyric-poems. The poems usually consist of one line, repeated, and then a third line that rhymes with the first. They are often full of melancholy, as the poets talk about rejection, poverty, and loneliness. Discuss these topics with students and ask them to come up with their own subjects for blues poetry. Students can "borrow" this blues pattern to write their poems.

More information about the blues is available from Alan Lomax's *The Land Where the Blues Began* (Bantam, 1993).

Poetry Challenges

Today, poets often read their work aloud in settings called *Poetry Slams*. Students can enjoy the same pleasure of oral performance and audience response when they compose poems orally. You might give everyone a topic on which to improvise or a first line to get them started. As students gain confidence, they will delight in trying to outdo each other, thinking on their feet. Groups can also perform oral poetry as one person thinks of a line with which to start, another takes up the challenge with a second line, and the poem continues thus around the group.

Cinquain

The cinquain is a poem consisting of five lines. There are many varieties of five-line poetry, but the cinquain is one that both teachers and students seem to enjoy. Easy to compose, the cinquain form follows these specification:

> Line one: one word (usually the title)
> Line two: two words (describing the title)
> Line three: three words (an action describing the title)
> Line four: four words (feelings describing the title)
> Line five: one word (refers back to the title)

Compose a class cinquain as the whole class contributes their ideas to the writing of one poem. Then students can compose cinquains independently.

Students at all grade levels are able to write cinquains successfully.

Puppies
Snuggly, cuddly
Jumping, rolling, chasing
They always love you
Dogs

Winter
Icy cold
Freezing, blowing, snowing
It lasts so long—
Spring?

Syllabic Cinquains

Another form of the cinquain is based on syllables, as outlined here:

Line one: two syllables
Line two: four syllables
Line three: six syllables
Line four: eight syllables
Line five: two syllables

The syllabic cinquain, illustrated in the poem that follows, provides an excellent lead-in to the writing of haiku, another syllabic form of poetry.

Today
Never ceasing
Passes sometimes hurting
Changing with every moment
Silent

Writing Haiku

A beautiful unrhymed poetry form, the haiku originated in thirteenth-century Japan. Haiku is a three-line verse form, with the three lines totaling 17 syllables, thus:

Line one: 5 syllables
Line two: 7 syllables
Line three: 5 syllables

The topic of Japanese haiku poetry is usually related to nature and the season. There is no rhyme, and articles and pronouns are rarely used. Like all poetry, haiku is subtle and symbolic. American haiku has been written by a variety of people on a number of topics.

The lines are not always the classic length. Paul R. Janeczko presents old and new haiku in his collection, *Stone Bench in an Empty Park* (Orchard, 1999), accompanied by black-and-white photographs by Henri Silberman.

Students are very successful with this brief form. Their poems are often as subtle as those of adults, as shown in these examples by students from Alberta, Canada:

> *Here comes a sunset**
> *Pulling a blind over me*
> *Making a dark orange.*
> —Geoffrey Delves

> *The sun goes to bed***
> *Leaving the scorched horizon*
> *To nurse its sunburn.*
> —Lauren Atkinson

Group Composing of Haiku

Begin composing haikus by working together as a group. Examine a classic haiku to observe the form it follows. Show children how the season is indicated and the way nature is stressed.

Suggest topics that children might find familiar, ones that are associated with the natural world—for example:

> *water:* stream, river, ocean
> *rain:* storm, drops, puddles
> *trees:* pine, roots, leaves

After selecting a topic, help the children develop the image before they write anything. Thinking of the pine tree, for instance, you can discuss where the tree is, what it looks like, and what might be happening around it. Then encourage children to suggest lines for the poem. Don't worry about the exact number of syllables at first, as this can be developed as part of polishing the poem. The group might gradually create a poem like this together:

> *Pine tree—tall, bold, strong;*
> *Lean into the wind*
> *Or you will be uprooted.*

---

*By Geoffrey Delves from *An Ice Cream Cone Feeling: In the Dark of December, An Anthology of Writing from the Students of Alberta* (Edmonton, Alberta: The Alberta Teachers' Association). Reprinted with permission.

**By Laura Atkinson from *An Ice Cream Cone Feeling: In the Dark of December, An Anthology of Writing from the Students of Alberta* (Edmonton, Alberta: The Alberta Teachers' Association). Reprinted with permission.

Humourous Haiku

One especially effective use of haiku is as a short, humorous poem. Students can take the point of view of an everyday situation and write their haiku from this perspective. Here are some examples:

> *Open the oven door.*
> *The aroma makes me smile.*
> *Grandma's hot cookies!*

> *Mittens, scarf, ear-muffs,*
> *snowboots, and wool hat—good-bye!*
> *It's summer at last!*

Tanka

The tanka is a five-line Japanese poem that contains a haiku in the first three lines. Similar to the haiku, the tanka's lines are unrhymed and contain a total of 31 syllables for the poem. Like the classic haiku, it usually has to do with nature. The form of the poem is:

> Line one: 5 syllables
> Line two: 7 syllables
> Line three: 5 syllables
> Line four: 7 syllables
> Line five: 7 syllables

Some people maintain that the original form was the tanka and that the haiku is, in effect, an abbreviation of this form. However, it is easier to teach the tanka as an advanced form of the haiku and an extension of it. After students have experienced writing haiku, they can go on to the tanka.

Diamante

The diamante, as its name indicates, is diamond-shaped. Created by Dr. Iris M. Tiedt, it follows this format:

> Line one: subject = one word
> Line two: adjectives = two words
> Line three: participles = three words
> Line four: nouns = four words, to begin the transition
> Line five: participles = three words
> Line six: adjectives = two words
> Line seven: noun = the opposite of the subject = one word

This seven-line poem gives students an opportunity to contrast two moods or two opposite ideas in one poem.

> ***Diamond***
> *Light*
> *all-colored, bright*
> *dazzling, flashing, flickering*
> *daybreak, dawn, sunset, twilight*
> *falling, slowing, dying*
> *heavy, awful*
> *Darkness*

Sneaky Poems

Children love writing sneaky poems because the subject "sneaks" up on the reader. These five-line poems are composed according to the following formula:

Line one: word related to the subject
Line two: adjective plus noun about subject
Line three: two action words
Line four: descriptive phrase
Line five: subject

Here are some examples written by sixth-graders.

> *Oval*
> *Unpredictable path*
> *Spiraling, flashing*
> *It's an odd shape*
> *Football.*
>   —Ryan

> *Steel*
> *Hesitant smile*
> *Binding, grinding*
> *Sparks off of teeth*
> *Braces.*
>   —Michelle

Discussion Questions

1. How much school time should be devoted to encouraging student creative thinking, or play, as in writing poetry?

2. What is the difference, if any, between reading and writing poetry and prose in the kind of thinking they foster?

3. With today's concern for teaching and testing the "basics," how can you justify taking the time to teach poetry?

Exploring Further

Barbara Chatton. *Using Poetry across the Curriculum: A Whole Language Approach.* Oryx, 1993.

Mary Kenner Glover. *A Garden of Poets: Poetry Writing in the Elementary Classroom.* NCTE, 1998.

William J. Higginson, with Penny Harter. *The Haiku Handbook: How to Write, Share, and Teach Haiku.* Teachers and Writers Collaborative, 1996.

Internet School Library Media Center. *Poetry for Children.* <falcon.jmu.edu/%7eramseyil/poechild.htm>

Paul B. Janeczko, comp. *Poetry from A to Z: A Guide for Young Writers.* Illustrated by Cathy Bobak. Bradbury, 1994.

Dave Morice. *The Adventures of Dr. Alphabet: 104 Unusual Ways to Write Poetry in the Classroom and the Community.* New York: Teachers and Writers Collaborative, 1995. (5 Union Square West, New York NY, 10003).

Ron Padgett. *Handbook of Poetry and Poetic Forms: 10 Audio Programs.* Teachers and Writers Collaborative, 1995.

Semantic Rhyming Dictionary. <www.cs.cmu.edu/~doughb/rhyme.html>

References

Jack Collom and Sheryl Noethe. *Poetry Everywhere: Teaching Poetry Writing in School and in the Community.* New York: Teachers and Writers Collaborative, 1994.

Lee Galda. "Children's Poetry." In *The Reading Teacher, 43,* no. 1 (1989).

Kenneth Koch. *Rose, Where Did You Get That Red? Teaching Great Poetry to Children.* Vintage, 1990.

Kenneth Koch. *Wishes, Lies, and Dreams.* Harper, 2000.

Judith Michaels. *Risking Intensity: Reading and Writing Poetry with High School Students.* NCTE, 1999.

Bill Moyers. *The Language of Life: A Festival of Poets.* PBS Video.

Marc Polonsky. *The Poetry Reader's Toolkit.* NTC Publishing, 1996.

Davi Walders. "Rhyme and Reason: How a Good Poem Can Change the Rhythm of a Class." *Education Week,* April 28, 1999.

Using the Language Arts across the Curriculum

Two plus two equals four.... When two plus two doesn't equal four, anything can happen.
—Louis Sachar, *Sideways Stories from Wayside School*

Oral and written language skills are best learned within an integrated curriculum that engages students with all kinds of interesting information. Students who are excited about a science experiment, for example, can teach the rest of the class about their findings, using a written pretest, an oral explanation, and diagrams on transparencies. A group of children who are investigating what life was like for slaves living on a plantation in 1800 could plan a readers' theater presentation using quotations, poetry, and excerpts from literature to share their study with others. Music and art can be incorporated to enhance the enjoyment of both presenters and the audience. Such activities provide a reason for using language arts in meaningful yet pleasurable ways.

Research shows that children learn most effectively in small working groups as they interact with each other and share their knowledge and abilities. At the same time, such interactive activities support students' learning to understand and respect each other. These activities also may give each child that much needed sense of belonging that engenders self-esteem and successful learning. Learning activities that cross the curriculum involve children in such thinking processes as comparing, evaluating, and synthesizing as well as generating original ideas. This kind of integrated approach to curriculum and instruction fits well with thematic units of study in the elementary school classroom, permitting the full participation of all students, with each working at his or her ability level.

Teaching and Learning in the Social Studies

This section features learning activities that engage students in using oral and written language as they learn about concepts from social science. Role playing, writing scripts, and reading historical novels are but a few of the ways that language skills can play an integral part in the social studies program.

287

Who's Who in Room 14?

Have your students interview each other to practice collecting different kinds of information and asking questions. For example:

- Who was born in this state?
- Who is the oldest person in the room?
- Who has a birthday this month?
- Who has lived in another country?

Each student selects one specific question to cover. After obtaining this information, investigate with students different ways to represent their data visually (charts, graphs, or maps). Display the results on a large bulletin board as an innovative way to get acquainted.

Collect the information the students have gathered into a class directory. You can use the directory for further activities to practice language skills, such as:

- Find names with double letters (for example, Bill).
- Find which letter is the most frequent in student names.
- Determine the average number of letters in students' names.

English Is Not the Only Language

Many different languages are spoken in the United States and throughout the world. Ask the students in your class what languages they speak. Some students may know more than two languages. Where do these languages come from? Have students locate these areas on the map. Encourage students to see their knowledge of different languages as an asset to the class by asking them to supply a few simple words in that language. Have students create a poster that features *WELCOME* in all the languages represented in the classroom or have students teach the others how to say *hello* in a different language every week.

History in Our Lives

Ask students to interview an adult they know well (for example, one of their parents, a neighbor, or grandparents) in order to learn about change in people's lives. Students can develop a list of questions as a group. Possible questions to ask include:

- How long have you lived here?
- What changes have you seen in the area?
- What was it like when you were a child?
- Is life different for children today?
- What kind of work do you do?
- Is it easier or harder than when you first started? Why?

- Has technology changed what you do? Did you have this 10, 20, 30 years ago?
- What's the most significant change that's taken place in your lifetime?

Students will practice important listening and writing skills as they ask questions, take notes, and write up their report. Discussion afterwards can focus on categorizing types of changes or describing how the local neighborhood has changed as students summarize their findings. Older students can assemble their findings into a book to distribute to the community, in appreciation of the people they interviewed.

Comparing Accounts

As students begin to read varied types of texts (called *genres*), outside the traditional social studies textbook, they need to learn how to interpret, evaluate, and compare these different kinds of accounts. They will have to ask questions such as "What's the difference between primary sources and secondary sources?" and "How is history pieced together from conflicting reports?" One approach to teaching these important skills is to provide texts from two different genres for the students to compare: a historical diary or letters (first person account) and a description of the same period by a modern historian (third person). After students have read both texts, discuss the strengths and weaknesses of each account. For example, reading a diary makes the reader feel a part of that time, whereas reading a historian's version can give the reader a larger context in which to understand the period.

Students can make a chart to list the characteristics of each text. They can also use a Venn diagram as a graphic representation to compare and contrast their own lives with the person they are reading about, as shown in Chapter 7.

The following are examples of diaries, real and fictionalized, to explore with students:

> Marlene Targ Brill. *Diary of a Drummer Boy.* Millbrook, 1998. Civil War, based on fact.
>
> Kristiana Gregory. *The Royal Diaries: Cleopatra VII Daughter of the Nile.* Scholastic, 1999. Fiction.
>
> Kathryn Lasky. *Dear America; A Journey to the New World. The Diary of Remember Patience Whipple.* Scholastic, 1998. Fiction.
>
> Lillian Schlissel. *The Way West: Journal of a Pioneer Woman Based on Diaries of Mrs. Amelia Stewart Knight.* Simon and Schuster, 1993. Family travels from Iowa to Oregon in 1853.
>
> Elvira Woodruff. *Dear Levi: Letters from the Overland Trail.* Random, 1998. Boy's letters to his brother as he travels from Pennsylvania to Oregon in 1851.

After students have read several of these diaries or letters, they can explore using this format, individually or in small groups, to express what they have learned about a place or period. The *Dear America* series is also available on videotape from Scholastic.

What's My Line?

Describe the format of this classic television show to students. A panel of people attempt to guess the identity or a significant fact about a person that they cannot see. To adapt this to the classroom, begin by selecting a group of five to seven students, and somebody to be the "mystery person." The "expert" panel sits facing the class so its members cannot see the board. The mystery person signs the name of the individual that he or she represents on the board, and the panel tries to determine who this person is by asking questions that can only be answered "yes" or "no." The mystery person can be an individual from history, a person from literature, or a contemporary individual.

Provide sufficient practice with this game so that all students have the chance to ask questions. They need an opportunity to evaluate the questions asked by the panel in order to learn how to ask more effective questions, instead of random ones.

This activity reinforces the importance of asking good questions. It also provides a good review for the class studying a particular period of history to select a person from that time.

The People's Museum

After studying famous people in history, experiment with alternatives to the written report as a means of sharing the information gathered with the class. Ask students, "If you could be anyone from history, who would you like to be?" After they have completed their investigation into this person's life, students present what they have learned in the form of an oral performance: Several students stand in front of the class as if they were the actual person that they studied, now a figure in a wax museum of famous people. Their audience can select which figure will "speak" by pulling a string, pressing a button, or winding them up.

A Checkup on Women

Ask students to list the names of 10 famous women, past or present, not including actresses, TV personalities, or sports stars. Discuss their responses and put some of the names on the board. Was it easy to think of 10 names? Did most students name the same people? This activity can be used to assess what students already know about women in history and what they need to learn. Based on student knowledge and interests, have them develop their own list of topics to investigate or questions to answer as a focus for further study of women in history.

Women Put Their Stamp on History

Ask if students have noticed the images featured on postage stamps. Stamps are issued to commemorate many things, including famous people. Women who have been honored with a stamp for their achievements are as diverse as Ruth Benedict (anthropology), Virginia Apgar (medicine), and Maria Mitchell (astronomy). Bring in stamps to show students or display the poster, *Putting Our Stamp on America* (available from National

Women's History Project, 7738 Bell Road, Windsor CA 95492-8518, 707-838-6000 <nwhp@aol.com>), which features 47 women on stamps. Do students recognize any of the names? Challenge students to discover why these women have appeared on stamps. Where would they look to find out more information about these people? Internet sites to start with include <www.greatwomen.org> and <www.legacy98.org>.

Stamps are issued for a person only after he or she is dead. Ask students whom they might like to see on a stamp and why. If your class uncovers a good candidate, you can begin a stamp campaign by writing to the U.S. Postal Service. Submit stamp proposals to:

Citizens' Stamp Advisory Committee
Stamp Development
U.S. Postal Service
475 L'Enfant Plaza, SW, Room 4474E
Washington DC 20260-2437

Women's Hall of Fame

What do these people have in common? List the following names on a chart:

Eleanor Roosevelt   Charlotte Perkins Gilman
Jane Addams   Betty Friedan
Rosa Parks   Barbara Jordan
Margaret Sanger   Helen Keller
Margaret Mead   Alice Paul

These women were all voted into the Women's Hall of Fame. Small groups of students can research the story of these women from history. For more information, write to:

The National Women's Hall of Fame
76 Fall Street
Seneca NY 13148

Calendar People

Create a calendar on which important dates can be noted. Each month, a committee can make a large calendar on the bulletin board on which to feature birthdays of famous people, as shown on page 292.

Students can research the birthdates for a specific group of people, as in the following:

Great American Women
April 3—Jane Goodall (1934–)
June 24—Amelia Earhart (1898–1937?)
June 27—Helen Keller (1880–1968)

S	M	T	W	Th	F	S
		1	2	3	4	5
6	7	8	9	10	11	12
13	14	15	16	17	18	19
20	21	22	23	24	25	26
27 HELEN KELLER 1880-1968	28	29	30			

October 11—Eleanor Roosevelt (1884–1962)
December 25—Clara Barton (1821–1912)

Each student can report on one person, explaining to the class why that person is considered important.

Here are a few biographies to get your students started:

Especially for Primary Students

Kathleen Krull. *Wilma Unlimited: How Wilma Rudolph Became the World's Fastest Woman.* Harcourt Brace, 1996.

Especially for Older Students

Tonya Bolden. *And Not Afraid to Dare: Stories of Ten African-American Women.* Scholastic, 1998. Includes women from Ellen Craft to Toni Morrison.
Russell Freedman. *Eleanor Roosevelt: A Life of Discovery.* Clarion, 1993.
Caroline Lazo. *Gloria Steinem: Feminist Extraordinaire.* Lerner, 1998.
Della Yannuzzi. *Mae Jemison: A Space Biography.* Enslow, 1998.

Note that all of the materials listed can be used as resources at any grade level.

The calendar can also include quotations from people whose birthdays are being celebrated. For example, feature this quote by Helen Keller:

> "We could never learn to be brave and patient,
> if there were only joy in the world."

Students can respond to these quotations orally or use them for a writing prompt.

Web of Literature

Explore different types of visual representations, ranging from brainstorming webs and idea clustering to task-specific organizers *(graphic organizers)* and thinking process maps, to help students see the internal organization or processes involved in any complex topic. These "maps" help students see what they need to learn about the topic and also serve as guidelines for writing. You can model developing a map at the beginning of a unit with the whole class. Later, have students use maps to focus their thinking individually or in small groups.

The simplest kind of mapping is the web, as illustrated on page 294 for *Number the Stars* by Lois Lowry, a novel about a family helping Jews escape from Denmark in World War II. Looking at this web, you can easily see the possibilities for organizing a thematic unit of study around this book.

Show students how to develop their own maps for reviewing a unit of study or organizing a research report.

For help in using map structures in the classroom, see:

Inspiration Software
PO Box 1629
Portland OR 97207

MacMapper
St. Johns University
Grand Central and Utopia Parkways
Jamaica NY 11439

Student to Student

Students are always interested in communicating with other people of their age, in this country and around the world. Some may already have penpals who live in other places. The students you contact do not have to be in other countries; some rural schools have developed an exchange with urban schools, for example. You can arrange for the class to participate in a penpal exchange by contacting one of the following organizations:

From *Multicultural Teaching: A Handbook of Activities, Information, and Resources,* 5/e by Pamela Tiedt and Iris Tiedt, Copyright © 1999 Allyn & Bacon. Reprinted by permission.

Fujifilm PhotoPals Nation of Neighbors
(for grades 3–6)
<www.scholastic.com/photopals>

National Geographic Society
Dept. GeoMail Pen Pal Network
PO Box 96088
Washington DC 20090-6088
<www.nationalgeographic.com/kids>

In addition, the international spread of the Internet allows students to make connections easily with others who have similar interests but who live far away.

On the Map

As you share children's literature with students, take the time to point out where in the world these books are set. Students can prepare ID tags or passports for every book they read and use string to pin them to the world map. They learn more and remember better when they can connect what they are reading with geography and information about different places. The following list of classic children's books demonstrates the range of possible locations:

Jean Craighead George. *Julie of the Wolves.*	Alaska
Virginia Hamilton. *The House of Dies Drear.*	Ohio
Lois Lowry. *Number the Stars.*	Denmark
Scott O'Dell. *Island of the Blue Dolphins.*	Channel Islands, California
Katherine Paterson. *Of Nightingales That Weep.*	Japan
Gary Soto. *Baseball in April and Other Stories.*	California Central Valley
Suzanne Fisher Staples. *Shabanu.*	Pakistan
Theodore Taylor. *The Cay.*	West Indies

Bon Voyage

Offer students a trip anywhere in the world for one month. Where would they like to go? Brainstorm together where students can find pictures, maps, information about the population, weather, geography, and history for the city or country they have selected. What else might they like to know about this place—the popular music, the food, the languages spoken? Once they have collected their information, they will need to write themselves a ticket, specifying the mode of transport and the length of journey. Remind them they only have a month. Next, they can prepare an itinerary, listing where they plan to go and what they want to see. The report of their trip can take the form of a travel journal, letters back home, or a talk accompanied by pictures.

You can increase the difficulty of this activity by having blindfolded students point to a location on a world map. The point that they select, land or ocean, will be their destination.

Print atlases for students to consult include:

National Geographic World Atlas for Young Explorers. National Geographic Society, 1999.

The Reader's Digest Children's Atlas of the World. Reader's Digest Young Families, 1999.

Ultimate Panoramic Atlas. DK Publishing, 1998.

Students might also investigate some of the CD-ROMs available, such as:

EnCarta Virtual Globe. Microsoft. For Windows.
Eyewitness World Atlas. DK Multimedia. For Windows.
My First Amazing World Explorer 2.0. DK Multimedia. For Windows, Macintosh.

Timeline of History

Students will have a clearer perspective on the length of historical time and be able to visualize the relationship of events and people in the past if you create a physical timeline, running a line of paper horizontally around the room, marked for every 50 years or so. Prepare a number of cards with interesting events, inventions, or people written on one side, and the year when they took place on the other. Students can draw a card from a basket and decide where to place it on the timeline. You can also have students draw two cards and ask them "Which came first?" Advanced students will enjoy creating more cards as they discover interesting facts.

Robin Hood	1190
cocoa beans imported to Europe	1520
walk on the moon	1969
Columbus reaches West Indies	1492
first telephone	1876
French invent metric system	1791
eyeglasses	1268
first vaccination (against smallpox)	1796
Pasteur—no more spoiled milk	1856
first television	1926
mechanical clock	1360
first world series (baseball)	1903
dynamite	1866
printing press (Gutenberg)	1452
first jeans	1873
Edison invented light bulb	1879
electronic pocket calculator	1971
first postage stamp	1840
Copernicus—earth rotates around sun	1530
first heart transplant	1967
South African blacks vote	1994
Newton's theory of gravity	1687

Working Together

This is a small-group activity that requires students to focus on cooperation. As described here, five people may play. If you want to use the game with more students, produce multiple sets of these materials.

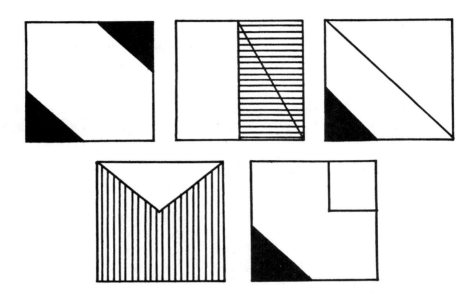

Each of the five players is given an envelope containing several pieces of construction paper. The shapes in all five envelopes potentially can make five squares, as shown in the illustration. The object of the game is to assemble the squares.

No one player, however, has enough pieces to form one square; therefore, all players must cooperate in order for each one to succeed. Rules for the game are:

- There is absolutely no talking.
- A player may give away pieces *only*. No player may take another player's pieces.

After the game is over, have a class meeting and discuss how players felt during this experience and the problems they encountered. Talk about when it is appropriate to cooperate with other people to solve a problem. What are the advantages and disadvantages of cooperation? When is *competition* effective or ineffective?

Taking a Time Machine

After studying a particular time period, plan a trip in a time machine with the class. Decide what date to set on the machine—for example, April 15, 1861. When students walk into the class, they will enter that day in history. Discuss beforehand how to prepare for the trip: what the classroom will look like, what clothes the students should wear, what books to read, and so on. When they take the time machine the next day, back to their usual time, the students can write a description of their experiences for that day as a diary entry.

A model for this trip is the Magic School Bus, which seems to be able to travel anywhere. Students will be interested in *The Magic School Bus: The Busasaurus* (video), which shows the class going back to visit the dinosaurs.

All the News

The daily newspaper is a rich source of teaching material for all the content areas. Some papers have a program for newspapers in the schools; others may be willing to donate class copies.

Primary students can tell stories about the pictures and cut out examples of words they can read. Talk about newspaper vocabulary, such as *headlines* and *bylines.* Cut the news pages apart for older students so they can match the story with its headline or write their own. Divide the newspaper into sections and have groups of students analyze each one. What can be found in the paper? Interviews, photographs, classified ads, crosswords, graphs and tables, editorials, letters, and movie reviews are a few examples. The question of what is *not* included in the newspaper is more challenging. Students can analyze whether the paper offers adequate news coverage of their school or neighborhood, for example.

Students may decide to create their own newspaper. *The Furry News: How to Make a Newspaper* by Loreen Leedy (Holiday House, 1990) shows how to go about putting a newspaper together and explains the terminology involved.

The newpaper format is also appropriate as a culminating project for a unit of study. Students can assemble what they have learned into feature stories, comic strips, advice columns, recipes, fashion, maps, and entertainment coverage. In addition, they will be practicing writing in a variety of genres, such as exposition and persuasion, and communicating in different media, such as drawing and photography. *The Stone Age News* by Fiona MacDonald (Candlewick, 1998) is an excellent example of what can be done with this format.

Social Studies Categories

This game can be adapted to review whatever subject the class is studying. For instance, use the word *History* to send children exploring books and other resources.

The object of the game is to fill in as many spaces as possible with a word beginning with the letter on the left. Encourage students to think of different possible answers. You can increase the difficulty by limiting the answers to a particular period or place.

	Countries	*People in History*	*Cities*
H	Hungary	Hitler	Helsinki
I	Ireland		
S	Spain		Seattle
T	Turkey	Thoreau	Toledo
O	Oman		
R	Romania	Roosevelt	Rome
Y	Yemen		

Classroom Time Capsule

With all the interest in the beginning of the new millennium, students will be motivated to talk about the next 100 years and what they might bring. What would students want to tell the young people of the future about the life of today? Explain that people often create *time capsules* in order to preserve memories and artifacts of the world in their time. Brainstorm with students what they might include in a time capsule for people a century from now. Decide what kind of container they will use that can last for 100 years. Where can the time capsule be kept so that it is retrievable in 100 years? Because the space in the container will be limited, it is important that students discuss their choices carefully in order to reach a consensus on the contents.

Teaching and Learning in Science and Math

Teachers sometimes have the mistaken impression that science and mathematics have little to do with learning language arts skills. Yet, scientists do write and mathematicians do discuss theories, so communication is an integral aspect of any field of study. The following activities demonstrate ways to integrate language arts into science and math.

Class Word Wall

Before beginning a science topic, list some related vocabulary words on the board. For example:

> tide
> bathysphere
> oceanographer
> current
> scuba

Ask the students what these words have in common. If they guess that the words are all related to the *sea,* does that help them figure out what *oceanographer* means? Challenge students to uncover the meaning of any new words. As they look up the words, they will run across others to add to the list. Post these examples on the Word Wall for students to refer back to later. The class can prepare a poster or a book showing the words and definitions, which can be consulted during their study of this topic.

Let's Classify

Once the class has developed an extensive list of vocabulary, talk about how to classify these words. What concepts tie some words together? Help students associate related words with a label for that class of words: occupations, technology, and measurement, for example. Do all of the words fall into a class or category? Do some words belong in more than one classification? Students will see the importance of classification in organizing a large amount of information.

Observing and Recording

Students can learn to collect and analyze data by looking at their environment for examples of nature and seasonal changes. Have them record their observations as a group in a Class Nature Log or individually in a journal or diary. Students can note changes in plants and animals according to the seasons, and record weather data such as temperature, rainfall, and wind direction from appropriate instruments. At the end of the school year, students can review their data and chart the seasonal variation,. What was the coolest day? The warmest day? On what day did the first leaves fall? If you keep a journal each year, students can compare their information to that of previous years.

I've Got the World on a String

Teach students important observation skills through this activity. Give each student a piece of string approximately two feet long. When each student has tied the ends together to make a circle, the class goes outside to a grassy area or anywhere on the playground. Each person chooses a place to lay his or her string to form a circle. The task for each student is to study and observe the world within this circle. Depending on the maturity of the student and the time available, students can observe what's going on not only on the surface but below the surface. Challenge them to record how many things there are in this little world. On returning to the classroom, they can describe either orally or in written form what they have just observed in their circles. They can also draw a picture or map of their world.

A Bug's Eye View

Following the previous activity, inform the class that they are to be an insect, a worm, or any small animal. They are to *become* that animal and tell what their world would look like: where they would live, what they would eat, what they might see and do. Students can use the first person as they take on the perspective of their chosen bug. Possible topics include:

> My Life as a Fly
> If I Were a Grasshopper

Create an Animal

After discussing what animals need in order to live, ask students to consider the question of animals that live on other planets. Your discussion might take the following path: "Most animals we know have two eyes. Can you imagine an animal with five eyes, or one eye? How would this animal make use of its eye(s)?" After discussing some ideas as a group, have students begin to sketch their imagined animal. Continue the discussion as students decide how their animal will move, eat, and communicate.

When students have finished inventing their animal, they can give it a name and write a story about where it lives and how it behaves.

Air, Land, or Sea!

Play this game in pairs or small groups. A student selects one of the categories: *air, land,* or *sea*. Then she or he points to another student and counts to five. The person pointed to must name an animal, for example, that lives on land (rabbit, pig, elephant, etc.) If the person names an appropriate animal before the number five is reached, then she or he is the next one to select the category. A particular animal or creature or species can be named only once. This activity can be developed on different levels of sophistication and can be played on a point basis if the group plays for some time.

Pet Animals

Ask if anyone in the class has a pet animal at home. What different kinds of animals are represented? Have students discuss which animals might make good pets. Each student selects an unusual animal to investigate and reports the findings to the class on the topic of "Why (or why not) you should choose _____ for a good pet." As a conclusion, the class can vote on which animal would be their favorite pet.

Preparing this presentation will require students to assemble and analyze information about their chosen animal as well as create persuasive strategies to influence the opinion of their audience. For example, students might pretend that they have this particular animal for sale.

Animal Idioms

Talk with students about animals used in the English language. People often compare others to animals or associate animals with certain qualities, as in these similes, for example:

eats like a horse	busy as a bee
walks like a cat	quiet as a mouse
roars like a lion	slippery as an eel

What characteristics of the animal are represented in each expression? Have students research the animals and determine whether the comparison has any validity in nature.

Some books to share with students are:

Stephanie Calmenson. *Shaggy, Waggy Dogs.* Clarion, 1998.
Lori Coleman. *My Pet Fish.* Lerner, 1998.
Patricia Lauber. *The True-or-False Book of Cats.* National Geographic, 1998.

Animal Stereotypes

Many idioms or expressions that refer to animals are based on prejudice rather than scientific observation. For instance, as students learn about the clean habits of a pig, they might decide that using the word *pig* in negative phrases—such as "eats like a pig" and "has a room like a pigsty"—is not a useful comparison. In fact, many animals have been associated with stereotypes in this way. Ask students if they can think of other animals that have a similarly negative reputation. Examples that they might mention are *rat* and *snake*. What images or impressions do we associate with these animals? Do these ideas have a factual basis or do they represent stereotypes? Perhaps a student who keeps a rat or snake as a pet can share information about their true nature. Students can also investigate how different animals are given positive or negative characteristics when they are portrayed in literature, video, and folklore.

Study Color

Utilize your students' interest in color to motivate writing and speaking. The following are suggestions that you might use to elicit student reactions to color:

- What color makes you feel good?
- What color makes you feel bad?
- What color is happiness?
- What color is pain?
- What color is Sunday?

Use these questions to begin a study of color as a science unit.

Flannelboard Review

Students will enjoy reviewing basic concepts in science when you illustrate them with flannelboard figures. For example, make a flannelboard cut-out for each stage of the butterfly's life cycle and use it to teach students the sequence. Then students can use the same figures to retell the story to each other or to other classes.

Combining oral language tasks with objects that can be manipulated helps key students' memories and reinforces concepts learned.

Fact or Fiction?

Research can help students learn to distinguish between science facts and common misconceptions. Is Mt. Everest really the tallest mountain? Students will find out by reading *The Dinosaur Is the Biggest Animal That Ever Lived, and Other Wrong Ideas You Thought Were True,* by Seymour Simon (New York: Lippincott, 1984). Students can prepare a "Science Trivia" bulletin board with questions such as "What's the biggest animal that ever lived?" written on cards that they turn over to find the answer.

Individual Lists

Have students choose one topic that interests them, about which they will collect words. For one week, the children search diligently, using varied sources, to develop their individual word lists. They can also help each other. For example, if everyone knows that Henry is collecting horse words, they will pass any they happen to find on to him.

These lists can be used to develop word collages including pictures related to the theme chosen. Or each student can copy his or her list on pages for a class book entitled "Master Word Lists."

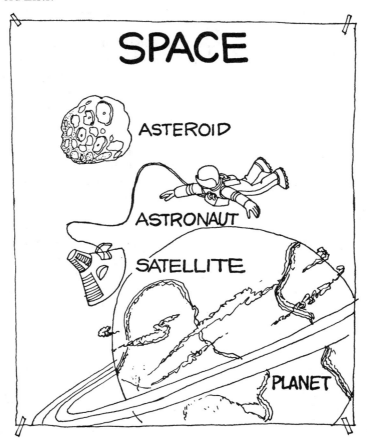

Word Brackets

Motivating students to explore the dictionary is easy with this game. Students can work by themselves and with each other to think up longer and more obscure words. The game is set up by writing a word vertically down the left side of the paper and then reversing it up the right side. The object is to think of words that begin with the letter in the first column and end with the letter in the other column.

S impl **E**
P icni **C**
A rom **A**
C atni **P**
E xactnes **S**

The word that forms the frame can be chosen to fit a school subject, such as *Science,* or a particular topic like *Mexico* or *Winter.* Vary the difficulty of the game by limiting the meaning of the words used to fill in. If your class is studying the sea, use *Ocean* for your bracket, and ask students to think of the sea's inhabitants, ocean-related occupations, and descriptive terms for the ocean.

Score this game by adding up the number of letters between the vertical columns. You may also wish to develop a way of rewarding the more unusual responses. Students are encouraged to develop their vocabulary by looking for longer and longer words and they will become interested in the meaning of these words.

Another advantage of this game is that students become more aware of spelling rules and word endings. Most people are accustomed to thinking of the beginnings of words but not of how they end. The letter *s* at the end is easily seen as a plural. Letters *g* and *d* can be used for *ing* and *ed.* Knowing suffixes (and prefixes) adds to the skill of playing the game. Students will begin to pay attention to less obvious suffixes such as *al* (seasonal), *ment* (enjoyment), and *tion* (exploration). Students will observe that the same letter can represent different sounds; for example, an *h* at the end can be preceded by *c* (church) or by *g* (rough).

Display the longest and most creative solutions to motivate further vocabulary development. Students can discuss the meaning of these words and the patterns of spelling and suffixes. This activity adapts well to different levels because everyone will have an opportunity to learn words that are new to them.

This game can also be made easier by allowing students to use words that include the letter in the right-hand bracket without ending in it. In this case, the score includes only the letters inside the brackets. The letters extending beyond them do not count.

Word People in Science

One of the ways of improving students' knowledge about science and also enlarging their vocabulary at the same time is to introduce them to the concept of Word People. Many terms and labels in science come from the name of the person who developed or discovered them. For example, Alexander Garden, a botanist, developed the *gardenia* flower, which is named after him. The *volt,* a measure of electricity, is named after Alessandro Volta, an Italian physicist.

As an activity, you might develop a list of people and have the students research what terms came from the people's names. Here are a few more examples of people and the word they gave their name to, also called an *eponym.*

- J. G. Zinn, German botanist   (zinnia)
- George Ohm, German physicist   (ohm)
- James Watt, Scottish inventor   (watt)
- Joel R. Poinsett, U.S. Ambassador to Mexico   (poinsettia)
- John McAdam, Scottish engineer   (macadam)

Science Is Multicultural

Although science is often presented as the province of white European males, many people from different cultures, both men and women, have contributed to scientific knowledge. Use resources such as the following to provide examples of significant scientific developments that come from different ancient cultures:

> George Beshore. *Science in Ancient China.* Franklin Watts, 1998.
> George Beshore. *Science in Early Islamic Cultures.* Franklin Watts, 1998.

Women in Science Today

Students can investigate the work that scientists who happen to be female are doing right now. Focus student attention on the role of women in many different fields by reading and discussing some of the following biographies:

> Carole Ann Camp. *Sally Ride.* Enslow, 1997.
> Kathryn Lasky. *The Most Beautiful Roof in the World: Exploring the Rainforest Canopy.* Harcourt Brace, 1997. Story of Meg Lowman, field scientist who works in Belize, Central America.
> Virginia Meachum. *Jane Goodall.* Enslow, 1997.
> Laurence Pringle. *Elephant Woman: Cynthia Moss Explores the World of Elephants.* Atheneum, 1997.

Robots Are Wonderful

Probably many students have wished that they had a machine or robot that did homework or completed their chores so that they would not have to. The word *robot* comes from the Czech *robota*, to work. As robots become more and more complex today, students can almost see their wishes come true. Ask students what they would like to have a robot do for them—maybe turn spinach into chocolate? Pick up clothes and make the bed? Play all the positions in baseball? Primary students can draw pictures of their robot, showing what it can do, and older students can describe the different parts (gears, levers, whistles) that will be required for the robot or other kind of machine to operate (see page 306).

Science and Creative Thinking

One excellent device for challenging students to think about their world in different ways is to ask them some provocative "What ifs": What if the oceans started drying up? What if dolphins could talk? Some additional examples are given here to help your students get started on this activity. They will, of course, be able to think of many more once they are started. Some can be used in oral discussions; others can be written about in a creative writing period. The important thing is that this activity rewards divergent thinking, or thinking "outside the bounds."

What if...

- it was always cloudy?
- you were a dolphin?
- all the planets switched positions?
- you could talk to birds?
- there was no gravity on earth?
- the world was flat instead of round?
- all plants began to die?
- all the rivers dried up?
- you discovered the skeleton of an unknown animal?
- you could grow a fantasy garden?

This activity adapts well to different levels, because students can use a variety of media through which to express their ideas: creative drama, art, oral discussion, writing, and so on.

The Question Box

The purpose of the Question Box is to encourage children to ask questions, which is an important skill to develop in science as well as in other areas. Provide a box where students can place questions that they want answered. They can also indicate topics that they want to know more about. These questions can be signed or unsigned. Provide opportunities for students to write questions.

These questions provide information to you about the areas of interest and concern to students. Periodically, questions should be pulled from this box and used as class discussions or as suggested areas for further study. This is an activity that can be conducted throughout the year.

Group Decision Making

This task requires group decision making, which involves individual decisions, group discussion, and group consensus. It is very important that students have this type of small-group experience. Although this is a somewhat artificial situation, it stimulates the type of activity that students will be involved in throughout their lives: decision making within groups.

Decision by Consensus
Prepared by NASA

1. Individual Decision

Instructions:
You are a member of a space crew originally scheduled to rendezvous with a mother ship on the lighted surface of the moon. Because of mechanical difficulties, however, your ship was forced to land at a spot some 200 miles from the rendezvous point. During the landing, much of the ship and the equipment aboard were damaged, and since survival depends on reaching the mother ship, the most critical items still available must be chosen for the 200-mile trip. Below are listed the 15 items left intact and undamaged after landing. Your task is to rank them in order of their importance in allowing your crew to reach the rendezvous point. Place the number 1 by the most important item, the number 2 by the second most important, and so on through number 15, the least important.

_____Box of matches
_____Food concentrate
_____50 feet of nylon rope
_____Parachute silk
_____Portable heating unit
_____Two .45-caliber pistols
_____One case of dehydrated milk
_____Two 100-pound tanks of oxygen
_____Map of the stars as seen from the moon
_____Life raft
_____Magnetic compass
_____5 gallons of water
_____Signal flares
_____First-aid kit containing injection needles
_____Solar-powered FM receiver-transmitter

2. Group Consensus

This is an exercise in group decision making. Your group is to employ the method of group consensus in reaching its decision. This means that the prediction for each of the fifteen survival items *must* be agreed upon by each group member before it becomes a part of the group decision. Consensus is difficult to reach. Therefore, not every ranking will meet with everyone's complete approval. Try, as a group, to make each ranking one with which *all* group members can at least partially agree. Here are some guides to use in reaching consensus:

a. Avoid arguing for your own individual judgments. Approach the task on the basis of logic.

b. Avoid changing your mind only in order to reach agreement and eliminate conflict. Support only solutions with which you are able to agree to some extent, at least.

c. Avoid conflict-reducing techniques such as majority vote, averaging, or trading in reaching decisions.

d. View differences of opinion as helpful rather than as a hindrance in decision making.

On the Group Summary Sheet place the individual rankings made earlier by each group member. Take as much time as you need in reaching your group decision.

	1	2	3	4	5	6	7	8	9	10	11	12	**Group Predictions**
Box of matches													
Food concentrate													
50 feet of nylon rope													
Parachute silk													
Portable heating unit													
Two .45-caliber pistols													
One case of dehydrated milk													
Two 100-pound tanks of oxygen													
Map of the stars as seen from the moon													
Life raft													
Magnetic compass													
5 gallons of water													
Signal flares													

Group Summary Sheet / Individual Predictions

First-aid kit containing injection needles												
Solar-powered FM receiver-transmitter												

Group _____

Key: Take the difference between your ranking and the ranking on the key. Add the differences. The lower the score the better. These answers are based on the best judgments that are now available. They are not absolute answers.

15	Box of matches	Little or no use on moon.
4	Food concentrate	Supply of daily food required.
6	50 feet of nylon rope	Useful in tying injured together; helpful in climbing.
8	Parachute silk	Shelter against sun's rays.
13	Portable heating unit	Useful only if party landed on dark side of moon.
11	Two .45-caliber pistols	Self-propulsion devices could be made from them.
12	One case of dehydrated milk	Food; mixed with water for drinking.
1	Two 100-pound tanks of oxygen	Fills respiration requirement.
3	Map of the stars as seen from the moon	One of the principal means of finding directions.
9	Life raft	CO_2 bottles for self-propulsion across chasms, etc.
14	Magnetic compass	Probably no magnetized poles; thus useless
2	5 gallons of water	Replenishes loss by sweating, etc.
10	Signal flares	Distress call when line of sight possible.
7	First-aid kit containing injection needles	Oral pills or injection medicine valuable.
5	Solar-powered FM receiver-transmitter	Distress-signal transmitter— possible communication with mother ship.

3. Critique

Following the exercise, discuss the sources of the problem-solving techniques. How often did individuals use the *affective* domain in working out the problem? How often did the *cognitive* domain dominate? What kind of balance existed? How did their knowledge of the familiar world allow them to work with the unknowns? What did they learn about their own learning styles? Did they work better in groups or alone? Did they score higher as a group, or was the individual score better? How did the scores compare with the group average? Did they enjoy the individual work more than the group work?

Science Acrostic

At the end of a unit, give students a thematic word or phrase and ask them to make an acrostic and construct sentences beginning with each letter. Here is an example done by students who completed a unit study on seasons:

> *Seasons change according to nature's timetable.*
> *Each season is about three months long.*
> *Autumn is when plants die and animals store food to prepare for winter.*
> *Spring is the season of new life.*
> *Old Man Winter brings cold weather and ice and snow.*
> *Nice, sunny weather makes summer the favorite season.*
> *Seasons are different in different parts of the world.*

The acrostic form can also be used to write poetry. Students can suggest ideas for a collective poem such as the following:

> *Wild winds blowing,*
> *Icicles hanging from the roof,*
> *Noses are red from the cold.*
> *The tinkle of sleigh bells is heard.*
> *Eagerly children await*
> *Reindeer and vacation, too.*

Students enjoy creating their own acrostics. Have students make acrostics to fit a book they have read, seasons, or current events. Acrostics relate spelling and vocabulary development to student interests.

Another format for science acrostics is the ABC book. *Spring: An Alphabet Acrostic,* by Steven Schnur (Clarion, 1999) and illustrated by Leslie Evans, includes an acrostic poem for each letter, such as DAWN for D and NEST for N.

Scrambled Words

For a quick review of words learned in a science unit, mix up some familiar words and put them on the board for students to unscramble.

losra tesysm	solar system
aletspn	planets

leecospet	telescope
apecs	space
ultop	Pluto
onortasym	astronomy
uoatstrna	astronaut

Students can prepare examples to stump their classmates. If you divide the class into two teams, all students will benefit from the vocabulary review.

Animal Poems

Read students several poems by Douglas Florian, from books such as *Mammalabilia* (Harcourt, 1999) and *Insectolopedia* (Harcourt, 1998). This poet enjoys using language in surprising ways to portray a range of animals. Students can use Florian's poems as models in order to write their own poems about the animals that interest them.

Cinquain Summaries

The cinquain poetry form lends itself to concise presentations of science topics—for example, ecology and pollution. This type of writing is a good way of summarizing what students have learned in a particular science unit. The students can write the cinquain poem and then illustrate it with their own pictures or pictures they select from magazines. A collage used to illustrate and summarize the end of a science unit might include this poem:

> *Pollution*
> *Unhealthy Litter*
> *Human Garbage Heaps*
> *Man's Inhumanity to Life*
> *Ugly*

Picture This

One creative way to end a science unit is to have students draw a picture of what they have studied and then write related words around the picture. For example, after studying whales, students can draw a picture and write words (adjectives, nouns, and verbs) such as *baleen, humpback, plankton, minke, playful,* and *spraying* (see page 312).

More resources for teaching about whales are available from the following website: <curry.edschool.Virginia.EDU/go/Whales>.

Humor and Science

Students will enjoy writing silly poems about complex science topics. The limerick is a natural form to use, as in this example by an anonymous writer:

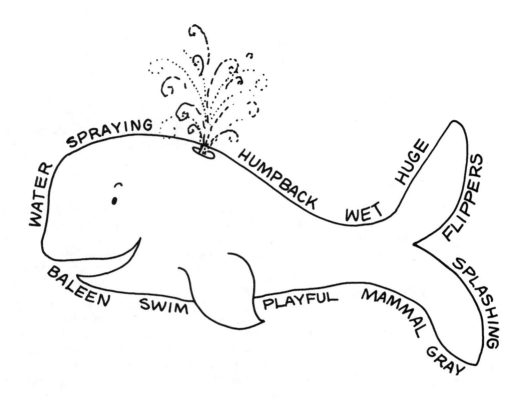

Relativity

There was a young lady named Bright,
Who traveled much faster than light,
She started one day
In a relative way,
And returned on the previous night.

Word Bingo

Use this game to review difficult vocabulary. Provide students with a list of at least 30 words you wish to practice. Have the students write 24 words at random on a bingo grid. Students can place a marker on the appropriate square as you pronounce the words, give definitions, or provide synonyms (see page 313).

Calendars and Time

The study of calendars and how people measure time integrates science and math topics. Students can examine calendars historically and explore how different ancient cultures, such as the Babylonians and the Aztecs, measured the length of the lunar month and the

BOTANY BINGO

STEM	OVARY	ZYGOTE	CORK	RHIZOME
LEAF	FLOWER	BULB	SEED	OSMOSIS
NODE	PETAL	FREE	NEEDLE	FRUIT
SPORE	BARK	BUD	ROOT	PITH
TUBER	CLONE	PISTIL	POLLEN	VEIN

solar year. Students can also look at how the ability to observe changes in the moon and the sun depended on advances in astronomy and technology. In addition, many different calendars are still in use around the world. Ask students to calculate today's date in calendars such as the Chinese, the Jewish, and the Islamic.

Pose students questions such as the following:

- What were some of the reasons that people needed to know the month or the year?
- How do astronomers measure time?
- Why does the New Year occur on different days in some calendars?

- Why do we have a 12- or 24-hour day?
- How does the atomic clock work?

Tell students that you expect them to use a variety of resources and not just one article, book, or Internet site as they research these questions. To introduce the subject of time, offer students *The Story of Clocks and Calendars: Marking a Millennium* by Betsy Maestro (Lothrop, Lee, Shepard, 1999), illustrated by Giulio Maestro.

Numbers Play Tricks

There are many tricks that students can learn to do with numbers that will make the unsuspecting think they are mental wizards. Show students how to guess another person's age, for example:

- Multiply your age by 10.
- Now multiply 9 by any lower number.
- Subtract this product from the first product.
- What's the answer?

(To get the person's age, you add the two digits of the answer together. If it is three digits, the first two digits are one number that is added to the third digit, to get the age.) Challenge students to analyze this process and figure out the trick.

Super-Calculators

These two sequences always produce the same number, no matter what number the person starts with. Tell someone that you will guess his or her secret number by guessing the result of a series of calculations.

- Choose a number from 1 to 8.
- Add 9.
- Double the sum.
- Subtract 4.
- Divide by 2.
- Subtract the chosen number.
     (The answer is always 7.)

- Choose any number.
- Multiply it by 5.
- Add 25 to the product.
- Divide the sum by 5.
- Subtract the chosen number.

• Multiply the remainder by 3.
    (The answer is always 15.)

Students can amaze their friends with these simple mental math tricks. They will be so enthralled to see these tricks work that they will be motivated to learn *how* they work.

Lucky Numbers

Another aspect of the power of numbers is that people think some numbers are lucky and others unlucky. Ask students to provide examples, such as, Why is the number 13 considered unlucky? Some numbers have mathematical powers. There is always something special about *primes,* for example, and *squares.* Introduce these concepts to students and discuss some examples.

Prepare a bulletin board featuring a number. "All about 7" could include expressions featuring the number 7 and facts about 7.

> ***All about 7***
> 7th heaven
> 7 league boots
> the 7 Wonders of the World
> at 6s and 7s
> 7 is a prime
> the square of 7 is 49

Adventures of a Number

Ask the students to pick a favorite number and write an adventure about that number. You may wish to help students begin the adventures of their numbers by asking questions such as:

> How is your number special?
> Is your number old or young?
> Does the shape of your number influence its movement?
> How was your number invented?
> What is your number's favorite operation? (+, −, ×, ÷)
> Where does your number work?
> Is your number lucky or unlucky?
> What does your number do in its time off?

The Magic of Doubling

The power of numbers is often a feature in folklore, where the number of tasks to complete or the number of wishes to be granted is always *three. One Grain of Rice: A Mathematical*

Folkltale by Demi (Scholastic, 1997) demonstrates another power of numbers. In this traditional Indian tale, the hero's reward is a single grain of rice, to be doubled each day. Have students calculate how much rice he will have after 30 days.

Numbers Count

Many picturebooks for primary readers are designed as counting books, to introduce and reinforce numbers. Share one of these books, such as *Arlene Alda's 1, 2, 3, What Do You See?* by Arlene Alda (Tricycle Press, 1998), or *1, 2, 3, to the Zoo* by Eric Carle (Putnam, 1998), with students and talk about the characteristics of a counting book. Have students brainstorm what they might put in a counting book. Primary students can choose items to make their own counting book, whereas older students can work together to design a counting book appropriate for younger students.

Students working with larger numbers will enjoy *Miss Bindergarten Celebrates the 100th Day of Kindergarten* by Joseph Slate (Dutton, 1998). Like Miss Bindergarten's class, your class can bring in objects (real or imaginary) to celebrate the day of school, the day of the month, or the day of the year. The students can also draw pictures of their contributions.

Students will learn more about numbers from Denise Schmandt-Besserat in *The History of Counting,* illustrated by Michael Hays (Morrow, 1999).

Math-a-Phobia

Some students in your class may have learned to hate math. Use a story, such as *The Number Devil* by Hans Magnus Enzensberger (Metropolitan/Holt, 1998), to introduce the topic of Math Phobia and then talk with students about their dreads and anxieties. Enlist the whole class in generating strategies for dealing with these fears. Students can draw pictures of how they feel during math activities and share them in small groups.

Another book to share about overcoming math phobia is Cindy Neuschwander's *Amanda Bean's Amazing Dream* (Scholastic, 1998).

Number Hunt

Divide your class into small groups to investigate the numbers in your classroom. Give each group a list of categories to fill, such as:

- List 3 things that come in pairs.   (shoes, socks, barrettes)
- List 1 thing that comes in 16s.   (crayons)
- List 1 thing that comes in 12s.   (numbers of a clock, eggs)
- List 1 thing that comes in 6s.   (jacks)

Expensive Words

Motivate interest in both spelling and math by giving letters monetary values, as follows:

A	1	J	6	R	1
B	2	K	4	S	1
C	4	L	2	T	1
D	2	M	2	U	1
E	1	N	2	V	7
F	5	O	1	W	6
G	3	P	1	X	10
H	4	Q	9	Y	5
I	1			Z	8

Because the less commonly used letters are given higher values, students will be encouraged to spell more difficult words. Longer words also carry higher values just because they contain more letters. A word such as *xylophone* would be a very high-priced word, worth 27 cents.

Give students assignments designed to use this monetary system. For example:

- What is the most expensive holiday you can think of?
- Spell at least three animals worth more than one dime.
- How much is this lunch worth: peanut butter and jelly sandwich, milk, orange.
- You have $1.00 to buy four words. List your four words and the price of each.

Compute This Riddle!

Students enjoy riddles and will quickly learn to recheck their computations if the numbers do not translate into a sensible answer. After students become familiar with the format, you may wish to organize a Riddle Workshop by providing riddle books and asking pairs of students to create computation riddles for the rest of the class. Note that each letter must have a unique value, like a code.

A	12	N	21
B	4	O	14
C	1	P	26
D	18	Q	11
E	9	R	24
F	23	S	7
G	2	T	20
H	16	U	13
I	5	V	22
J	25	W	8
K	10	X	19
L	15	Y	6
M	3	Z	17

Riddle

How many elephants can you put in an empty boxcar?*

| 19 | 7 | 16 | 17 | | 6 | 30 | 12 | 7 | 12 | | 6 | 30 | 6 | | 21 | 8 | 5 | 30 | 9 | 24 | 28 | 14 |
| +3 | +7 | +5 | −8 | | +6 | −7 | +8 | +2 | +12 | | +8 | −9 | +1 | | −12 | +7 | +4 | −4 | +7 | −12 | −7 | +6 |

_____,   _____   _____   _____

| 14 | 11 | | 4 | 13 | | 17 | 16 | 13 | | 18 | 6 | 30 | 10 | 14 |
| −9 | +9 | | +1 | −6 | | +4 | −2 | +7 | | −9 | −3 | −4 | +10 | −8 |

_____   _____   _____   _____!

Secret Codes

Putting messages or other important information in code is a great motivator for practicing particular math skills. Older and more advanced students will especially enjoy this challenge to their skills, as they create codes and encode or decode "secret" transmissions. For more code activities, check Bob Hugel's *Secret Code Math: Kids Solve Math Problems to Crack Secret Codes and Reinforce Essential Math Skills* (Scholastic, 1999).

Celebrating Math

Students will always remember the value of *pi* if you have them celebrate Pi Days on March 14 at 1:59 P.M. precisely. They can eat pie, cut circles out of paper, measure balloons, make beads to wear and so on while you talk about the relationship between the circumference of a circle and the diameter.

Math Vocabulary

Help students learn new vocabulary by having them compare a math dictionary with definitions of terms written in their own words. Writing a definition for themselves will clarify their understanding of the terms and they will find their own definition easier to remember than those memorized from a book. For example:

- Triangle: It always has three sides but can be different shapes.

Creative Math Writing

Have students write letters explaining the concept or process they are learning. These letters can be addressed to real or imaginary beings. The letters should be used to monitor concept comprehension and not be corrected for spelling or grammar.

*Answer: None, after one elephant it is not empty!

Dear Hamlet Hamster,

This is a picture of a right triangle. The little square means that the angle is exactly 90°, like one of the corners of a square. The other two angles also add up to 90° since all three angles of a triangle must equal 180°.

Personalized Math

To maintain student interest in written and oral word problems, create problems featuring your students' names.

The sunflower Demian planted in his garden began growing this morning. If Demian's sunflower grows an average of 3 cm a day, how tall will it be in two weeks?

Rava and her family are going to Disneyland during vacation. Rava's father will wake her up at 6:00 A.M. Rava's mother will serve breakfast 30 minutes later. Write the time that Rava should be at the breakfast table on your paper.

Students will enjoy suggesting new situations for word problems and creating problems of their own.

Divergent Problems

Challenge your students by presenting them with problems that require careful reading and thinking. Practice strategies for identifying and solving each type of problem before expecting students to solve these problems on challenge worksheets.

- *Problems with extra information:* Ask students to cross out the unnecessary details and to circle the important ones.

  Michael and Vincent went to the store to buy vegetables for supper. Artichokes were 4 for $1.00. Corn was 8 ears for $1.50. Celery was 49 cents a bunch. Radishes were 39 cents a bunch. Lettuce was 79 cents a head. How much change did Michael and Vincent get if they paid $5.00 for 2 heads of lettuce and 6 artichokes?

- *Insufficient information:* Ask the students to identify what additional information is needed to solve the problem.

  Emily rode her bike to the store to buy supplies for her birthday party. She bought 20 balloons for 2 cents each, 2 packages of paper plates for 79 cents each, 3 bags of peanuts for $1.29 each, and 2 sacks of mints for 89 cents each. How much change did Emily get?

- *More than one answer:* Show your students that some problems have several right answers.

David got a 10-gallon fish tank for his birthday. He can put about 1 inch of fish per gallon in his new tank. David wants to buy some Pearl Gourami and some Bala Sharks. The Pearl Gourami are about 1 inch long and the Bala Sharks are about 1 ½ inches long. How many of each should he buy?

Estimation Game

Give the students oral or written problems to demonstrate the importance of estimation. Use examples that show the value of this process in daily life. How can you answer the question without doing all the computation?

The PTA will give out juice bars to celebrate our first 2-mile jog. They have 400 juice bars and want to know if that will be enough for everyone. Here is the enrollment for each class: 28, 23, 29, 27, 24, 32, 29, 26, 28, 31, 27, 23, 22, 28. Does the PTA have enough juice bars?

Kipp saw that he had exactly $10.00 when he opened his wallet. Does he have enough money to buy all of this?

orange juice	$1.29
apples	$1.89
crackers	$1.85
carrots	$.79
soap	$2.19

Graphing Your School

Divide your class into small groups to survey another class or the entire student body. After the data have been collected, conduct a workshop to decide the best visual format for presentation of each topic (bar graph, pie graph, etc.). Display the results in a central location. Topics might include:

number of students in each grade
favorite school lunch
favorite subject in school
hours spent on homework
favorite weekend activity
age of students (years and months)

Pesos or Pounds?

Provide your students with a currency conversion chart from the newspaper and a list of problems, such as:

- Would you rather have 100 pesos or 100 pounds?
- How many Canadian dollars would you get for 10 U.S. dollars?
- How many French francs would you get for 150 lira?

Invite students to bring in examples of money from other countries. Prepare tags listing the name of the money and the country of origin. Include a sample of U.S. currency. Ask students to rank the money by value. Provide conversion charts (or display U.S. equivalents for younger children) and discuss relative values.

England: pence, pound	France: centime, franc
Mexico: peso	Italy: lira
India: rupee	Austria: shilling
Japan: yen	Germany: mark

The Decimal System

When Americans count money, they use the decimal system (based on 10) so that 100 pennies equals 1 dollar. Can students think of other systems that Americans use to count or measure things? (3 feet in a yard, 12 months in a year, 2 pints in a quart might be examples.) In addition, students may have noticed that parallel systems are used in science (inches and centimeters) and speed (miles and kilometers). Discuss with students the advantages and disadvantages of different systems. Have students hypothesize how this complicated system of measurement might have arisen. Students can then check their hypotheses by investigating the background to these different systems. Look for books—such as Kathryn Lasky's story of Eratosthenes, *The Librarian Who Measured the Earth* (Little, Brown, 1994)—to show students how measurement developed.

Challenge older students to explore the reasons why the United States continues to use its idiosyncratic measures of inches and miles and has not officially adopted the decimal system used elsewhere.

Math Practice

The computer can be especially helpful in providing additional practice for students who need assistance and challenging problems for advanced students. Check out these recommended CD-ROMs:

> *Awesome Animated Monster Maker Math.* Houghton.
> *Math FactMaster.* Curriculum Associates. Mac/Windows.
>   <www. curriculumassocates. com>
> *Math Word Problems.* Optimum Resource. Mac/Windows.
>   <www.stickybear.com>

Teaching and Learning in Art and Music

The fine arts can do much to enhance learning language arts skills. Conversely, the language arts have much to offer students as they acquire a knowledge base related to art and music. This section presents activities designed to support the integration of language arts into the study of both art and music. Students will be able to practice reading and writing, speaking and listening in meaningful contexts as they explore learning about video, collage, and dance, for example.

Video Stories

Check your library to see what classics of children's literature are available on video for your grade level. Students can watch a video after they have read the story and analyze the differences between the two experiences. Ask them to think about the visual images presented. How did these images compare to the descriptive language of the book? What sounds and music were used for the soundtrack? What effect did that have on their experience?

Students will enjoy being taken behind the scenes of a video production in *Take a Look, It's in the Book: How Television Is Made at Reading Rainbow* by Ronnie Kraus (Walker, 1997).

The Power of Visual Images

The power of images is not limited to moving pictures. Even still pictures—photographs—can influence people. Many photographers have become famous, not only for artistic ability but also because their photographs have illuminated social problems and led to social change. *Restless Spirit: The Life of Dorothea Lange* by Elizabeth Partridge (Viking, 1998) is a biography you can use to introduce students to this photographer noted for her sensitive photographs of migrant farmers.

Documentary

In a documentary, one documents or provides concrete evidence of something. Have students design a poster or a presentation using visual images to document a problem in their community. They will need to consider the use of persuasive language, as well. When would visual images be more powerful? When might they need text to explain their concern?

Examples of successful class projects are:

Molly Cone. *Come Back Salmon.* Illustrated by Sidnee Wheelwright. Sierra Club, 1994.
Dyanne Disalvo Ryan. *City Green.* Morrow, 1994.

Museums

Many students are unfamiliar with art museums or find them intimidating, yet they are familiar with the principle of a collection or classification of objects. Introduce them to the features of an art museum through these examples from children's literature:

> J. Otto Seibold and Vivian Walsh. *Going to the Getty: A Book about the Getty Center in Los Angeles.* J. Paul Getty Museum, 1997.
> Jacqueline Preiss Weitzman and Robin Preiss. *You Can't Take a Balloon into the Metropolitan Museum.* Dial, 1998. For primary students.

ABC Art

Letters of the alphabet can be considered visual symbols and art forms as well as letters to be used in writing and reading. Groupings of letters or words can be used to produce pictures of animals, people, or whatever students can imagine.

Students can use letters to develop fascinating pictures or designs. Begin by having students bring in newspapers and magazines. They can cut out letters and words of varying sizes and shapes. Give students large sheets of construction paper and paste to see how they can incorporate these letters and words in pictures. The goal of this assignment is to have students become involved with letters so that they are aware of the abstract symbols but they also see letters and words as having artistic value, as shown in these illustrations.

ABC Letters

After discussing letters as graphic images, have students create their own ABC book from the letters they have drawn. Share with students the creations of Mordecai Gerstein in *The Absolutely Awful Alphabet* (Harcourt, 1999) as the letters turn into monsters, or Stephen T. Johnson's discoveries in *Alphabet City* (Viking, 1995).

An alphabet book can also be used as a review of the vocabulary at the conclusion of a unit on art or music.

Make a Letterhead

A simple computer, graphic software, and printer are all students need to design a *letterhead* for stationery. This can be used for notes from the teacher or the school, or for letters the students write. Students can draw, import images, or use clip art to create an attractive letterhead or border. If you don't have a color printer, students can color the designs afterwards if they wish. Discuss with students how to create an effective image. Why do they like some designs better than others?

Older students can expand this activity into creating a newsletter for the class or school.

What Is It?

This creative writing idea involves both art and creative writing. Have the children make a blot figure out of thinned poster paint and then pass it to the person next to them to write about it. Blowing on the blot will make interesting spike patterns. You may want to guide them with questions such as:

- Where did you find it?
- What was it doing?
- How does it move?
- What does it eat?
- Where do you keep it?
- Where does it sleep?
- What would happen if it got wet?
- What does it do when you go to school?
- Can it fly?
- Can it change shape?
- Is it magical?
- Does it need your help?
- Is it lost?

- Is it in danger?
- What is it afraid of?

The Illustrator

Show students the work of one illustrator, such as Thomas Locker, Pat Mora, or John Steptoe. Let them compare the different styles of art used in various books illustrated by one author. They may discover that an illustrator uses a very distinctive style or chooses particular media they can recognize.

Ezra Jack Keats is one illustrator with a consistent style. He uses a technique called *collage* to create colorful images. Students can practice making similar collages to illustrate their own writing. Keats was one of the first illustrators to include pictures of African American children in his books, such as *Snowy Day* (Viking, 1962), which won the Caldecott Medal. Talk about the reasons why this was unusual. Should artists include pictures of different kinds of people when illustrating books?

Investigate his life and technique in *Ezra Jack Keats: A Biography with Illustrations,* by Dean Engel and Florence B. Freedman (Silver Moon Press, 1995). An illustrator who uses collage very differently from Keats is David Diaz, who won the Caldecott Medal for *Smoky Night* by Eve Bunting (Harcourt, 1994). Can students find examples of painters who have used a collage technique?

Collage Art

Even primary students can experiment with making collages. Students will need pictures and paper to cut or tear into smaller pieces. They can arrange these elements into patterns, overlapping them and attaching them with glue to a tagboard backing. Once they have assembled their picture, they can embellish it with pens, crayons, and so on. Eric Carle, another well-known illustrator who uses collage, describes his technique in *You Can Make a Collage: A Very Simple How-To Book* (Klutz, 1998).

Illustration as Art

Illustrations play an important part in the reader's reaction to a story. Select several editions of familiar works illustrated by different people to share with students (*Grimm's Fairy Tales* or *A Child's Garden of Verses,* for example). Discuss how the illustrations made them feel. What was each illustrator trying to do? Compare the illustrators' styles, use of color, subject matter, and emotional tone. Which did the children prefer and why?

Two recent books to compare, based on the same text, are:

Bob Barner. *To Everything.* Chronicle, 1998.
Leo and Diane Dillon. *To Every Thing There Is a Season.* Blue Sky Press, 1998.
    The words in these books come from the Bible and have also been set to music. Students can learn the song after they read these books.

Caldecott Awards

Every year the Caldecott Medal is awarded to an illustrator for the illustrations in a particular children's book. In addition, Honor books may be selected. Most libraries have a list of the winners. Also see Chapter 10. Students might select an illustrator or a book to study from this list and then report to the class about their illustrator.

Characters with Pizazz

Students can create a papier-mâché model of their favorite character from children's literature. They will have to read the descriptive passages closely to determine what their figure should look like. They can decorate the figure with paint and then present it to the class. Other students will guess which character is represented.

Art Is a Universal Language

Art can help bridge the gulf between strangers and between cultures. Students who are struggling to learn English can benefit from expressing themselves through art, a medium that doesn't need translation. If students were unable to speak the language of those around them, how would they communicate? How might they show themselves in their art? Show students the way Aliki, the well-known children's author, has shared her memories of being an outsider, because she was not able to speak English. Turn the book one way and the story is in text; turn the book the other way, and the story is in pictures.

> Aliki. *Marianthe's Story: Painted Words* and *Marianthe's Story: Spoken Memories.* Greenwillow, 1998.

What's Your Color?

Ask the students to choose their favorite color. Provide watercolors (and color wheels or paint test strips for unusual colors) and show students how to make a wash of the color they have selected. While the watercolor backgrounds are drying, have students compose a first-person account of their color's experience and feelings.

> My name is Yellow. I am bright and happy. I am the color of the moon and the sun. I am the color of the first flowers in spring and new baby chicks. I am the color of the banana peels that clowns slip on.

These essays can be copied onto the watercolor washes, or shapes can be cut from the washed paper and used to border the essay. Some students may prefer to turn their essays into cinquains or free verse before copying onto the colored paper.

> *Yellow*
> *Sun bright*
> *Soft baby chicks*
> *Banana peels tripping clowns*
> *Golden*

Young fuzzy chicks
Endless desert sands
Long summer days
Lovely bright moons
Old faded books
Windows at night

Students of all ages will appreciate the video, *Dr. Seuss's My Many Colored Days* (Notes Alive! Story Concert Video Series), in which a child experiences a range of feelings through color and music.

Words with Texture

Help students become more aware of the shapes of letters by making the letters with something that they can feel. Use scraps of carpet, sandpaper, burlap, glue, or anything with a distinct texture to make the letters. Attach the letters to a surface that is the same color so that students do not rely solely on the outline contrast. Younger students can work with textured letters to support letter recognition skills. Older students can talk about the shapes and describe the texture.

Colorful Book Covers

As students write original stories or reports, have them create beautiful book covers as art projects. Try a variety of these activities:

- Fold a sheet of white construction paper in half. Place bits of yarn dipped in different colors of tempera randomly on one half. Fold the other half over and press firmly while pulling the yarn out. Unfold and let dry.
- Use bright crayons to draw heavy lines or an abstract shape on a sheet of 9" × 12" paper. Then cover the sheet with thin black tempera paint. The bright crayon shows through.
- Drop several colors of oil-based paint, diluted in a little paint thinner, on water in a pie pan. Stir. Lay a sheet of paper (9" × 18") on the water to pick up the enamel. Fold into a booklet.
- Drop several colors of tempera on a dampened sheet of paper. Tip the paper to encourage the colors to run together and mix, creating attractive colored designs. Fold as a cover.

Books about Art and Artists for Students

The following books will introduce important painters and concepts about art to students. Share one to begin a special unit on art; students can use others to develop individual or group reports.

Michelle Dionetti. *Painting the Wind: A Story of Vincent Van Gogh.* Little, Brown, 1996.

John Duggleby. *Story Painter.* Chronicle, 1998. Biography of Jacob Lawrence.

Faith Ringgold, Linda Freeman, and Nancy Roucher. *Talking to Faith Ringgold.* Crown, 1996.

Jeanette Winter. *My Name Is Georgia: A Portrait.* Harcourt, 1998. Biography of Georgia O'Keeffe.

Gillian Wolfe. *Oxford First Book of Art.* Oxford University Press, 1999.

Especially for Primary

Anthony Browne. *Willy the Dreamer.* Candlewick, 1997.

Nina Laden. *When Pigasso Met Mootise.* Chronicle, 1998.

Art Software for Children

Now that art software is readily available to schools, all students have greater opportunities to see what happens when they manipulate color, line, shape, and texture. When they see the result and modify their creations accordingly, they are benefiting from the computer's ability to give immediate feedback. Encourage students to incorporate art into all their school activities. Everyone can be an "artist," not just a few talented exceptions. The following are some of the possibilities:

Crayola Art Studio. Micrografx. (800) 326-4576.

Flying Colors. Davidson. (800) 545-7677.

The Incredible Coloring Kit. Creative Pursuits. (800) 653-8298.

A Music Wall

Students will encounter a variety of vocabulary associated with music. As the students learn musical terms and the names of the instruments, include the words on a poster or a class Word Wall especially for music. Then you can help students to find patterns and make generalizations about these words. For example, many of the musical terms are of Italian origin. You might note that these words are pronounced differently from similar English words.

cello

andante

etude

vivace

flugelhorn

aria

The Sounds of Music

Instruments have distinctive sounds, and composers combine instruments in particular ways for distinctive sound effects. Teach students to listen to music with discrimination by explaining how to listen for a particular instrument. Before you play a piece of music, write the names of some of the instruments on the board. Ask students to think of what these instruments remind them of. What feelings and images does a trumpet call up? Then have them list words that describe the sounds these instruments make. Is a trumpet shrill or brassy? After you have developed a list for each of the instruments, discuss the differences between these instruments. Why would some instruments be used for certain effects and not others?

Now have students listen to a piece of music. Have them shut their eyes to listen to the music better and name an instrument for them to listen for. When they hear the instrument, they are to raise their hands. After the listening period, discuss how they recognized the instrument. Was it by the visual or emotional images evoked by the instrument or did they recognize the instrument by the words that describe its sound?

Instruments

As students listen to music and become familiar with the instruments, they will be curious to find out more about particular instruments. They can research the history of an instrument such as the guitar, drum, trumpet, or flute, and answer the following questions:

- Where does the name come from? What does it mean?
- How has the shape changed over the years?
- When and where was it invented?
- How is it used?
- What kind of sound does it make?

This kind of research is most effective when students are divided into small groups and each group takes responsibility for an instrument. When the groups have completed their reports, they can decide on an interesting way to present the information to the class—play the instrument, play a record, make a poster, design a bulletin board, and so on. Later, each group develops an exercise to check students' understanding of the information presented. Having to construct a true-false, matching, or question-and-answer exercise reinforces students' grasp of the concepts involved.

The following book will introduce students to the instruments:

Saint Saens with Barrie Carson Turner. *Carnival of the Animals.* Illustrated by Sue Williams. Holt, 1999. This picturebook, based on classical music, includes a CD.

A humorous approach that will appeal especially to primary students is:

Kathryn Meyrick. *The Musical Life of Gustav Mole.* Childs Play, 1990. Features homemade instruments.

Word People in Music

What do the following people have in common?

> Adolph Sax
> John Philips Sousa
> Nellie Melba
> Luisa Tetrazzini

They're all people from the world of music whose names have entered the language. Ask students if they know what instruments are named after the first two people. Do they know the foods named after the other two people? Investigate how *saxophone, sousaphone, melba toast,* and *turkey tetrazzini* got their names.

Who's Who in Music

Whenever you play a particular piece of music, tell the students about the composer—his or her name, nationality, and date and place of birth. After the class has heard a selection, discuss the music. Ask them what would help them listen to the music. Would knowing more about the composer's life help them understand or appreciate the music better? What would they like to know?

Divide the students into groups and have each group use a different source to research and read about the composer and the piece of music. Ask them to answer these questions:

- Where and when was the composer born?
- Who or what was the music composed for?
- Where and when was it first performed?

Assemble the information gathered by the students into a report. Discuss whether the groups found different answers in their research. Why might this be? Share the results and then listen to the music again.

Some biographies to start with are:

> Gloria Kamen. *Hidden Music: The Life of Fanny Mendelsohn.* Simon & Schuster, 1996.
> Susanna Reich. *Clara Schumann, Piano Virtuoso.* Clarion, 1999.
> Jeanette Winter. *Sebastian: A Book about Bach.* Harcourt Brace, 1999.

Favorite Songs

For practice with writing capital letters, encourage students to write song titles. This not only provides practice for handwriting but it also helps students learn which words require capitalization in a title. Have students create lists of their favorite songs to display on the board. Everyone will have a number of titles to share. This list will introduce new vocabulary, too, and may lead to an interesting exchange of music as students bring in their own music.

Write Poetry to Music

Music has an affinity with poetry. After your students have had some experience with music, talk with them about what they think music and poetry have in common. Some musical selections are *tone poems,* which describe a setting and/or a feeling; some represent stories; and others are complex, combining all elements. Play music for the class—a dreamy fantasy like Debussy's *La Mer,* or something emotional like Stravinsky's *The Rites of Spring.* Ask students to write a poem about what the music made them see. They can list the images that the music conjured up for them or express the musical themes in words.

After students have written their poems, discuss how the music made them feel. Did some people react very differently? Why? Trying to capture the spirit of the music in a poem helps students to understand the richness of feeling expressed in music.

Play the record again. Ask if anyone notices new aspects of the music that they had not heard before. A piece of music can be a new experience every time it is played. You may want to have students read their poems to the class while you play passages from the music. In this way, the music is illustrating the poem and the poem is illustrating the music.

Setting Poems to Music

Help children create a melody for poems they enjoy. Have a simple keyboard available to aid them in choosing the notes that match their singing. Several students may work together on this project.

Encourage students to select short poems to produce songs such as that found on page 332, which you may enjoy playing and singing together.

Students' Songs

Students can make up their own songs, using familiar melodies. Play examples of vocal music, such as folksongs, to stimulate student thinking. What topics are folksongs usually about? Why do people write songs? What's the difference between singing about being unemployed, for example, and talking about it? Contemporary music usually reflects the concerns of the day. Ask students what topics they would like to put into song. Some suggestions might be pollution, violence, and friendship. As a class or in small groups, students can develop new words to a song and then sing it for the school. *Songs for Social Justice* (NECA, 1994) includes song lyrics and teaching ideas.

Books That Sing

There are many books that will encourage students to sing along. Share the story silently while the class listens to appropriate music or invite students to chime in with the book's

Who Has Seen the Wind

Christina Rossetti   Iris M. Tiedt

Who has seen the wind?
Who has seen the wind?

Nei-ther you nor I
Nei-ther I nor you

But When the leaves hang trem-bl-ing
But When the trees bow down their heads

The wind is pas-sing by.
The wind is pas-sing through.

chorus as you read to them. For longer pieces, divide the class into sections that will sing different parts. Here are some books that show the possibilities of matching literature and music:

Dominic Catalano. *Frog Went A-Courting: A Musical Play in Six Acts.* Boyds Mills, 1998. The familiar song is presented as if in an animated movie. Students can use it as a model for acting out songs.

Ann Grifalconi. *Tiny's Hat.* HarperCollins, 1999. This story about the power of song could be accompanied by a recording of Billie Holiday.

Deborah Hopkinson. *A Band of Angels: A Story Inspired by the Jubilee Singers.* Illustrated by Raúl Colón. Atheneum, 1998. Story of a chorus that was formed to sing black songs. Play a recording of Mahalia Jackson singing spirituals for the students.

Margaret Read MacDonald. *Pickin' Peas.* Illustrated by Pat Cummings. HarperCollins, 1998. A rhyme for telling, acting out, and singing in parts.

Music in History

The history of different musical forms is an important part of our past. In the history of the United States, music from ragtime to jazz and blues has been a significant aspect of the important trends of the day. Students may have favorite musical groups but they don't always know the ancestry of that music. The class can embark on a project to learn more about the sources of today's music. The following are books that will start students thinking about these topics:

> Debbi Chocolate. *The Piano Man.* Illustrated by Eric Velasquez. Walker, 1998. Based on the history of ragtime music and players such as Scott Joplin, Jelly Roll, Fats Waller.
> Toyomi Igus. *I See the Rhythm.* Illustrated by Michele Wood. Children's Book Press, 1998. Covers music through this century, from blues to rock.
> Sallie Ketcham. *Bach's Big Adventure.* Illustrated by Timothy Bush. Orchard, 1999. Story set in Bach's time.

Studying Jazz

Jazz has been called "America's classical music." Students may not be aware of the impact that American jazz (and blues) has had worldwide. They can research some of the notable composers, musicians, and types of this music, and present their findings to the class, accompanied by musical examples. There are many excellent books for students that will introduce them to jazz, the blues, and the people who play it, such as the following:

> Linda England. *The Old Cotton Blues.* Illustrated by Teresa Flavin. McElderry, 1998.
> Ann Grifalconi. *Tiny's Hat.* HarperCollins, 1999.
> Roxane Orgill. *If I Only Had a Horn: Young Louis Armstrong.* Illustrated by Leonard Jenkins. Houghton Mifflin, 1997.
> Andrea Pinkney. *Duke Ellington: The Piano Prince and His Orchestra.* Illustrated by Brian Pinkney. Hyperion, 1998.

Older students will appreciate *Bud, Not Buddy,* a novel by Christopher Paul Curtis (Delacorte, 1999), and *Miles Davis,* a biography by George R. Crisp (Watts, 1997).

Keeping the Beat

Often, the first aspect of music that students attend to is the rhythm. You don't need any special equipment to bring rhythm into the classroom. Many simple household objects can be adapted to make a beat. For an activity showing the role of rhythm, have students put their hands over their ears and then play music. What can they hear, if anything? Do deaf people hear music in the same way that hearing people do? Share Isaac Millman's *Moses Goes to a Concert* (Farrar Straus, 1998), which features a deaf boy who attends the concert of a deaf percussionist, who "hears" music through bare feet. For more suggestions that incorporate rhythm in the classroom, see Avery Hart and Paul Mantell's *Kids Make Music: Clapping and Tapping from Bach to Rock* (Williamson, 1993).

Dance to the Music

It is not surprising that students would want to move and dance to the music that they hear. Explore some of the many types of dance around the world as well as the people (men and women) from different cultures who create these dances, to express themselves and their communities.

> George Ancona. *Let's Dance.* Morrow, 1998.
> Rives Collins. *Creative Drama and Improvisation.* Videorecording. Video Communications, 1990.
> Russell Freedman. *Martha Graham: A Dancer's Life.* Clarion, 1998.
> Savion Glover. *Savion: My Life in Tap.* Morrow, 2000.
> Rachel Isadora. *Isadora Dances.* Viking, 1998.
> Bill T. Jones and Susan Kuklin. *Dance.* Hyperion, 1998.
> Andrea Davis Pinkney. *Alvin Ailey.* Hyperion, 1995.
> Kate Waters and Madeline Slovenz-Low. *Lion Dancer: Ernie Wan's Chinese New Year.* Scholastic, 1990.
> Chamroeun Yin. *In My Heart I Am a Dancer.* Philadelphia Folklore Project, 1996.

Creativity and the Artist

Because students are often hard on people who are nonconformists and stand out from the crowd, it is worthwhile to initiate a discussion of these issues in the classroom. After talking about many different kinds of artists, from painters to musicians and dancers, have students switch focus to thinking about art in their own lives. Ask students what comes to mind when they hear the word *creative* or *artist.* Can anybody be an artist? Students may have heard the words used in different contexts, but what does being creative really mean—in school, for example? Does there have to be a connection between creativity and being different? What does it feel like to be different? After opening up these topics, students may be interested in exploring how children like themselves deal with being creative. Suggest these books:

For Older Students
Sharon Creech. *Bloomability.* Joanna Cotler, 1998.

For Younger Students
Libba Moore Grey. *My Mama Had a Dancing Heart.* Orchard, 1995.
Allen Say. *Emma's Rug.* Houghton Mifflin, 1996.

Discussion Questions

1. If you are teaching social studies with traditional text materials, how can you integrate them with children's literature and language arts activities?

2. How can you make science and math exciting for students of low ability as well as challenging for students of high ability?

3. With the cutback in school funding and the lack of resources, how do you make sure that children have a chance to experience the arts?

Exploring Further

Ancient World 2000+ (intermediate) and *Social Science 2000* (primary). Decision Development. Program features facts, video, Internet resources, database, and maps.

C. S. Evans. "Writing to Learn in Math." *Language Arts, 61* (1984): 825–835.

Exploring Ancient World Cultures. Maps, timelines, essays, images about India, China, Greece, and the Near East available from <http://eawc.evansville.edu/index.htm>.

Karolynne Gee. *Visual Arts As a Way of Knowing.* Galef/Stenhouse, 1999.

Green Teacher. Magazine published quarterly on-line. <www.web.net/~greentea/>.

The JASON project site for explorations featuring expedition leader Bob Ballard: <http://sea-wifs.gsfc.nasa.gov/JASON.html>.

Janet Rubin and Margaret Merrion. *Drama & Music: Creative Activities for Young Children.* Humanics Learning, 1995.

Science and Children. Journal of the National Science Teachers Association. 1840 Wilson Blvd., Arlington VA 22201-3000.

Ken Winograd and Karen Higgins. "Writing, Reading, and Talking Mathematics: One Interdisciplinary Possibility." *The Reading Teacher, 48,* no. 4 (1994/1995).

References

Bill Bigelow and Bob Peterson (Eds.). *Rethinking Columbus: The Next 500 Years.* Rethinking Schools, 1998.

Jane Buchbinder. "The Arts Step Out from the Wings." *Harvard Education Letter, 15,* no. 6 (November/December, 1999): 1–4.

Michael J. Caduto and Joseph Bruchac. *Keepers of the Earth: Native American Stories and Environmental Activities for Children.* Fulcrum, 1997.

Bernice Cullinan, et al. *Three Voices: An Invitation to Poetry across the Curriculum.* Stenhouse, 1995.

Maureen McLaughlin and MaryEllen Vogt (Eds.). *Creativity and Innovation in Content Area Teaching.* Christopher-Gordon, 2000.

Young Voices from the Arab World. Video. Amideast, 1999.

Claudia Zaslavsky. *The Multicultural Math Classroom: Bringing in the World.* Heinemann, 1996.

Planning Ahead

Harriet never minded admitting she didn't know something. So what, she thought, I could always learn.
—Louise Fitzhugh, *Harriet the Spy*

This chapter focuses on supporting the teacher through the next steps of becoming a more effective language arts teacher. A few recommended lists are presented—just a sampling of the resources and support that is available to help any teacher continue to develop professionally. Based on the experience of the authors, professional books and journals have been selected that will enrich everyone's teaching. In addition, the chapter includes lists of recommended children's literature to build a library. Resources are also provided to aid you in accessing information via the Internet as well as utilizing varied media—for example, video and CD-ROM.

Continuing to Develop Professionally

As more and more is demanded of today's teachers, they are expected to be education *professionals*. Once it may have been enough to complete the training needed for a credential; today, teachers must stay involved in learning their profession, just as they expect students to continue learning. This section contains material that will help you stay sharp in the rapidly changing world of education. We include professional organizations and journals to keep you well informed, language arts resource books with practical ideas and information that every language arts teacher needs, and Internet connections for further professional development.

Professional Organizations as Resources

Today, professional organizations are more necessary than ever before to meet the needs of educators. Teachers can no longer depend on a set curriculum that determines their lesson plans or basal readers and textbooks that come with a teacher's edition telling you what questions to ask. Through attending meetings and being involved in these organizations, you will have the support of other teachers who share your goal of becoming a more effective language arts teacher. Two highly regarded professional organizations are:

- National Council of Teachers of English. 1111 W. Kenyon Rd., Urbana IL 61801. NCTE meets in March and November. Publishes numerous journals and includes different interest groups. Contact NCTE for information about the state level and regional councils in your area <www.ncte.org>.
- International Reading Association. 800 Barksdale Rd., Newark DE 19714. IRA meets in May. Publishes several journals for audiences from elementary teachers to reading researchers. Contact IRA for information about the state and regional councils in your area <www.reading.org>.

Professional Journals to Keep You Up to Date

These journals are recommended because they deal with timely topics in the field. All include reviews of children's literature and present articles about teaching methods as well as research. Because it is impossible to subscribe to all of the journals individually, you might suggest that your school subscribe to these journals or share with fellow teachers by each subscribing to a different one. Check to see if your state reading or English organization also publishes a journal or newsletter.

> *Book Links; Connecting Books, Libraries, and Classrooms.* American Library Association, 50 Huron St., Chicago IL 60611. Directed to teachers and librarians.
>
> *Journal of Children's Literature.* Children's Literature Assembly, National Council of Teachers of English, 1111 W. Kenyon Rd., Urbana IL 61801. Lengthy articles on topics related to children's literature.
>
> *Language Arts.* National Council of Teachers of English, 1111 W. Kenyon Rd., Urbana IL 61801. Directed to elementary and middle school teachers.
>
> *The New Advocate.* Christopher-Gordon Publishers, Inc. 480 Washington Street, Norwood MA 02062. Articles and interviews with children's literature writers.
>
> *The Reading Teacher.* International Reading Association. 800 Barksdale Rd., Newark DE 19714. "Children's Choices" (a list of children's literature) appears in October issues; "Teachers' Choices" (a list of children's literature) appears in November issues. The compilation is available from <www.bookstore.reading.org>.
>
> *The Bulletin of the Center for Children's Books.* This is now published on-line <edfu.lis.uiuc.edu/puboff/bccb/>.

Recommended Books about Teaching the Language Arts

Following are books that provide information every language arts teacher needs. A number of titles share practical ideas that you can implement immediately in your classroom.

Others provide an overview of recommended teaching methods and materials designed to give you a strong rationale for what you are doing. Selected titles are also included that review the research that has shaped this field.

JoBeth Allen (Ed.). *Class Actions: Teaching for Social Justice in Elementary and Middle School.* Teachers College Press, 1999.

J. J. Beaty. *Building Bridges with Multicultural Picture Books.* Merrill, 1997.

Susan Benedict and Lenore Carlisle (Eds.). *Beyond Words: Picture Books for Older Readers and Writers.* Heinemann, 1992.

Gloria Blatt (Ed.). *Once upon a Folktale: Capturing the Folklore Process with Children.* New York: Teacher's College Press, 1993.

Bette Bosma and Nancy D. Guth (Eds.). *Children's Literature in an Integrated Curriculum: The Authentic Voice.* International Reading Association, 1995.

California Curriculum Development and Supplemental Materials Commission. *Reading/Language Arts Framework for California Public Schools; Kindergarten through Grade Twelve.* California Department of Education, 1999.

Committee to Revise the Multicultural Booklist. *Kaleidoscope: A Multicultural Booklist for Grades K–8* (2nd ed.). National Council of Teachers of English, 1997.

Cathie H. Cooper. *ABC Books and Activities: From Preschool to High School.* Scarecrow Press, 1996.

I. Forte and S. Schurr. *Using Favorite Picture Books to Stimulate Discussion and to Encourage Critical Thinking.* Incentive Publishers, 1995.

Evelyn Freeman and D. Person (Eds.). *Using Nonfiction Trade Books in the Elementary Classroom: From Ants to Zeppelins.* National Council of Teachers of English, 1992.

Jeffrey Golub. *Activities for an Interactive Classroom.* National Council of Teachers of English, 1994.

Susan Hall. *Using Picture Storybooks to Teach Literary Devices.* Oryx Press, 1994.

Linda Hart-Hewins and Jan Wells. *Real Books for Reading: Learning to Read with Children's Literature.* Heinemann, 1990.

IRA Children's Literature Special Interest Group. *Notable Books for a Global Society.* IRA, 1997. An annotated list of picture books available from IRA SIG, c/o Siu-Runyan, 2591 Sumac Ave., Boulder CO 80304-0922. Include check for $6.00 made out to IRA Children's Literature SIG.

International Reading Association and Teacher's College Press. *Children's Literature in an Integrated Curriculum: The Authentic Voice.* Newark, DE: IRA and Teacher's College Press, 1995.

Gloria Ladson-Billings. *The Dreamkeepers: Successful Teaching of African American Children.* Jossey-Bass, 1994.

Carolyn W. Lima and John A. Lima. *A to Zoo: Subject Access to Children's Picture Books* (5th ed.). Bowker, 1998.

Patricia Phelan (Ed.). *Talking to Learn.* National Council of Teachers of English, 1989.

Michael Schiro. *Integrating Children's Literature and Mathematics in the Classroom.* Teachers College Press, 1997.

John Simmons and Lawrence Baines (Eds.). *Language Study in Middle School, High School, and Beyond.* International Reading Association, 1998.

John Stewig. *Looking at Picture Books.* Highsmith, 1994.

Barbara Taylor et al. (Eds.). *Reading for Meaning: Fostering Comprehension in the Middle Grades.* Teachers College Press, 1999.

Iris Tiedt. *Writing: From Topic to Evaluation.* Allyn and Bacon, 1989.

Iris Tiedt. *Teaching with Picture Books in the Middle School.* IRA, 2001.

Iris M. Tiedt et al. *Reading/Thinking/Writing: A Holistic Language and Literacy Program for the K–8 Classroom.* Allyn and Bacon, 1989.

Iris M. Tiedt et al. *Teaching Thinking in K–12 Classrooms: Ideas, Activities, and Resources.* Allyn and Bacon, 1989.

Pamela Tiedt and Iris M. Tiedt. *Multicultural Teaching: A Handbook of Activities, Information, and Resources* (5th ed.). Allyn and Bacon, 1999.

Chip Wood. *Yardsticks: Children in the Classroom, Ages 4–12.* Northeast Foundation for Children, 1994.

Internet Connections for Teachers

With the advent of the Internet, teachers have greater and easier access to the latest ideas, issues, and research, as education changes rapidly. For example, the new learning environments will incorporate new strategies.

Traditional Learning Environment *	*New Learning Environment*
teacher centered	student centered
single-sense stimulation	multisense stimulation
single-path progression	multipath progression
single media	multimedia
isolated work	collaborative work
information delivery	information exchange
passive learning	active/exploratory/inquiry-based
factual, knowledge-based	critical thinking and informed decision making
reactive response	proactive/planned action
isolated, artificial context	authentic, real-world context

Organization and Institutional Sites

Educational Resources Information Center (ERIC) (contains an extensive body of education-related articles and research)
<www.accesseric.org:81/>

ERIC Clearinghouse on Elementary and Early Childhood Education

*List from National Educational Technology Standards for Students, 1998, p. 2 <ww.iste.org>.

The Children's Literature Web Guide
<www.ucalgary.ca/~dkbrown/index.html>

National Association for the Education of Young Children

American Library Association (sponsors Newbery and Caldecott awards)
<www.ala.org/booklist/index.html>

News from the Department of Education

New Mexico State University menu of children's literature, electronic resources
<gopher://lib.nmsu.edu:70/11/.subjects/Education/.childlit>

Library of Congress Learning Page
<lcweb2.loc.gov/ammem/ndlpedu>

A collection of educational Web resources from the Franklin Institute
<sln.fi.edu/tfi/hotlists/hotlists.html>

Fairrosa Cyber Library of Children's Literature
<www.users.interport.net/~fairrosa/>

School and Teacher-Run Sites

Teachers Network collection of classroom projects
<www.teachnet.org>

Bantam Doubleday and Dell Teachers Resource Center
<www.bdd.com/teachers>

Hazel's Homepage
<www.marshall-es.marshall.K12.tn.us/jobe>

Loogootee Elementary West
<www.siec.K12.in.us/west/>

Gander Academy Theme-Related Resources
<www.stemnet.nf.ca/CITE/ themes.html>

Cinco de Mayo
<www.zianet.com/hatchelementary/Cinco.html>

Harriet Tubman and the Underground Railroad
<www2.Lhric.org/pocantico/tubman/tubman/.html>

An education search engine
<www.education-world.com>

Only the Best: The Annual Guide to the Highest-Rated Educational Software and Multimedia, 1990-98. CD-ROM (Association of the Study of Curriculum and Development) for Windows, Mac

On-line ERIC Clearinghouse with ready-to-use lesson plans
<ericir.sunsite.syr.edu/Virtual/>

Education site

National Latino Children's Institute, Día de los Niños Kit
(512) 472-9971
<www.nlci.org>
National Clearinghouse for Bilingual Education (with lessons in Spanish and English)
<www.ncbe.gwu.edu>

Working with Students

As the teacher's role changes, so does the role of the student. Students are expected to take an active part in the learning process and to initiate projects and follow through in student-directed learning. This section includes materials that you can use directly with students. We present a list of Newbery Award Winners and Honor Books from 1980 to 2000, and a list of Caldecott Award Winners and Honor Books from 1980 to 2000. These books, recognized for the quality of their illustrations and writing, would make an excellent foundation for your collection of children's literature. In addition, we list journals that publish student writing.

Two Decades of Newbery Winners

The Newbery Medal is given annually to a children's book that is judged by the American Library Association to represent the finest writing in any book published that year. Honor books are also selected. Named for John Newbery, an early publisher of children's books, this highly coveted medal is placed on each copy of the award-winning book. Newbery winners are often reprinted in paperback editions or are available through school book clubs at reduced prices. Because of the emphasis on text, these books tend to be for upper-grade students. Although the award has been presented since the 1920s, we have chosen to include only the books from the past 20 years.

2000 *Medal Winner:* *Bud, Not Buddy* by Christopher Paul Curtis (Delacorte)
   Honor Books:
   Getting Near to Baby by Audry Couloumbis (Putnam)
   25 Fairmount Ave by Tomie de Paola (Putnam)
   Our Only May Amelia by Jennifer Hom (Harper)

1999 *Medal Winner:* *Holes* by Louis Sachar (Frances Foster)
   Honor Book:
   A Long Way from Chicago by Richard Peck (Dial)

1998 *Medal Winner:* *Out of the Dust* by Karen Hesse (Scholastic)
   Honor Books:
   Ella Enchanted by Gail Carson Levine (HarperCollins)
   Lily's Crossing by Patricia Reilly Giff (Delacorte)
   Wringer by Jerry Spinelli (HarperCollins)

1997 *Medal Winner:*   *The View from Saturday* by E. L. Konigsburg (Jean Kari/Atheneum)

> ***Honor Books:***
> *A Girl Named Disaster* by Nancy Farmer (Richard Jackson/Orchard Books)
> *Moorchild* by Eloise McGraw (Margaret McElderry/Simon & Schuster)
> *The Thief* by Megan Whalen Turner (Greenwillow/Morrow)
> *Belle Prater's Boy* by Ruth White (Farrar Straus Giroux)

1996 *Medal Winner:*   *The Midwife's Apprentice* by Karen Cushman (Clarion)

> ***Honor Books:***
> *What Jamie Saw* by Carolyn Coman (Front Street)
> *The Watsons Go to Birmingham: 1963* by Christopher Paul Curtis (Delacorte)
> *Yolonda's Genius* by Carol Fenner (Margaret K. McElderry/Simon & Schuster)
> *The Great Fire* by Jim Murphy (Scholastic)

1995 *Medal Winner:*   *Walk Two Moons* by Sharon Creech (HarperCollins)

> ***Honor Books:***
> *Catherine, Called Birdy* by Karen Cushman (Clarion)
> *The Ear, the Eye and the Arm* by Nancy Farmer (Jackson/Orchard)

1994 *Medal Winner:*   *The Giver* by Lois Lowry (Houghton)

> ***Honor Books:***
> *Crazy Lady* by Jane Leslie Conly (HarperCollins)
> *Dragon's Gate* by Laurence Yep (HarperCollins)
> *Eleanor Roosevelt: A Life of Discovery* by Russell Freedman (Clarion Books)

1993 *Medal Winner:*   *Missing May* by Cynthia Rylant (Jackson/Orchard)

> ***Honor Books:***
> *What Hearts* by Bruce Brooks (A Laura Geringer Book, a HarperCollins imprint)
> *The Dark-thirty: Southern Tales of the Supernatural* by Patricia McKissack (Knopf)
> *Somewhere in the Darkness* by Walter Dean Myers (Scholastic Hardcover)

1992 *Medal Winner:*   *Shiloh* by Phyllis Reynolds Naylor (Atheneum)

> ***Honor Books:***
> *Nothing But The Truth: a Documentary Novel* by Avi (Jackson/Orchard)
> *The Wright Brothers: How They Invented the Airplane* by Russell Freedman (Holiday House)

1991 *Medal Winner:*   *Maniac Magee* by Jerry Spinelli (Little, Brown)

> ***Honor Book:***
> *The True Confessions of Charlotte Doyle* by Avi (Jackson/Orchard)

1990 *Medal Winner:*   *Number the Stars* by Lois Lowry (Houghton)

> ***Honor Books:***
> *Afternoon of the Elves* by Janet Taylor Lisle (Jackson/Orchard)
> *Shabanu, Daughter of the Wind* by Suzanne Fisher Staples (Knopf)
> *The Winter Room* by Gary Paulsen (Jackson/Orchard)

1989 *Medal Winner:*   *Joyful Noise: Poems for Two Voices* by Paul Fleischman (Harper)
    Honor Books:
    In The Beginning: Creation Stories from Around the World by Virginia Hamilton
      (Harcourt)
    Scorpions by Walter Dean Myers (Harper)

1988 *Medal Winner:*   *Lincoln: A Photobiography* by Russell Freedman (Clarion)
    Honor Books:
    After The Rain by Norma Fox Mazer (Morrow)
    Hatchet by Gary Paulsen (Bradbury)

1987 *Medal Winner:*   *The Whipping Boy* by Sid Fleischman (Greenwillow)
    Honor Books:
    A Fine White Dust by Cynthia Rylant (Bradbury)
    On My Honor by Marion Dane Bauer (Clarion)
    Volcano: The Eruption and Healing of Mount St. Helens by Patricia Lauber (Brad-
      bury)

1986 *Medal Winner:*   *Sarah, Plain and Tall* by Patricia MacLachlan (Harper)
    Honor Books:
    Commodore Perry In the Land of the Shogun by Rhoda Blumberg (Lothrop)
    Dogsong by Gary Paulsen (Bradbury)

1985 *Medal Winner:*   *The Hero and the Crown* by Robin McKinley (Greenwillow)
    Honor Books:
    Like Jake and Me by Mavis Jukes (Knopf)
    The Moves Make the Man by Bruce Brooks (Harper)
    One-Eyed Cat by Paula Fox (Bradbury)

1984 *Medal Winner:*   *Dear Mr. Henshaw* by Beverly Cleary (Morrow)
    Honor Books:
    The Sign of the Beaver by Elizabeth George Speare (Houghton)
    A Solitary Blue by Cynthia Voight (Atheneum)
    Sugaring Time by Kathryn Lasky (Macmillan)
    The Wish Giver: Three Tales of Coven Tree by Bill Brittain (Harper)

1983 *Medal Winner:*   *Dicey's Song* by Cynthia Voigt (Atheneum)
    Honor Books:
    The Blue Sword by Robin McKinley (Greenwillow)
    Doctor DeSoto by William Steig (Farrar)
    Graven Images by Paul Fleischman (Harper)
    Homesick: My Own Story by Jean Fritz (Putnam)
    Sweet Whispers, Brother Rush by Virginia Hamilton (Philomel)

1982 *Medal Winner:*   *A Visit to William Blake's Inn: Poems for Innocent and Experienced Travelers* by Nancy Willard (Harcourt)

Honor Books:
Ramona Quimby, Age 8 by Beverly Cleary (Morrow)
Upon the Head of the Goat: A Childhood in Hungary 1939–1944 by Aranka Siegal
(Farrar)

1981 *Medal Winner:*   *Jacob Have I Loved* by Katherine Paterson (Crowell)
Honor Books:
The Fledgling by Jane Langton (Harper)
A Ring of Endless Light by Madeleine L'Engle (Farrar)

1980 *Medal Winner:*   *A Gathering of Days: A New England Girl's Journal, 1830–1832*
by Joan W. Blos (Scribner)
Honor Book:
The Road from Home: The Story of an Armenian Girl by David Kherdian (Greenwillow)

Two Decades of Caldecott Winners

The Caldecott Medal is given annually to a children's book that is judged by the American
Library Association to display the finest illustrations of those books published that year.
Named for Randolph Caldecott, a nineteenth-century author and illustrator, this highly
coveted medal is placed on each copy of the award-winning book. Because the award
focuses attention on the quality of the illustrations, winners are often considered appropriate only for the youngest readers. This misperception, however, obscures the fact that
these books can also be used profitably with students in the upper grades. Although the
Caldecott has been awarded since 1938, we have selected only the past 20 years of award
winners and honor books.

2000 *Medal Winner:*   *Joseph Had a Little Overcoat* by Simms Taback (Viking)
Honor Books:
Sector 7 by David Weisner (Clarion)
The Ugly Duckling by Jerry Pinkney (Morrow)
When Sophie Gets Angry–Really, Really Angry by Molly Bang (Scholastic)
A Child's Calendar illustrated by Trina Schart Hyman Text: John Updike (Holiday)

1999 *Medal Winner:*   *Snowflake Bentley* illustrated by Mary Azarian; text: Jacqueline
Briggs Martin (Houghton)
Honor Books:
Duke Ellington: The Piano Prince and the Orchestra illustrated by Brian Pinkney;
text: Andrea Davis Pinkney (Hyperion)
No, David! by David Shannon (Scholastic)
Snow by Uri Shulevitz (Farrar)
Tibet Through the Red Box by Peter Sis (Frances Foster)

1998 *Medal Winner:*   *Rapunzel* by Paul O. Zelinsky (Dutton)

    Honor Books:

    The Gardener illustrated by David Small; text: Sarah Stewart (Farrar)

    Harlem illustrated by Christopher Myers; text: Walter Dean Myers (Scholastic)

    There Was an Old Lady Who Swallowed a Fly by Simms Taback (Viking)

1997 *Medal Winner:*   *Golem* by David Wisniewski (Clarion)

    Honor Books:

    Hush! A Thai Lullaby illustrated by Holly Meade; text: Minfong Ho (Melanie Kroupa/Orchard Books)

    The Graphic Alphabet by David Pelletier (Orchard Books)

    The Paperboy by Dav Pilkey (Richard Jackson/Orchard Books)

    Starry Messenger by Peter Sis (Frances Foster Books/Farrar Straus Giroux)

1996 *Medal Winner:*   *Officer Buckle and Gloria* by Peggy Rathmann (Putnam)

    Honor Books:

    Alphabet City by Stephen T. Johnson (Viking)

    Zin! Zin! Zin! a Violin, illustrated by Marjorie Priceman; text: Lloyd Moss (Simon & Schuster)

    The Faithful Friend, illustrated by Brian Pinkney; text: Robert D. San Souci (Simon & Schuster)

    Tops & Bottoms, adapted and illustrated by Janet Stevens (Harcourt)

1995 *Medal Winner:*   *Smoky Night,* illustrated by David Diaz; text: Eve Bunting (Harcourt)

    Honor Books:

    John Henry, illustrated by Jerry Pinkney; text: Julius Lester (Dial)

    Swamp Angel, illustrated by Paul O. Zelinsky; text: Anne Isaacs (Dutton)

    Time Flies by Eric Rohmann (Crown)

1994 *Medal Winner:*   *Grandfather's Journey* by Allen Say; text: edited by Walter Lorraine (Houghton)

    Honor Books:

    Peppe the Lamplighter, illustrated by Ted Lewin; text: Elisa Bartone (Lothrop)

    In the Small, Small Pond by Denise Fleming (Holt)

    Raven: A Trickster Tale from the Pacific Northwest by Gerald McDermott (Harcourt)

    Owen by Kevin Henkes (Greenwillow)

    Yo! Yes? illustrated by Chris Raschka; text: edited by Richard Jackson (Orchard)

1993 *Medal Winner:*   *Mirette on the High Wire* by Emily Arnold McCully (Putnam)

    Honor Books:

    The Stinky Cheese Man and Other Fairly Stupid Tales, illustrated by Lane Smith; text: Jon Scieszka (Viking)

    Seven Blind Mice by Ed Young (Philomel Books)

Working Cotton, illustrated by Carole Byard; text: Sherley Anne Williams (Harcourt)

1992 *Medal Winner:*   *Tuesday* by David Wiesner (Clarion Books)
Honor Book:
Tar Beach by Faith Ringgold (Crown Publishers, Inc., a Random House Co.)

1991 *Medal Winner:*   *Black and White* by David Macaulay (Houghton)
Honor Books:
Puss in Boots, illustrated by Fred Marcellino; text: Charles Perrault, trans. by Malcolm Arthur (Di Capua/Farrar)
"More More More," Said the Baby: Three Love Stories by Vera B. Williams (Greenwillow)

1990 *Medal Winner:*   *Lon Po Po: A Red-Riding Hood Story from China* by Ed Young (Philomel)
Honor Books:
Bill Peet: An Autobiography by Bill Peet (Houghton)
Color Zoo by Lois Ehlert (Lippincott)
The Talking Eggs: A Folktale from the American South, illustrated by Jerry Pinkney; text: Robert D. San Souci (Dial)
Hershel and the Hanukkah Goblins, illustrated by Trina Schart Hyman; text: Eric Kimmel (Holiday House)

1989 *Medal Winner:*   *Song and Dance Man,* illustrated by Stephen Gammell; text: Karen Ackerman (Knopf)
Honor Books:
The Boy of the Three-Year Nap, illustrated by Allen Say; text: Diane Snyder (Houghton)
Free Fall by David Wiesner (Lothrop)
Goldilocks and the Three Bears by James Marshall (Dial)
Mirandy and Brother Wind, illustrated by Jerry Pinkney; text: Patricia C. McKissack (Knopf)

1988 *Medal Winner:*   *Owl Moon,* illustrated by John Schoenherr; text: Jane Yolen (Philomel)
Honor Book:
Mufaro's Beautiful Daughters: An African Tale by John Steptoe (Lothrop)

1987 *Medal Winner:*   *Hey, Al,* illustrated by Richard Egielski; text: Arthur Yorinks (Farrar)
Honor Books:
The Village of Round and Square Houses by Ann Grifalconi (Little, Brown)
Alphabets by Suse MacDonald (Bradbury)
Rumpelstiltskin by Paul O. Zelinsky (Dutton)

1986 *Medal Winner:*   *The Polar Express* by Chris Van Allsburg (Houghton)
> *Honor Books:*
> *The Relatives Came,* illustrated by Stephen Gammell; text: Cynthia Rylant (Bradbury)
> *King Bidgood's in the Bathtub,* illustrated by Don Wood; text: Audrey Wood (Harcourt)

1985 *Medal Winner:*   *Saint George and the Dragon,* illustrated by Trina Schart Hyman; text: retold by Margaret Hodges (Little, Brown)
> *Honor Books:*
> *Hansel and Gretel,* illustrated by Paul O. Zelinsky; text: retold by Rika Lesser (Dodd)
> *Have You Seen My Duckling?* by Nancy Tafuri (Greenwillow)
> *The Story of Jumping Mouse: A Native American Legend,* retold and illustrated by John Steptoe (Lothrop)

1984 *Medal Winner:*   *The Glorious Flight: Across the Channel with Louis Bleriot* by Alice & Martin Provensen (Viking)
> *Honor Books:*
> *Little Red Riding Hood,* retold and illustrated by Trina Schart Hyman (Holiday)
> *Ten, Nine, Eight* by Molly Bang (Greenwillow)

1983 **Medal Winner:**   *Shadow,* translated and illustrated by Marcia Brown; original text in French: Blaise Cendrars (Scribner)
> *Honor Books:*
> *A Chair for My Mother* by Vera B. Williams (Greenwillow)
> *When I Was Young in the Mountains,* illustrated by Diane Goode; text: Cynthia Rylant (Dutton)

1982 *Medal Winner:*   *Jumanji* by Chris Van Allsburg (Houghton)
> *Honor Books:*
> *Where the Buffaloes Begin,* illustrated by Stephen Gammell; text: Olaf Baker (Warne)
> *On Market Street,* illustrated by Anita Lobel; text: Arnold Lobel (Greenwillow)
> *Outside Over There* by Maurice Sendak (Harper)
> *A Visit to William Blake's Inn: Poems for Innocent and Experienced Travelers,* illustrated by Alice & Martin Provensen; text: Nancy Willard (Harcourt)

1981 *Medal Winner:*   *Fables* by Arnold Lobel (Harper)
> *Honor Books:*
> *The Bremen-Town Musicians,* retold and illustrated by Ilse Plume (Doubleday)
> *The Grey Lady and the Strawberry Snatcher* by Molly Bang (Four Winds)
> *Mice Twice* by Joseph Low (McElderry/Atheneum)
> *Truck* by Donald Crews (Greenwillow)

1980 *Medal Winner:* *Ox-Cart Man,* illustrated by Barbara Cooney; text: Donald Hall (Viking)

> ***Honor Books:***
> *Ben's Trumpet* by Rachel Isadora (Greenwillow)
> *The Garden Of Abdul Gasazi* by Chris Van Allsburg (Houghton)
> *The Treasure* by Uri Shulevitz (Farrar)

Journals That Publish Student Writing

The following are recommended magazines that feature student writing. Send for a sample copy for information on subscription and submission guidelines.

Chart Your Course!
PO Box 6448
Mobile AL 36660
For gifted and talented, includes a variety of genres.

Children's Album
1320 Galaxy Way
Concord CA 94520
Creative writing, arts, and crafts.

Cobblestone: The History Magazine for Young People
30 Grove St.
Peterborough NH 03458
Theme-related, includes a variety of texts on the topic.

Creative Kids
PO Box 637
100 Pine Ave.
Holmes PA 19043
Stories, poetry, art, puzzles, photos, and so on.

Daybreak Star: The Herb of Understanding
United Indians of All Tribes Foundation
PO Box 99100
Seattle WA 98199
Written and edited by Native American students and adults.

Faces: The Magazine about People
30 Grove St.
Peterborough NH 03458
Theme-related, publishes work on the topic.

Free Spirit: News and Views on Growing Up
123 N. Third St.
Minneapolis MN 55401
Bimonthly, for gifted and talented.

Merlyn's Pen: The National Magazine of Student Writing
98 Main St.
East Greenwich RI 02818
email: merlynspen@aol.com
Encourages young authors.

National Geographic World
17th and M Sts. NW
Washington DC 20036
Stories, puzzles, and contests about children around the world.

Prism
Box 030464
Ft. Lauderdale FL 33303
Stories and penpals for gifted and talented.

Shoe Tree
National Association of Young Writers
PO Box 452
Belvedere NJ 07832
Encourages young authors.

Stone Soup
PO Box 83
Santa Cruz CA 95063
A literary magazine of young authors.

Zillions
PO Box 51777
Boulder CO 80321-1777
Consumer Reports-style magazine for children.

Incorporating Technology in the Classroom

More and more, teaching and learning take place in a variety of media. Teachers use visual images, print, and sound to create a multisensory environment in order to communicate information to students; students use Internet and CD-ROM sources for their research in order to have access to the most up-to-date information. How does teaching and learning change when NASA makes the latest images from Mars available to all, elementary students and planetary researchers, through the Internet at <msss.com/mocgallery>? Given the appropriate technology, isolated schools will be able to tap the same resource advantages as schools in populated areas. Through technology, students have a greater chance of individualized learning, being able to move at their own pace, and being treated as equals by other learners, even adults. Effective multimedia learning environments will need to connect traditional learning approaches with alternative ones offered by the new technology. These learning environments should prepare students to*

- Communicate using a variety of media and formats
- Access and exchange information in a variety of ways
- Compile, organize, analyze, and synthesize information
- Draw conclusions and make generalizations based on information gathered
- Use information and select appropriate tools to solve problems
- Know content and be able to locate additional information as needed
- Become self-directed learners
- Collaborate and cooperate in team efforts
- Interact with others in ethical and appropriate ways

*List from National Educational Technology Standards for Students, 1998, p. 2 <www.iste.org>.

Internet Basics

A major concern for teachers and parents considering use of the Internet is student safety and control over student access to particular sites. Ideally, computer-assisted technology will enable students to be more interactive, motivated, and able to solve problems. On the other hand, "safe surfing" requires that students on the web be supervised by a teacher or other adult. Before your students go on the web, discuss these basic safety rules with the class.

- Do not give out personal information (address, phone number) to anyone on-line.
- Do not plan to meet in person alone with someone you have met on-line.
- Do not respond to email or chat invitations from anyone you do not know.

If you are beginning to think about or use the Internet in your classroom, the following are some resources that will help you negotiate your way through this process:

America Links Up: Internet Safety for Kids, links to child-friendly sites, gives safety tips
<www.americalinksup.org>

Evaluation Center
<www.EDsOasis.org/Guidelines.html>

From Now On: The Educational Technology Journal

Guide for Educators, by Kathy Schrock
<www.capecod.net/schrockguide/eval.htm>

Internet for People Project, University of California at Berkeley
<infopeople.berkeley.edu:8000/bkmk/select.html>

Kids' Internet Gateway, University of Texas, Austin
<volvo.gslis.utexas.edu/~kidnet>

Kids Online: Protecting Your Children in Cyberspace
<www.protectkids.com>

Librarian's Guide to Cyberspace
<www.ala.org/parentspage/great sites/guide.html>

*South Central R*TEC*
<www/4Kids.org>

Tips for searching the net

Web66: A K12 World Wide Web Project
<web66.coled.umn.edu>

See also:

Jessica Morton. *Kids on the 'Net: Conducting Internet Research in K-5 Classrooms.*
Heinemann, 1999.

Students on the Net

Students frequently use the Internet for obtaining information, facts, and figures. However, just because it is on the net does not make the information accurate. Students need to exercise the same critical judgment with Internet data that they would apply to materials that appear in print. Before planning a large project in which students will depend on the net for gathering information, discuss these questions with students:

1. What do you know about the site? What do *.edu, .com,* and *.org* mean? Is the sponsor an Internet service provider (such as America On-Line), an organization, or an individual? Has this site been recommended by other sources?

2. Who is the author of this information? What is the information based on—facts or opinions? Does the information make sense? How does it compare to what you have gathered from other sources?

3. Is the site updated frequently? Do the links to other sites still work?

4. Is the site easy to navigate or does it take too much time to load? Is the information organized clearly and concisely?

Students should be prepared to evaluate their sources according to these questions and to justify their decisions about the accuracy of the information acquired on the Internet.

Here are a few Internet sites that students can use:

American Library Association (collection links)
<www.ala.org/parentspage/greatsites/amazing.html>

Electric Library (where you can search in plain English)
<www.k12.elibrary.com/classroom>

The Holiday Page
<wilstar.net/holiday.htm>

Just for Kids
<www.yahooligans.com>

For research on U.S. states
<www.ipl.org/youth/stateknow>

For more information, try the following:

Nyla Ahmad. *Cybersurfer: The OWL Internet Guide for Kids.* Owl, 1996. Paperback with Mac/Windows disk.

Preston Gralla. *Online Kids: A Young Surfer's Guide to Cyberspace.* Wiley, 1996.

Multimedia: Videos and CD-ROMs

Computer resources for teaching include more than surfing the Web. Increasingly, videos for teaching and learning are accompanied by extensive use of CD-ROM technology that replaces standard print reference works and brings more information and materials into the classroom that will not go out-of-date so quickly. Some examples of videos for classroom use:

The Arab Americans, Multicultural Peoples of North America series. Schlessinger Productions, 1993.

My Brown Eyes, the story of a Korean boy's first day at school, and other films about the Asian American experience. NAATA, 1994 (415) 552-9550 <www.naatanet.org>.

Debra Chasnoff and Helen Cohen. *It's Elementary: Talking about Gay Issues in School: The Elementary Training Version.* New Day Films, 1997. (888) 367-9154 <www.newday.com>. Also see their video *In Whose Honor: American Indian Mascots in Sports.*

The Essential Blue-Eyed and other videos about the African American experience. California Newsreel (415) 621-6196 <www.newsreel.org>.

Video Resources

Keith Kyker and Christopher Curchy. *Video Projects for Elementary and Middle Schools.* Libraries Unlimited, 1995.

Jerry Martin. *Active Video: A Teaching Tool for Every Classroom.* Good Year, 1998.

CD-ROMs and Other Software

Asian-American Experience. From the Asian-American Studies Center at UCLA. American Journey, 1997. Mac/Windows

Choices, Choices. Role play and problem-solving simulations. Tom Snyder Productions. (800) 342-1236 or <www.teachtsp.com>.

Crossword Studio and *Wordsearch Studio.* Helps you put together puzzles to print out or solve on screen. Nordic, 1997. Mac/Windows.

Dr. Seuss ABC (1995), *Green Eggs and Ham by Dr. Seuss* (1996), *Stella Luna by Cannon* (1996). Living Book Series. Random House: Broderbund.

Encarta Africana. Microsoft, 1999. Windows.

The Factory Deluxe. Students can build with different tools. Sunburst. Mac/Windows. (800) 321-7511 or <www.sunburst.com>.

Hollywood and *Hollywood High.* Students write and direct animated scripts. Theatrix, 1996. Mac/Windows.

Hyperstudio 3.1. Software used to produce "talking books" for the classroom. Roger Wagner, 1997.

Kid Pix Studio Deluxe. One of the top graphics programs, use for independent writing or learning centers. Broderbund/Learning Company. Mac/Windows. (800) 548-1798.

Simpletext. Use this to write text and computer will read text aloud. Apple, 1995.

SuperPrint V.1.2. For making banners, cards, and so on. Scholastic. (800) 541-5513. Mac.

Index